D0081290

DATE DUE

10/19/04			
10-31-07			

Demco No. 62-0549

THE
NAVAJO
NATION

Contributions in Ethnic Studies
Series Editor: Leonard Doob

NATIONS REMEMBERED: An Oral History of the Five Civilized Tribes,
1865-1907
Theda Perdue

OPERATION WETBACK: The Mass Deportation of Mexican Undocumented
Workers in 1954
Juan Ramon García

6336613

E
99
N3
I9

THE NAVAJO NATION

Peter Iverson

SE 20 '83

DISCARDED

CONTRIBUTIONS IN ETHNIC STUDIES, NUMBER 3

Greenwood Press

WESTPORT, CONNECTICUT • LONDON, ENGLAND

Copyright Acknowledgments

The author wishes to thank the following for permission to use material from his earlier articles. Portions of this book appeared in:

"Legal Counsel and the Navajo Nation Since 1945," in *American Indian Quarterly*, Vol. 3, No. 1, 1977, pp. 1-15. Reprinted by permission of the Society for American Indian Studies & Research.

"Legal Assistance and Navajo Economic Revitalization," in *The Journal of Ethnic Studies*, Fall 1976.

American Indian Leaders: Studies in Diversity, edited by R. David Edmunds (Lincoln: University of Nebraska Press, 1980).

Library of Congress Cataloging in Publication Data

Iverson, Peter.
  The Navajo Nation.

  (Contributions in ethnic studies ; no. 3 ISSN 0196-7088)
  Bibliography: p.
  Includes index.
  1. Navajo Indians—History. 2. Navajo Indians—
Tribal government. 3. Indians of North America—
Southwest, New—Tribal government. I. Title.
II. Series.
E99.N319   970.004'97   80-1024
ISBN 0-313-22309-2 (lib. bdg.)

Copyright © 1981 by Peter Iverson

All rights reserved. No portion of this book may be reproduced, by any process or technique, without the express written consent of the publisher.

Library of Congress Catalog Card Number: 80-1024
ISBN: 0-313-22309-2
ISSN: 0196-7088

First published in 1981

Greenwood Press
A division of Congressional Information Service, Inc.
88 Post Road West
Westport, Connecticut 06881

Printed in the United States of America

10 9 8 7 6 5 4 3 2 1

To William
and Adelaide Iverson

The author's proceeds from this book will be given to the college scholarship fund of the Navajo Nation.

CONTENTS

ILLUSTRATIONS

TABLES

SERIES FOREWORD

"Contributions in Ethnic Studies" focuses upon the problems that arise when peoples with different cultures and goals come together and interact productively or tragically. The modes of adjustment or conflict are various, but usually one group dominates or tries to dominate the other. Eventually some accommodation is reached: the process is likely to be long and, for the weaker group, painful. No one scholarly discipline monopolizes the research necessary to comprehend these intergroup relations. The emerging analysis, consequently, inevitably is of interest to historians, social scientists, psychologists, and psychiatrists.

Primarily Professor Iverson's scholarly study offers the history of an important ethnic group from its arrival in the American Southwest, probably at the end of the fifteenth century, until the late 1970s. Part of the story is well known and hence is briefly recapitulated: the Navajo much more eagerly accepted horses and sheep than Catholicism from the Spanish explorers; they were finally defeated by the United States Army (Kit Carson et al.) at the time of the Civil War and, having been forcibly moved from their homeland, they were cruelly imprisoned in Fort Sumner, New Mexico; four years later they were released and confined to a semi-arid reservation. Until Roosevelt's New Deal, The People, as they call themselves, were by and large neglected by American authorities, they were exploited by traders and other intruders, and their culture appeared to be gradually perishing. The present volume concentrates upon events during the last five decades.

It was then that the Bureau of Indian Affairs sought to rescue and re-vive the Navajo by providing medical, educational, and other public services. At first these efforts essentially failed because federal authorities attempted more vigorously than previously to curb the overgrazing of the land, whereas the Indians believed it vital to possess large herds of live-stock. Since World War II, however, the Navajo have revived and have become an important, self-conscious minority. The Indian men who participated in that war discovered some beneficial aspects of Western civili-zation; many returned to the reservation with a determination to change and yet preserve their cultural heritage. The land itself has become a fertile economic resource: it provides water, lumber, coal, oil, and most recently uranium. Anglo companies and politicians have tried to continue to exploit the wealth and its owners, a second invasion generally resisted by the Navajo, often with the help of the federal government. Most sig-nificant has been the growing awareness of the Indians themselves that, on the American continent and in spite of the location of their lands in three states (Arizona, New Mexico, and Utah), they constitute a distinct Nation with a capital N and possess their own institutions and way of life. Even their Community College has a Navajo flavor. In his inaugural address at the beginning of his first term as the elected leader of his people, the "Navajo Chairman" (an electrical engineer with experience as a Marine and in an aircraft factory) brilliantly summarized his program and antici-pated what indeed has more or less occurred:

First, what is rightfully ours, we must protect; what is rightfully due us, we must claim. Second, what we depend on from others, we must replace with the labor of our own hands and the skills of our own people. Third, what we do not have, we must bring into being. We must create for our-selves. . . . We must do better. We must do it in our own way. And we must do it now.

In these respects our Indian contemporaries resemble other ethnic groups, whether they be as widely different as the Basques and the Zulus, which are struggling to retain their national identity in an interdependent world and which, when they achieve greater independence, develop factions within their own ranks.

That the Navajo program has not been completely successful leads Professor Iverson to transcend his own scholarly discipline. Anthropologists and sociologists can find here the sequel to the appealing, provocative analysis of social change and stability among the Navajo provided by Clyde Kluckhohn and Dorothea Leighton in 1946; the penchant for field research is followed since Professor Iverson's family has had a long association with the Navajo, and he and his wife lived among The People for almost three years and gathered data for this account. Political scientists and especially lawyers are offered details concerning the rise of a political and legal structure derived from both Indian and American society; the relation of that structure to the rest of American society, the legal battles, and the skulduggery are copiously described. Economists and others concerned with this country's current energy problems can observe how the Navajo affect, and have been affected by those very problems; industrial development on the reservation lags and has been fraught with scandals and swindles; emphasis is now being placed upon small businesses and cooperatives.

Here, in short, is history brought up to date. The Navajo are not a "vanishing race," indeed their population is rapidly increasing. Like the rest of us, they face an uncertain future, yet it appears, as a result of "their strength, resilience, and persistence" that their future is likely to be more satisfying to them than the past once inflicted upon them by the invaders from the civilization of Europe and the Atlantic seaboard.

Leonard W. Doob
June 9, 1980

PREFACE

My interest in Navajo history began when I was a young child, when I
heard stories from my grandmother and grandfather about the Navajos
and their land. During the 1930s my grandfather had worked in Navajo
country as a principal in Indian Service schools. An aunt had been married
at St. Michaels; I had cousins in Santa Fe. Toadlena and Lukachukai
seemed real to me long before I ever saw them.

As a graduate student in history at the University of Wisconsin I learned
about the new college the Navajos had started in January 1969. Soon
thereafter I applied for a position at this institution, which was called
Navajo Community College and located in Many Farms, Arizona, but the
college officials hired someone with more impressive credentials. That
summer though, while visiting my wife's parents in South Dakota, I received a phone call. At the last minute, the person hired by the school
had decided not to come, and the college needed someone foolish enough
to be there immediately. Could we be in Many Farms in a week?

Fortunately, Kath and I had the good sense to say that we could. We
rushed back to Madison, packed our belongings, and drove to Many Farms.
As we drove north from Ganado, we wondered whether a friend of ours
had impersonated a college administrator. Perhaps we would arrive to
find the job had been taken after all. In fact, upon arrival we were asked
if we were there for an interview. Things could only get better. If nothing
else, we did have the benefit of supportive, if slightly incredulous families;
I can still hear Kath's grandfather saying, "Many *What*?"

From September 1969 to June 1972 we were residents in the Navajo Nation. Since that time I have returned to the area, both to continue my research and to be with old friends. Such a residency and degree of familiarity with a land and its people guarantee neither sensitivity nor perception, but it did have a major effect on this study and my work in Native American history. I learned something, at least, about the perduring quality of Navajo life. While I saw the problems and difficulties of the Navajo present, I could understand the Navajo pride in their heritage and their hope for the future. This book has been influenced, thus, not only by more traditional academic research but by life experience as well.

I have attempted a history for both Navajos and non-Navajos. If I have been at all successful, I have many people to thank and will take this opportunity to express my appreciation to some of them. My wife, Katherine Jensen Iverson, provided essential assistance. Her training in the social sciences and special interest in Native American education proved especially helpful. Robert F. Berkhofer, now of the University of Michigan, advised me during the initial phases of my work. My work also benefited immeasurably from the thorough criticism of Allan G. Bogue. A former colleague at Navajo Community College, Navajo anthropologist Priscilla Kanaswood helped me at various stages. Robert W. Young improved this study by his careful, sympathetic reading of the manuscript. He is an acknowledged authority in Navajo language and history, and I was fortunate to have his assistance. My editors at Greenwood Press also deserve thanks for their interest, support, and aid.

In the 1973-74 academic year, I held a doctoral fellowship at the Newberry Library Center for the History of the American Indian. I learned from my peers, from visiting scholars, from members of the Indian community in Chicago, and perhaps most of all from D'Arcy McNickle, the center's first director. As I commuted between my family in Wisconsin and the center in Chicago, a number of people made my life richer by their friendship and hospitality, including Bob Bieder, Fred McTaggart and Donna Carroll, Calvin and Jean Martin, Bob and Ann Masur, and John and Sarah Wilson.

During the past decade, countless people in the Navajo area taught, féd, housed, and helped me. I cannot name them all, but I would like to acknowledge my indebtedness to Anagilda and Mort Abromowitz, Francis Becenti, J. Lee Correll, Larry Emerson, Scott Fisher, Gene Gade, Joe and

Lou Gelt, Bill and Marsha Harbison, Nancy Hilding, Bob and Lucy Hilgendorf, Keith Leafdale, Peter Ludwig, Mike Luther, Richard Mike, William Morgan, Eric Natwig, Agatha Yazzie Spencer, Soge Track, Bea Yazzie, and Ray Young. They may not agree, of course, with my interpretation and analysis.

I am indebted to the University of Wisconsin and the Newberry Library for fellowship and travel funds. During the revisions of the manuscript, the history departments at Arizona State University and the University of Wyoming provided additional assistance. Diane Alexander of Wyoming patiently typed the final draft. My colleagues at Wyoming and Arizona State and other associates here and there have been most supportive.

Finally, I thank my wife, Kath, my children, Erika and Jens, and all the members of our extended family for their love and encouragement. I am happy to be able to dedicate this book to my parents, William and Adelaide Iverson. As they know, it is also for all who have shared in its creation.

INTRODUCTION

This is a history of continuity within and through change in Navajo life, as seen in Navajo efforts to determine the use of their resources and the course of their lives. It deals with the reasons for the institutionalization of the Navajo national idea and analyzes the extent to which sovereignty has been and can be achieved for a people who are both Diné—roughly, The People, as the Navajos call themselves—and Americans. On a larger scale, this history explores additionally, the degree to which the United States will tolerate, let alone approve, a significant separation from some elements of American life for not merely a people, but a people whose land holds great wealth.

Some time ago, when I first began this research, I encountered a photograph by Edward Curtis entitled "The Vanishing Race." It shows a group of Navajos on horseback, each figure less distinct, with the final rider barely visible in the distance. This image typified the prevalent American attitude of the late nineteenth and early twentieth centuries that Native Americans no longer would be unique and important participants in American life.[1]

The Navajos have not vanished. Today they are the most populous Native American people with the largest land base. Their population is now at least 150,000; their land base is 25,000 square miles. Covering a large portion of northeastern Arizona, a part of northwestern New Mexico, and a small section of southeastern Utah, the Navajo Nation is slightly larger than West Virginia.

But the Navajos have done more than increase in number and claim a portion of the Southwest. They have maintained a way of life, flexible and changing, which is identifiably Navajo. Moreover, as Clyde Kluckhohn and Dorothea Leighton observed in their classic study, *The Navaho,* a steadily growing "tribal" or "national" consciousness has arisen among The People. Kluckhohn and Leighton, more than thirty years ago, saw it only as a "beginning" but noted, "The People are becoming increasingly conscious of common background, common problems, a common need to unite to protect their interests against the encroachment of whites."[2]

The Navajo Nation is part of the Navajo effort to maintain a working ethnic boundary. Through Navajo nationalism we see the persistence of Navajo determination to remain Navajo. As Edward Spicer would argue, the nation's boundary cannot be represented simply on a map. It is more than a territorial limit:

Situations of interaction among people . . . situations which have a location, are characterized by the use of artifacts, and in which roles are activated and ideas expressed . . . situations in which the sense of identity receives some kind of expression and where individuals align themselves in some manner as members of one ethnic group.[3]

In understanding the growth of Navajo nationalism, we must note some of the ironic consequences of greater Anglo encroachment and demand for the use or changed use of once isolated Navajo land resources. As Diné have come into increasing contact with Anglo institutions, ideas, and pressures, they have had ample reason to reinforce their designation as The People. The resolution passed in 1969 by the Navajo Tribal Council's Advisory Committee officially calling for the use of the term "Navajo Nation" reads in part:

The Deneh [Diné] —the Navajo People—existed as a distinct political, cultural and ethnic group long before the establishment of the States of Arizona, Colorado, New Mexico, and Utah, and
The Government of the United States of America recognized this fact and entered into treaties with the sovereign Navajo Tribe, and down through the years both the Congress of the United States and the Supreme Court of the United States have recognized the inherent right of the

Navajo People to govern themselves, and

When the geographical area occupied by the Navajo People was incorporated into the Union of states of the United States of America, no one asked the Navajo People if they wished to be so included, and

It is becoming increasingly difficult for the Navajo People to retain their identity and independence, and

It appears essential to the best interests of the Navajo People that a clear statement be made to remind Navajos and non-Navajos alike that both the Navajo People and Navajo lands are, in fact, separate and distinct.[4]

This history thus is an examination of the effort to maintain this separation and distinction—an assertion which has meant the creation of the Navajo Nation.

To many Americans, the idea of a Navajo Nation existing within the United States seems paradoxical, if not contradictory. Our reaction to this notion of a nation in our midst reveals in part an unwillingness to acknowledge the value that Navajos in particular and Native Americans in general place on maintaining identity. We have been reluctant to make distinctions among different tribal peoples—stubbornly using "Indians" as a blanket term, so to speak—let alone give them credit for being able to transmit differing cultural ways. For more than a century, in fact, Anglo Americans have been objecting to Navajo cultural patterns and trying to eliminate what they have perceived as conflicting ideologies and practices. Now the Navajos are moving from resisting these efforts to creating institutions responsive to their needs.

Navajo cultural distinction is one thing; a Navajo Nation another. By consciously employing the term, Navajos emphasize their uniqueness: their special language, territory, cultural traditions, and political institutions. It is a way of saying "we are different and we shall endure." It does not mean, however, that Navajos see themselves as totally self-sufficient or completely separate from the United States. There is collective pride, for example, in the Navajo Codetalkers, whose linguistic skills baffled the Japanese in World War II, and there is the Navajo pick-up truck with two bumper stickers: "I'm Navajo and Proud of It" and "America: Love It or Leave It."

Yet the term "nation" is important. The Navajo Nation exists as a formal entity, so created by Navajo declaration. But it is in the process of evolution, having gone beyond the state of a tribe, but not yet to the stage we generally associate with a nation. The Navajo Tribal Code states that the Navajo Nation is seeking "to work out the relationship of its nation to the United States and the surrounding states" and to require "these governmental systems to recognize the extent to which the Navajo Tribe has become a truly sovereign entity."[5] The precise nature of this relationship remains to be determined.

Some sense of Navajo history as Navajos have perceived it must be established, for The People's version of their history has strongly influenced Navajo actions of the present. However, anyone interested in Navajo or Native American history quickly discovers unique problems in evaluating evidence on that perspective. Navajo testimony is crucial but hard to obtain, and, once obtained, it must be analyzed for accuracy. Before worrying about the substance, one has to wonder about translation from Navajo to English.

Another problem is that by and large non-Navajos have written most of Navajo history as well as the records needed for new histories, and there are definite limitations to the outsider's view. Non-Navajos in the Navajo Nation are restricted, some more than others, in what they can do, be, and perceive. In addition, "Navajo" sources have not always been free from Anglo influence. The *Navajo Times,* for example, has had Anglo editors; Anglos have been involved in the publications of the Navajo Community College Press. Still, such sources largely succeed in providing more of a Navajo perspective than has been available and enhance our understanding of Navajo history and Navajo nationalism.

They serve as well to revise or eliminate widely held beliefs about the nature of Native American history: that Indians do not have a history because they usually did not have a written language, that there is little factual evidence available in Native American traditional stories, that Indian history is merely a response to white presence and institutions, and that Indians are vanishing Americans with dying cultures. A careful examination of Navajo history, however, reveals a most different picture. It shows not only a people confident they will endure but also much available evidence to flesh out the image of the Navajo past. However, to gain a dynamic view of this adaptive, creative nation, one must be willing to accept new forms of evidence.

A central element of Navajo history comes from what some have termed mythology. The very word "myth" has taken on a pejorative connotation in the popular usage: something false or misleading. But myth may also mean a body of traditional or legendary stories dealing with the creation of a particular world and the growth of particular values and beliefs. Such a search for legendary people and places, after all, is a normal attempt to understand our world and ourselves. Such materials provide a rich storehouse of collective knowledge informing the researcher and guiding The People. They blend with Navajo history in such a way that the Navajo artist Carl Gorman truly might say, "Navajo history and mythology are intertwined like strands of a rope."[6]

Navajo mythology is part of an alternate perspective that deemphasizes time in history. A review of the Navajo emergence story, recently published for the first time by Navajos themselves, and a modern adaptation of it by Larry Emerson, Navajo, may help to illustrate this point. These stories and others have an immediacy and pertinence that make them instructive today.

The emergence story recounts how The People came to be. It begins in the First World, the Black World, "where only spirit people and Holy People lived." Here First Man (Áłtsé Hastiin) is formed through the meeting of the white cloud and the black cloud, and with him is formed a perfect ear of white corn (Doo Honoot'ínii). Similarly, in the west, First Woman (Áłtsé Asdzą́ą́) is created when the yellow cloud and the blue cloud meet; she is joined by a perfect ear of yellow corn, white shell, and turquoise. Different beings live in this first world, primarily Insect Beings (Wóláz-hiní Diné'é), who "had developed a way of life because they recognized the value of making and carrying out plans with the approval of one another." These beings quarrel among each other and all eventually move upward into the Blue World.[7]

In the Second World, the Blue World, they find other beings, including blue-feathered beings, such as Blue Hawks (Ginítsoh Dootł'izh) and Blue Jays (Joogii). Larger insects could be seen as well as animals, including Wolves (Mą'iitsoh) and Mountain Lions (Náshdóítsoh). There is quarreling and suffering here, too, and First Man presents proper rituals so that the beings may be allowed to leave for the Third World, the Yellow World.

The Yellow World had six mountains and no sun. Here lived Turquoise Boy (Doot'iizhii Ashkii) and White Shell Woman (Yoołgai Asdzą́ą́); here lived Squirrels (Dloziłgai), Deer (Bįįh), and Snakes (Na'ashǫ́'ii). Coyote has accompanied First Man and First Woman to this world, and now, typically, he creates a dilemma. He successfully begs for a small piece of white shell from First Man. Coyote takes the white shell to the water, where it makes the river rise and fall. Coyote discovers the child of Water Monster (Tééhoołtsódii) as the river goes down for the fourth time. He hides the child. A flood then comes, and, as it threatens to engulf all, First Man tries to find a method of getting to the next world. His fourth effort, planting a female reed, succeeds. All climb up it into the Fourth World, the Glittering World.

It is in the Glittering World where First Man and First Woman form the four sacred mountains in the East, South, West, and North. Here the Holy People make the first fire, using flint on fir, pinon, spruce, and juniper. The first sweat bath is taken and then the first hogan built, following the instructions of Talking God (Haashch'ééłti'í). The stars are put in the sky, the sun and moon are formed from turquoise and white shell, and the Sun Carrier and the Moon Carrier begin their journeys. After the moccasin game is played, day and night are created. The seasons are decided upon and the first harvest occurs. Then men and women are separated following the first adultery. Reunited when separation proves harmful to all, the people prosper, but their prosperity is threatened by monsters, many of whom had been created by the Sun's adultery.

Fortunately, the twin sons of Changing Woman (Asdzáá Nádleehé) are able to slay these monsters. Changing Woman, born of darkness and dawn, is discovered as a baby by First Man and First Woman near Governador Knob (Ch'óol'í'í) in northwestern New Mexico. When she reaches puberty, the first Kinaalda is held for her. Later, the Sun visits her while she is sleeping and "in time, she had twins." The boys became known as Monster Slayer (Naayéé' Neizgháni) and Child Born of Water (Tó Bají́sh Chini). They learn of their father's existence from Spider Woman (Na'ashjé'ii Asdzáá) and undertake a long and dangerous visit to see him. He tests them and finally gives each a weapon to use in killing the monsters. The older brother receives Lightning That Strikes Crooked (Atsinit'ishk'aá) and the younger brother obtains Lightning That Flashes Straight (Hatsoo'algha k'aa'). The twins return and slay the monsters, including One Walking Giant (Yé'iitsoh Ła'i Naagháii), whose dried blood near Grants, New Mexico, "is called the lava beds by white people." However, they allow several monsters to live, who personify old age, hunger, lice, and death.

The twins then go again to visit their father, who gives them gifts from the four directions, in exchange for the Sun's being able to "destroy those who live in houses," since many of the monsters had been his children. Before a great flood covers the earth and destroys most living things, the Holy People save a man and a woman and pairs of all animals. Following the flood, Monster Slayer "became very tired and concerned. He felt distressed and lacked peace and harmony." To restore this balance, the people hold a meeting, from which comes the first Squaw Dance ceremony.

The final two chapters of the emergence story relate the creation of the first four clans (Kiiyaa'áanii, Honágháahnii, Tó Dích'íi'nii and Hashtl'ishnii) by Changing Woman and the wandering of the people. Some of the people split off from the people who became known as the Navajos, including the Paiutes (Báyóodzin), the Chiricahua Apaches (Chishi), the Mescalero Apaches (Naashgalí Diné'e), and the Jicarilla Apaches (Beehai). Finally, the Holy People decide upon the home for The People within the area of the four sacred mountains. It is said that "there is a god (Yé'ii) whose body starts at the foot of Mount Taylor (Tsoodzil) and curves all the way around on the outside of the four sacred mountains, with the head stopping at Blanca Peak (Sis Naajiní)." The People are protected by this body, but today's population increase beyond these boundaries may mean "they will run into difficulties with nature and will be out of harmony with the plan of the Gods." So ends the Navajos' published version of their beginnings.[8]

Larry Emerson's adaptation of the emergence story is set in the area of Gallup, New Mexico, the self-proclaimed Indian capital of the world. The story takes place in a time of great difficulty and turmoil, when white businessmen, traders, and employees of the Bureau of Indian Affairs are taking advantage of Indian peoples. All of a sudden, a prophet appears. A Navajo, Natani Man, he bids Native Americans from all over the continent to gather in Gallup. Once they assemble, he leads them to the heart of the Navajo country, to Canyon de Chelly, where they go back to the previous world through a small hole in the canyon wall.

All goes well for a period of time. The Indians are delighted with their new state, and the Bureau of Indian Affairs, unencumbered at last, flourishes as never before. Eventually, though, the Indians quarrel. The gods grow weary of the disagreements and sentence the Indians to return to the world from which they had escaped. The Native Americans make their way back, most reluctantly, only to discover that the whites have vanished. Perhaps greed has vanquished them; perhaps war. In any event, they are gone, and the land remains again solely for Indian use. As the story concludes, the Indians are going about the business of forming their own governments.[9]

What may we learn from such stories? The emergence story surely is important as a means of instruction. Through it, Navajos learn not only about how things came to be, but what kind of world they live in and how they should live within it. As we shall see, Navajos bring this same kind of perspective to events of the recent historical past. So it is, too, with Emerson's story, which utilizes the ancient story of emergence in an attempt to resolve dilemmas of the present. As Fred McTaggart wrote in his study of the Mesquakies of Tama, Iowa:

To Mesquakies, the events of the present, and of the future, are the visions of a time long past. A Mesquakie historian looks not just back at the past but also forward into the future and he constructs from both past and future a meaning that is part of the present—a present that always has been and always will be.

For the Mesquakies, McTaggart found, "History teaches rather because it allows us to live and relive basic experiences. It brings us closer to our ancestors and to those things which unite us as a people."[10] This is the way it is with the Diné.

The emergence story readily yields places of importance to present-day Navajos: the four sacred mountains, in particular. But the full account reveals dozens of easily recognizable places where specific episodes took place. The glossary to the version published by the Navajos provides a list of canyons, mountains, and places clearly identified in the course of the story. Thus the story provides a sense of place—surely an important element of nationalism.

But the story does more. It summarizes how things came to be: the stars, the sun and moon, hunger, and old age. It tells The People something about their place in the universe. There are gods and nature to be reckoned with. The character of these gods, as Katherine Spencer has pointed out, is hardly all-powerful or all good: they are capricious, somewhat unpredictable beings to whom proper ceremonies must be directed.[11] Man is understood as part of nature along with animals, insects, and features of the land; he is not seen as necessarily superior or destined to dominate.

In addition, the origin story mirrors a great deal about Navajo social organization and Navajo values. One learns how things should be. For example, there is an emphasis upon the maintenance of harmony. Beings are forced to go upward from one world to the next because of quarreling (Emerson reverses the process); Insect Beings, however, develop a way of life because they are able to get along among themselves. Such a repetition of a particular theme or value is understandable in the context of harmony's central place in Navajo curing ceremonies and Navajo life generally.

The origin myth, finally, is the basis for the chantway myths, which form the heart of the great Navajo ceremonials or chants. These myths follow much the pattern of the Twins going to see their father, the Sun, to obtain aid to slay the monsters. As Katherine Spencer has observed, "A Navajo chantway myth describes the origin of the associated curing ceremony, how it was obtained from supernaturals and made available for the use of earth people." The myths are revealed as teachings to the Navajos about how they should relate to each other, families, and strangers. They learn the possible consequences for failing to live up to these standards. In sum, the stories provide a thorough education for those who will heed them.[12]

The stories remain widely known. Although Navajo students largely have been sequestered away from their elders' teachings by attendance at boarding schools, the stories endure for them with surprising vitality. For many, the stories continue to inspire and strengthen. Larry Emerson's work is but one case in point. One reads the poem of a Navajo girl, a high school senior, praying for her brother in Vietnam:

> Very early at dawn, with corn pollen in my hand,
> I raise my corn pollen to the East,
> Where Mt. Blanco is setting.
> I ask the White Stone to help my brother,
> to give him the courage to live again this day.

She turns to each of the other directions, continues, and concludes:

> I am within my four sacred mountains.
> I know the four sacred mountains will hear
> My daily prayer and answer me.

A boy writes of his grandfather who would "scare us with stories of the terrible ye'iitsoh" and "make us wonder with stories about how the proud Diné originated."[13]

In addition to Navajo mythology, there is a vast body of historical literature that Navajos have passed down from one generation to the next. The boy's grandfather just mentioned would also "excite us with stories of Diné warriors before the Bosque Redondo tragedy."[14] The forced march of The People in 1864 to incarceration at the Bosque or Fort Sumner—Hweeldi, the Navajos call it—is known by the Diné as "nináda' iishjidéedáá" (the time when people came straining back with packs on their backs), or, in English, the Long Walk. The Long Walk and the events surrounding it inspired a large number of stories. The other great threat to Navajo perseverance, the livestock reduction era of the 1930s and 1940s, also encouraged many oral accounts. Other situations, often confrontations with non-Navajos, have been recorded and shared: battles with other tribes, resistance to enforced schooling of Navajo children, and, more recently, experiences in World War II. I have utilized much of this storehouse of oral history in tracing the Navajo heritage.

Taken in sum, the Navajos' view of their history provides them with a usable past, a record of "common memories, sacrifices, glories, afflictions and regrets," which help to create and unite a nation.[15] One must look to what Scott Momaday once termed the living racial memory, the inspiration that informs Navajo oral historical accounts. These rich resources have been indispensable to the evolution of the Navajo Nation.

THE
NAVAJO
NATION

FROM THE EARLY DAYS TO THE EARLY TWENTIETH CENTURY

1

Anthropologists classify the Navajos as an Athapascan people. The Navajo language, diné bizaad, is placed within the family of Na-Dene languages. These affiliations link the Navajos, like the Apaches, with other groups to the north, in Canada and Alaska. Navajos tell some stories that are strikingly similar to tales told by some of these northern peoples. All of these indicators suggest to us that the Navajos migrated to the American Southwest from the north hundreds of years ago.

Precisely when they arrived we cannot say. Estimates for that time and projections on their subsequent movement within the area are based mostly on archaeological evidence. Work by Hall and others have placed the Navajos in the Gobernador Canyon area of northwestern New Mexico by the late 1400s or early 1500s. By the early 1600s, they believe, some of The People had migrated westward, as far as the Black Mesa country of northern Arizona. Reports from Arate Salmeron in 1626, and Father Benavides in 1630, provide the first written historical observations of the Navajo from the same period. In addition, Navajo stories of their origins place their emergence into this world and the first events of creation in the Governador area as well.

The various Pueblo peoples apparently exerted a strong influence on the evolution of Navajo culture in the new region. While the Navajo-Hopi land dispute and other conflicts of earlier generations incline us to view the Navajos and Pueblos as traditional foes, surely the historical record contains more than centuries of unremitting enmity. David Brugge recently suggested a number of instances of Navajos and one Pueblo village or another allying against the Spanish or other outside groups. Robert W. Young and others have argued that the initial period of contact between the Navajos and the Pueblos seemed marked primarily by peaceful rather than hostile relationships.[1] In any event, the Pueblos probably did change Navajo life in some crucial ways. Unlike the other Apachean peoples, the Navajos adopted the matrilineal clan system. This form of social organization, not unimportant even today, dictated that one inherit one's clan and thus one's lineage from one's mother. People from the same clan are considered relatives with varying responsibilities to one and other. The western Pueblos, where the clan tradition was strong, probably influenced the Navajos in this direction. These Pueblo peoples' sedentary, agricultural ways also had some effect on the Navajos, as the Navajos gradually adopted a way of life significantly less nomadic and with correspondingly less emphasis on hunting than the other Apachean groups. While the Navajos may have learned weaving and the art of agriculture from peoples en route to the Southwest, as some authorities believe, surely the Pueblo culture had a vital effect as well. The Navajos themselves credit Spider Woman with their instruction in weaving and may hasten to add that Pueblo men are weavers, whereas only very rarely will a Navajo man weave.

Politically, at the time of the Spanish contact, the Navajos must be seen as something very different from a nation in the sense of a political entity or even a relatively unified people. In this era, to the contrary, their allegiances were much more narrowly drawn—to family, clan, and immediate neighbors, but certainly not to all Navajos. The Navajos did not claim one supreme leader but rather acted in smaller, relatively autonomous groups, much to the dismay of the more rigidly organized Spanish. Spanish reports may not be terribly reliable in this realm, and anthropologists of more recent vintage are not sure about the kind of authority system that operated. There were naat'aani, headmen with oratorical ability and ceremonial knowledge, and there were others who served as leaders in war or in hunting or curing ceremonies. Hózhoojí naat'ááh served as peace leaders. But all held their positions at the discretion of their peers and had to perform in their interests and with proper consultation.[2]

The presence of the Spanish culture also vitally affected the Navajo way of life. While the Spanish missionaries won few Navajo converts, indirectly the Spanish altered Navajo society forever, for the Spanish had horses and sheep. It is impossible to imagine The People without either, so thoroughly have they integrated the possession and care of these animals into their everyday existence. "Since time immemorial our grandfathers and our grandmothers have lived from their herds—from their herds of sheep, horses and cattle, for those things originated with the world itself."[3] A Navajo world began and the Navajos earned their reputation as raiders— as distinct from warriors—in the days after the Spanish contact as they sought to further their collection of these animals. The Navajos, of course, were hardly the only tribe to do so; they often raided with other tribes, raided other tribes, and were attacked in turn by other tribes and by the Spanish.

Thus when we look to Navajo life in the American Southwest during the sixteenth, seventeenth, and eighteenth centuries we review a time of Navajo expansion, cultural acquisition, and social change. Yet, too, from the earliest reports there is no mistaking these people as Navajos. "The Apacheans, and especially the Navajo," writes Young, "have always had a great capacity to absorb and elaborate upon cultural traits which they have adopted from other peoples." Pueblo weaving, he notes, produced the Navajo blanket, unmistakably the product of the Diné. The language, though, remained distinctly Navajo; other Indians often learned Navajo, but few Navajos bothered to master a foreign tongue.[4]

By the time the Americans arrived in the nineteenth century, the Navajos had developed a diversified economy. Stockraising was an important but not the sole element within that economy. Both the early accounts of Spanish travelers and Navajo oral tradition tell us of the vital place of farming Navajo life. Father Benavides identified the Navajos as great farmers. Diné origin stories emphasize hunting and gathering and farming activities; care of livestock is included but secondary. W. W. Hill's work, recently augmented by that of William Adams, dispels the "current belief that the Navajo are nomadic." As Hill notes, "The Navajo have been since historic times primarily sedentary agriculturalists."[5]

Ethnological data corroborate the significance of hunting and gathering in the pre-reservation period. Increasing pressure from non-Navajo populations, restrictions imposed by the reservation boundary lines, and limitation of off-reservation hunting and gathering would curtail these activities, but the importance of hunting at one time is evidenced in a well-developed series of hunting rituals. The coming of trading posts reduced the importance of gathering, with the exception of piñon nut harvesting.

In sum, the care of livestock simply added another element of needed diversity to the Navajo economic picture. Livestock did not become an important segment of the economy until the late eighteenth century, long after initial Spanish settlement. The basically sedentary economic pursuits of the Navajo strongly influenced the kind of livestock raising they practiced. Seasonal movements of animals, particularly to higher, cooler grazing areas in the summertime, took place within a prescribed, narrow radius which in no way could be considered nomadic.[6]

Why did the Navajos need such a diversified economy? Why did livestock take on a steadily more essential role within that economy? The answers to these questions overlap and are mutually reinforcing. A diversified economy could make more thorough use of the different opportunities provided by various soils, altitudes, and vegetations. The Navajo landscape includes valleys, plains, mesas, and mountain areas, with altitudes ranging from about 4,500 to slightly over 10,000 feet. Canyons and prominences further divide these classifications. There are three climatic zones: the humid, mountain zone (roughly 8 percent of the Navajo area), the intermediate steppe climate of the mesas and high plains (37 percent), and the comparatively warm desert (55 percent). Winter temperatures thus range from an average minimum of 4 to 15 degrees in the humid zone to 10 to 25 degrees in the steppe and 11 to 30 degrees in the desert. Average summer maximum temperatures range from 70 to 80 degrees in the humid zone, 80 to 88 degrees in the steppe, and up to 100 degrees in the desert. In all three regions, rainfall is concentrated in a late summer period (July-September), with great variations in amount within each zone and from desert to humid (which receives in addition 41 percent of its precipitation in winter snow). Soils may be classified as excellent, good, fair, poor, and unproductive in terms of run-off, grass-producing ability, and erosion. Only a third of the area is considered excellent or good, though this percentage is higher than many casual observers would assume. Fifteen percent of the soil is unproductive, with little vegetative cover. Vegetation in the Navajo area includes grassland, meadow, weeds, sagebrush, browse (shrub), timber (inaccessible and barren) woodland, and aspen. The diversity is striking: more Navajo land is covered with coniferous timber than with sagebrush.[7]

Conflicts between the Navajos and their neighbors also contributed to economic diversification, particularly in the one hundred years preceding the Long Walk. Raiding by and against Diné grew in intensity, and complicated agricultural pursuits, and increased the need for mobility. Of course, livestock could often be obtained through raiding. Moreover, livestock could be used for meat, clothing, and many other material items.

Generally speaking, a lack of specialization and a flexibility about economic activity enabled The People to deal with changing circumstances.[8]

The steady growth of the Navajo population as well figured in economic diversification. As Diné increased in number so did the quantity of their livestock. This progression, however, was not related strictly to population increase, nor did all Navajos share equally in the growth of livestock numbers. There were in retrospect two principal periods of growth. The first came in the last years of the eighteenth century and during the nineteenth century prior to the Anglo American campaign against the Navajos. The second followed the Navajo return from Bosque Redondo. The first era of expansion established livestock as economically important and culturally significant.[9] Navajo leader Ganado Mucho, for example, must have gained his name as a tribute to the size of his holdings, which enhanced his prestige within Navajo society. When those Navajos who had been imprisoned at Hweeldi returned to their homeland, the United States government provided them with livestock to assist in the transition. Such actions by the government made the stock reduction stipulations years later all the more confusing.

The spectacular growth in Navajo population began in this post-Fort Sumner era. The Diné numbered perhaps as many as 15,000 in 1870, and their population has grown steadily ever since.[10] Livestock numbers increased enormously as well. Many economists contend population growth, however, may provide more consumers than producers, given the preponderance of the young. In a Navajo society keyed increasingly to the raising of livestock, this younger segment could be readily utilized as herders from a very early age. Herding in fact became a central part of the Navajo socialization process.[11]

The Navajos, of course, were not alone in their demographic expansion. During the last half of the eighteenth century, Spanish settlers started moving into Navajo country in northwestern New Mexico. A round of raiding and military retaliation followed, and many Spaniards were forced to leave their newly established ranches. Governor Juan Bautista de Anza of New Mexico concluded a treaty with the Navajos of the area in 1786, a pact generally followed for the remainder of the century. However, early in the 1800s the New Mexicans again tried to expand into Navajo country, initiating the same cycle. It was at this time that Navajo raiding increased markedly and the Navajos gained the reputation they possessed when the Anglo Americans arrived. The Mexican period of administration from 1821 to 1846 simply meant more of this pattern. Treaties would be made, then broken. Mexican officials could not enforce regulations in this frontier region. The Navajos continued as many political units and could not be bound by a tribal-wide agreement.[12]

The Anglo Americans who claimed the Navajo territory as a result of the Mexican War initially followed much of the same tradition as the Spanish and the Mexicans and with essentially the same results. The Navajos, to be sure, felt the Americans had little cause of complaint with them; the Anglos, after all, had just defeated the very people with whom the Navajos had been fighting. Almost from the outset, relations with the Americans were marked by mistrust and misunderstanding. Seven Navajos, including the famous Narbona, lost their lives in a conflict that flared up in 1849. A series of treaties signed had relatively little impact. The Navajos, perhaps, could not tell that this era would differ from others.

But the Anglos moved on other fronts. They built Fort Defiance, aptly named, in the heart of Navajo country, near present-day Window Rock. They also constructed Fort Fauntleroy, later to be rechristened Wingate after the fort's namesake joined the Confederate cause. By the end of the 1850s the movement toward war seemed irreversible. New Mexico citizens demanded that the Navajos be brought to heel; Navajos called upon each other to drive the Anglos from their homeland. In April 1860, Manuelito and Barboncito led about 1,000 Navajos in an assault on Fort Defiance. They did not quite succeed, and the cry resounded for a full-scale war to be waged against the Diné. Later in the year the enraged members of the militia went on the rampage, murdering many Navajos, capturing others, and destroying Navajo crops and livestock. It was another chapter in the long and tragic story of Indian-White confrontation. The Navajos would no longer be permitted to stay where they had been. As in the Jacksonian era, the "practical" answer eventually would appear to be removal.

The outbreak of the Civil War in 1861 delayed only slightly the final onslaught of the U.S. Army against the Navajos. In September 1862, Brigadier General James H. Carleton replaced General E. R. S. Canby as head of the New Mexico command. Carleton inherited not only Canby's position but Canby's plans for the forcible removal of the Navajos. Canby had not decided where the Navajos would have to go, only that they would have to be a long way from their home country, where they were to be reformed. Carleton eventually combined in one location, the Bosque

Redondo area in eastern New Mexico, where he could transform not only the Navajos but the Mescalero Apaches as well.[13]

Colonel Christopher "Kit" Carson spearheaded both campaigns to make the Mescaleros and Navajos move to the bleak surroundings of Bosque Redondo. Carson and his associates, together with a particularly bitter winter, helped to encourage Navajo surrender. They marched through the region of Canyon de Chelly and ranged through Navajo country. There were incidents, of course; Red Shirt, as the Diné call him, is not remembered with particular fondness. Diné storytellers emphasize killing by the soldiers and starvation as key factors in forcing surrender.[14]

Not all the Navajos went on the Long Walk. Those residing in some of the more isolated reaches of their homeland, to the west and to the north, managed to avoid the trek to Bosque Redondo. For those who went it must have been a time of great bewilderment and sorrow. "A majority of the Navajos," Curly Tso said, "didn't know the reason why they were being rounded up and different stories went around among the people." Many saw Hweeldi as a place "where they would be put to death eventually." The United States had claimed the region only recently. If they had raided other peoples, had not they been raided as well? If a few of their own bore some responsibility for American antagonism, need all The People pay such an awful price?[15]

General Carleton saw the imprisonment of the Navajos as absolutely necessary. Only "away from the haunts and hills and hiding places of their country," he contended, could their children learn to read and write and could the Navajos learn "the art of peace" and "the truths of Christianity." At their new home, the Navajos soon would "acquire new habits, new ideas, new modes of life"; the old Navajos would "die off and carry with them all latent longings for murdering and robbing," and "thus they will become a happy and contented people, and Navajo Wars will be remembered only as something that belongs entirely to the past." Peace, Carleton argued, "must rest on the basis that they move onto these lands and like the Pueblos become an agricultural people and cease to be nomads." So began the general's four-year program of enforced acculturation.[16]

If the Bosque Redondo experience did not exactly meet Carleton's expectations, it perhaps surpassed the Navajos' fears. They remember not only the Long Walk but the years at Hweeldi with great bitterness, and there was much to be bitter about: the forced march itself, the barren

surroundings in which they found themselves, the very fact of imprisonment, and the homesickness, illness, hunger, and discomfort that characterized life at the Bosque. At the same time, they remember the ability
of their forefathers to persevere, and they emphasize the role of traditional
Navajo religion in allowing them to return to their homeland. One man
recalled a special ceremony that immediately preceded the announcement
that the Navajos could return home; one woman stated that Navajo singers
performed several ceremonies "to find out whether they would be released," and "they could see their release in the near future."[17]

Fraud, alkaline soil, weather, bureaucratic bungling, and administrative factionalism all helped do in Carleton's experiment. In his new administrative history of the Bosque Redondo reservation, Gerald Thompson
terms the attempt a "successful failure." "It failed," he believes, "to make
the Navajos self-sufficient," and "it did not solve the age-old problem of
Indian depredations." It succeeded in changing the Navajo perspective on
the everyday white man's world, introducing them to many aspects of
white culture. It altered many Navajo ways of doing things, and "most
importantly the reservation fostered a sense of tribal unity."[18]

Thompson's final point is the most central and the most valid. It was
indeed at Bosque Redondo, or perhaps one might say in the context of
the whole Long Walk era, that the Navajos were dealt with as one people
by the U.S. government and equally that they began to view themselves
politically as one unit. Previously, the Navajos had had things in common
culturally, but politically there had been little centralization. They had
lived in widely scattered locations, and authority was vested solely in
local headmen. Their allegiances and frames of reference were based on
a far more limited area. But now things would be altered. They had gone
through the common crucible of the Long Walk experience. Now, through
the treaty of 1868, they would be returned to a portion of their old home
country, but they would return to a reservation with strictly defined
borders. Their political boundaries had been established: the Navajo Nation had begun.[19]

The Treaty of 1868 created a reservation of about three and a half
million acres straddling what would become the state line of Arizona
and New Mexico. Though only a segment of the territory they had occupied, the reservation at least represented continuity; unlike so many other
tribes, the Navajos would not be moved permanently to a foreign location. Their ability to remain and, indeed, expand their territory can be

explained primarily in terms of the value the U.S. government placed on their high desert terrain. It was poor farming country, quite obviously, and isolated from main non-Navajo populations. Had the government officials foreseen the great mineral wealth of the land for twentieth-century America, doubtless the Navajo reservation would not have emerged in its present size.

It would be more than a half-century before the Navajo tribe would have an official government of its own, and then only because of economic concerns by outsiders. Eventually the U.S. government would need a formal entity to approve mineral leases on Navajo lands. At Fort Sumner, Carleton had hoped to divide the Navajos into twelve villages, with a chief for each appointed by the commanding officer. This government did not materialize. After the treaty was signed, Special Indian Agent John Ward of Santa Fe suggested a council of headmen, appointed by the agent, be formed to represent reservation districts. Once in a while the government would summon various Navajo "councils," but with little impact. These appointed chiefs might be people of standing in their own community, but their role with the federal government had little meaning or significance for the Navajos as a whole, scattered across the expanding reservation.[20]

The period from 1868 to early in the 1900s featured impressive demographic expansion. The Navajos numbered perhaps as many as 15,000 in 1870; by early in the twentieth century their population had doubled. Following their return from Fort Sumner, the Navajos, with government assistance, soon brought their herds of livestock back to the numbers they had known in the 1840s. As David Aberle has noted, most of the estimates of livestock holdings in this era are precisely that; taken in sum they seem to be largely wild guesses. But surely there was a rapid rise in the number of livestock per capita during the first two decades after the creation of the reservation. After 1890 or so this figure probably stabilized, while the total number continued to increase. Though the reservation did grow, we have reports of overgrazing as early as 1883. While it was not a uniformly good time economically, in general Navajos fared far better than many other Native Americans in the final decades of the nineteenth century. They had relied less on hunting before Fort Sumner, and they could go back to farming, herding, and weaving. If hunting and gathering decreased and raiding all but vanished, livestock played the central role in the Navajos' new economy. Rugs and blankets, wool, hides, and meat all found a market by the 1870s. Not all Navajos shared equally in what prosperity was to be had. While kin ties and social pressure assured some redistribution of the wealth, some families held a great many sheep and others none at all.[21]

Traders proved vital to this nascent reservation economy. They provided a market for Navajo weaving, silverwork, and wool and in return added to the Navajos' store of material items from Anglo industrial society. More than any other single figure during these years the trader was the intermediary between the Navajo and the outside world. He helped to shape Navajo weaving and silversmithing designs and encourage their evolution into art forms that became justifiably famous. The Englishman Thomas Keam (after whom Keams Canyon takes its name) and Lorenzo Hubbell emerged as two of the early leading figures. Hubbell began his trading empire at Ganado—the post remains preserved as a classic example of the old-time trading post and is operated by the National Park Service— and for many years operated a chain of posts within a fifty-mile radius of Ganado. Other men left their mark around the turn of the century: Richard and John Wetherill, Sam Day, John B. Moore, David and William Babbitt, and the various sons of Joseph Lehi Foutz. Given their central role in economic affairs, the traders became influential in many spheres, including the political. They tried and often succeeded in coloring both local Navajo and U.S. government views and politics, to their advantage and to what they deemed the best interests of the Diné.[22]

Others besides the traders entered the Navajo land. Under the division of Indian country in the Grant administration, the Presbyterians claimed the Navajos. The Presbyterians came to use Ganado as a base for their operations, building in addition to a church a school and a hospital. The school was to enroll many Navajos who would play prominent roles in tribal affairs, and the hospital would be the initial purveyor of Anglo medicine to the Diné. This would be, of course, a long-term process; instant acceptance could not be expected. In addition to the Presbyterians, the Catholics also entered the picture. The Franciscans began a school at St. Michaels in 1902, four years after the founding of a mission at that site. Like Ganado Mission, St. Michaels Indian School played an important role in the education of Navajo leaders. The Franciscans also emerged in the twentieth century as leading scholars of Navajo life, and St. Michaels, under the direction of Father Berard Haile, became a center for the study of the Navajo language and culture. Off the reservation, finally, other denominations sponsored missions and schools. Two of the most important were located in Farmington, New Mexico, and just outside Gallup, New Mexico. The Methodists actually started their mission at Hogback, twenty miles west of Farmington in 1891, but moved it to its current location in 1912. The Christian Reformed Church started its mission at a site it named Rehoboth in 1898, with a school commencing five years later.[23]

Schooling also was instituted by the federal government under the terms of the Treaty of 1868. "In order to insure the civilization of the Indians entering into this treaty, the necessity of education is admitted," the treaty stated; therefore, the Navajos pledged "to compel their children, male and female, between the ages of six and sixteen to attend school." The United States agreed to provide "a house" and "a teacher competent to teach the elementary branches of an English education" for every thirty children who could be induced or compelled to attend. The Bureau of Indian Affairs hired Charity Gaston in 1869 as the first teacher on the Navajo reservation. She attempted in vain to teach in a room reserved for her at the agency headquarters at Fort Defiance. Few Navajo children attended through the 1870s. The bureau built a school at Fort Defiance in the early 1880s, but attendance remained minimal and sporadic. A few Navajos also attended government schools built at Keams Canyon in 1887 and Tohatchi in 1895, as well as off-reservation boarding schools constructed in Albuquerque (1886), Santa Fe (1890), and Phoenix (1891) and the better-known and distant boarding schools to the east, such as Carlisle in Pennsylvania and Haskell in Kansas.[24]

Most Navajos who went to these schools had to be coerced into scholarship. Police brought children to school and brought them back when they ran away. A Navajo agent in 1884 had concluded on the basis of his experience at the Fort Defiance school that "the children would come and stay a day or two, get some clothes, and then run away back to their hogans, but few of them attended regularly, consequently the school done [sic] but little good." One Navajo storyteller said that the Navajo of those days would not send the bright children to school, only the orphans and slaves: "They placed in school the children over whom no one would weep in case something might happen to them." Rather than the best and the brightest, "those who don't have homes and just roam around, the ones who are not well-mannered—they are the ones who are put in school." Parents and other relatives needed the children

MAP 1 Boundaries of the Navajo Reservation

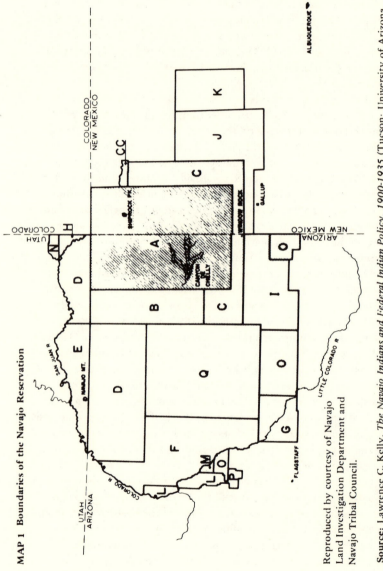

Reproduced by courtesy of Navajo Land Investigation Department and Navajo Tribal Council.

Source: Lawrence C. Kelly, *The Navajo Indians and Federal Indian Policy, 1900-1935* (Tucson: University of Arizona Press, 1968), pp. 18-19. Copyright 1968. Used by permission.

A   Original treaty reservation. June 1, 1868.

B   Executive-order addition. October 29, 1878.

C   Executive-order addition. January 6, 1880.

CC   Originally a part of "C"; withdrawn from the reservation by executive order, May 17, 1884; restored by executive order, April 24, 1886.

D   Executive-order addition. May 17, 1884.

E   The Paiute Strip. Originally a part of "D"; in 1892 restored to the public domain; in 1908 withdrawn for the use of various Indians; restored to public domain in 1922; in 1929 again withdrawn from entry; 1933 transferred permanently to the Navajo reservation.

F   Executive-order addition. January 8, 1900.

G   Executive-order addition. November 14, 1901.

H   Executive-order addition. March 10, 1905.

I   Executive-order addition. November 9, 1907.

J   Executive-order addition. November 9, 1907; restored to public domain by executive order of January 16, 1911.

K   Executive-order addition. November 9, 1907; restored to public domain by executive order of December 30, 1908.

L   Tusayan Forest addition. Act of May 23, 1930.

M   Executive-order addition. May 7, 1917.

N   Act of March 1, 1933.

O   Arizona Boundary. Act of June 14, 1934.

P   Tusayan Forest addition. Act of February 21, 1933.

Q   Hopi reservation. Executive-order reservation created on December 16, 1882.

to herd the livestock and help out at home. They resisted, sometimes politely and sometimes violently. In 1892, Black Horse spearheaded a revolt aimed against Agent Shipley, who had gone out to gather children for school, and the military had to be called out to calm things down.[25]

This resistance should have been expected. The traders, who were agents of acculturation, had something to offer the Navajo people, and their presence generally was tolerated in Navajo country. But the school-teachers provided little of utility. In this era of Americanization, the government schools clearly were trying to remake the character of their pupils. "Their training should be so thorough," wrote Commissioner of Indian Affairs Thomas J. Morgan in 1889, "and their characters so formed that they will not be dragged down by the heathenish life of the camp." Only English, "the language of the greatest, most powerful and enterprising nationalities beneath the sun," could be employed. There never seemed to be enough food. Homesickness reigned. School personnel punished children for speaking Navajo and for running away. So the Navajos fought back. After all, the parents and elders knew what one needed to know about how to make a living, how the world came to be, and how one should live in the world.[26]

That world seemed an increasingly good one in the years that followed the Navajos' return from Fort Sumner. The Navajo land base increased impressively (see map 1). From 1878 to 1886, five additions were made to the 1868 reservation, expanding it almost to its present western, northern, and eastern boundaries. Included in these additions was the executive order addition of December 16, 1882, jointly occupied by the Navajos and the Hopis. The Navajo reservation almost quadrupled in this period. Four smaller additions were made, primarily in the west, from 1900 to 1907; other additions were made in New Mexico in 1913 and in the west in 1918. Except for three final additions made in the 1930s, this would essentially conclude the expansion of the reservation. Not surprisingly, once Arizona and New Mexico joined the union in 1912, land additions became extremely hard to achieve.[27] This generalized picture omits various maneuverings that occurred even prior to 1912, which reveal the increasing interest in any land available in the American Southwest. But by and large the Navajos emerged reasonably well in this period, and, again, compared to most of their Native American counterparts, they were very fortunate indeed. Still, as the twentieth century dawned, the Navajos unmistakably were moving into a period when their heretofore privileged isolation was threatened. The expanding Anglo American presence in the southwest would have an effect not only on limiting demographic expansion but on internal questions involving the use of existing land and the consequent need for some kind of formal tribal governmental structure. In the previous decades the Navajos had grown accustomed to an expanding area for grazing their animals. With that avenue no longer open to them, pressure on existing grazing land obviously would increase. The Navajo population would not decline, nor would the size of their herds. At the same time, one hears of warnings about overgrazing. For example, in 1894, Agent Edwin H. Plummer wrote to the commissioner of Indian affairs: "The Reservation is not large enough or in condition to support the herds of the Navajos." Rather than reduce the livestock numbers, more land should be given to the Navajos, Plummer counseled. In 1914 Father Anselm Weber of St. Michaels Mission echoed Plummer: "The Navajo Reservation is stocked heavier and its range is more overgrazed and run down than the range in other parts of these States (New Mexico and Arizona)."[28]

By this time, a pattern of livestock grazing had developed which William Adams later characterized as being for many areas "not so much overdeveloped as it is inefficient. Areas close to camps and water sources are virtually denuded, while substantial tracts, particularly at higher elevations, are very inconsistently utilized." As Adams noted, stock corralled during the night and some hours of the day "eat voraciously and unselectively during their hours of liberty." The use of young children for herding contributed to the sedentary nature of Navajo pastoralism.[29] By the late 1920s the issue of overgrazing and soil erosion would at last begin to culminate in the policy of livestock reduction.

In the first decade of the twentieth century, too, we see the initial steps taken in the direction of more systematic administration of the reservation. The federal government created five Navajo agencies, with a corresponding agency headquarters in each: Southern (Fort Defiance), Northern (San Juan, then Shiprock), Western (Tuba City), a Western extension (Leupp), and Eastern or Pueblo Bonito (Crownpoint). The Hopi Agency also included some Navajos within its jurisdiction. If anything, as Young notes, this development retarded the evolution of tribal government for it increased bureau activity and segmented the reservation. It did, however, bring some tangible, if imposed, form of administration to different locations within Navajo country and therefore perhaps reduced the isolation of this administration.[30]

The government also instituted a Court of Indian Offenses at this time. Three Navajos served as judges, with a government agent supervising them. According to one agent, his role was a formality; the decisions made needed no correction. How much Navajos utilized this system marked at least to some extent a turning away from exclusive adjudication of internal disputes by local Navajo headmen. Indian police established after the return from the Bosque could bring offenders to this tribunal. The Navajos in this sphere, again, were having to deal with changing times and changing methods that affected the tribe as a whole.[31]

At the local level the Bureau of Indian Affairs encouraged the development of a new political organization: the chapter. To some extent, as Howard Gorman later put it, the chapter "built upon what was already present." Navajos would have to meet occasionally, and local headmen would direct consideration of important issues. In 1927 Superintendent John G. Hunter of the Leupp Agency established community councils to discuss the people's concerns and inform Indian Service employees of them. According to Gorman, "Hunter's ideas added some new things, such as Robert's Rules of Order, majority voting, elected officials, and the office of chairman." In addition to confronting matters of dispute or debate, chapters were to plan public works projects. In 1928, Hunter moved to head the Southern Agency and again instituted the chapter system in this region.[32] The idea soon spread throughout the reservation. While they have enjoyed periods of greater and lesser vitality, the chapters remain a viable and important political unit today. As will be discussed later they have become more fully integrated in the overall Navajo political system.

The West as a whole was changing. Los Angeles and other urban areas were growing remarkably. New mineral discoveries in many Western sites heightened national interest in the region. Early in the century Americans began to gaze anew at reservations heretofore deemed worthless—as they would again in the 1970s, in the heyday of the energy crisis and the insistence that America depend more upon its own mineral resources, many of them located on Indian lands—and the Navajo reservation would be no exception.

An 1891 law allowed for the exploitation of minerals on Indian land but only where Indians had bought and paid for the land. Executive order and treaty reservations did not fall under this provision. Various congressional representatives attempted to alter this situation through legislation introduced in the first two decades of the century. Arizona and New Mexico representatives led the movement. Arizona's Senator Henry F. Ashurst and Congressman Carl Hayden along with New Mexico Senator Albert B. Fall introduced bills designed to open reservations in general to mineral leasing. The eventual Metalliferous Minerals Leasing Act of 1918 permitted the secretary of the interior to lease Indian lands in order to mine "deposits of gold, silver, copper and other valuable metalliferous minerals." Indians would be entitled to at least a 5 percent royalty, but that money could be apportioned by Congress as it deemed proper.[33]

With the passage of the Metalliferous Minerals Leasing Act, all of the Navajo reservation could be exploited by mining interests. The original treaty portion already had been subjected to the searches of various prospectors, much to the displeasure of Navajos in the area. Under the terms of the 1891 law a council for the Navajos was supposed to sanction the prospecting. An occasional group of Navajos in the affected San Juan or Shiprock area would be summoned to rubber stamp an agreement authorizing such exploration. It became increasingly apparent that a more formal and more general council of all Navajos would be needed as outside interest in Navajo minerals intensified. The Metalliferous Minerals Leasing Act and the subsequent General Leasing Act of 1920 had opened the door. While the acts curbed prospecting and development, nonetheless by the 1920s prospectors and oil company officials were besieging the Navajos and the Bureau of Indian Affairs.[34]

Thus Navajos attended a series of Shiprock area councils to consider the possibility of oil leases in the early 1920s. While called by the federal government and at the behest of the persistent oil concerns, Navajos in attendance took the sessions seriously. Diné representatives rejected all proposed leases at the first and third council. The Midwest Refining Company, controlled by the Standard Oil Company of Indiana, did succeed in gaining a 4,800-acre lease for oil and gas in August 1922, but the Navajos rejected the overtures of all major companies in the fourth meeting and gave a lease instead to W. E. Lockhard and J. J. Hall for the Producers and Refiners Corporation. Superintendant Evan W. Estep of the San Juan Agency signed the leases for the government. The royalties designated were "for the use and benefit of the Indians of said reservation" and not, significantly, solely for the Navajos residing in the agency. Navajos of the Southern Agency approved three similar leases of 4,800 acres each approximately at the same time northern Navajos agreed to the Midwest lease.[35]

The government then turned to a business council to expedite the leasing process. In January 1922, a three-man council, probably appointed by the secretary of the interior, came into existence, whereby Chee Dodge, Charlie Mitchell, and Dugal Chee BeKiss could sign for the Navajo tribe as a whole. They promptly met in Fort Defiance on January 26, 1922, and, with Superintendent Peter Paquette of the Southern Agency supervising, they authorized three leases "on behalf of the Navajo Indian Tribe." But a business council hardly could be construed as a legislative body truly representative of the entire tribe. With the Midwest lease quickly yielding a large quantity of oil, pressures redoubled for such a tribal council to be created.[36]

As described by Robert W. Young, Charles Burke soon acted to bring the council into existence. The commissioner of Indian affairs issued *Regulations Relating to the Navajo Tribe of Indians* on January 27, 1923, in order "to promote better administration of the affairs of the Navajo Tribe of Indians in conformity to law and particularly as to matters in which the Navajo Tribe at large is concerned, such as oil, gas, coal, and other mineral deposits, tribal timber, and development of underground water supply for stock purposes." The regulations recognized the need for a "continuing body to be known and recognized as the Navajo Tribal Council with which administrative officers of the Government may directly deal in all matters affecting the Tribe." The council would consist of a chairman and a vice chairman plus a delegate and alternate from each agency. The council would elect its chairman at its first meeting. It would meet when the newly created commissioner of the Navajo tribe so desired, and the council could not convene without the commissioner in attendance. The secretary of the interior could remove any council member for cause. It almost goes without saying that the regulations, in sum, represented the government's overt desire to have a council that would suit the needs of the government.[37]

Three months later Acting Commissioner of Indian Affairs E. B. Meritt produced a revised set of regulations. He apportioned the council on the basis of population, giving greater representation to the Northern, South-ern, and Western districts. Merit specified the term of office—four years—for the chairman and vice chairman, though he neglected to say how long the delegates might serve. Meritt also wrote to Secretary of the Interior Hubert Work (who had recently replaced the infamous Albert Fall) suggest-ing that the secretary be empowered "where there is no lease" to "grant a least for any number of acres not exceeding 4,800, without advertise-ment." The Tribal Council, he added, should be able to consider any leases and indicate whether they would be "willing to pass a resolution authorizing the Interior Department to lease the land under the plan out-lined." Work concurred.[38]

Thus the first Navajo Tribal Council would meet in Toadlena, New Mexico, on July 7, 1923. The key government official at the gathering was Herbert J. Hagerman, a New Mexican appointed in January by Fall as "Special Commissioner to Negotiate with Indians." Hagerman met with the Navajo superintendents in March in Albuquerque after he had toured the reservation and become acquainted with various issues. Hagerman's findings prompted him to write to Washington urging several changes in Burke's original regulations. Meritt, as we have seen, agreed. Hagerman, now simply "Commissioner to the Navajo Indians," went on to schedule the various election dates through Navajo country.[39]

The first council meeting would fulfill the purpose for which it had been called. The members approved a resolution giving the commissioner to the Navajo tribe the power "to sign on behalf of the Navajo Indians all oil and gas mining leases which may be granted covering tracts on the treaty part of the Reservation." As Kelly has noted, the approval by the Navajos should not be viewed as mere obeisance to Washington's dictates. Hagerman stressed to them that only if the Navajos cooperated with the government would they have any chance of the government gaining them badly needed new lands. As we shall see, the government utilized this carrot-and-stick approach a number of times with the Navajos. But despite the promises held forth, the amount of land added proved minimal—at least from the Navajo perspective.[40]

Jacob Morgan and Chee Dodge, both of whom would figure prominently in Navajo politics for many years to come, were both very much in evidence at the first council session. Morgan, the conservative Christian graduate of Hampton Institute, represented the Shiprock region. He protested in vain against the recent dismissal of Shiprock Agency Superintendent

Evan Estep, a man not held in the highest regard by Dodge. Morgan likely advocated then the kind of position he would later adopt, one highly critical of the government and very protective of regional interests. The day belonged to Dodge, but Morgan's would come in the tumultuous years of livestock reduction.[41]

The "progressive" Morgan had to yield to the older, more "traditional" Dodge, for even before this time Dodge had firmly established himself as the unofficial leader of the tribe. Dodge's peers named him chairman of the first council, acknowledging his years of experience and storehouse of knowledge about the changing times in which the Navajos found themselves. He was then a man in his early sixties, a product of more traditional roots, though a less fundamentalist Christian than Morgan; Dodge was a Catholic. Born four years before the Long Walk, he had gone to Fort Sumner and returned near Fort Defiance. He learned English as a boy, worked as a clerk, and by the age of twenty had been named by the government as official interpreter for the Navajos. Gradually he built up his land holdings. He also served as mediator in some difficult situations, including the incident between Black Horse and Agent Shipley at Round Rock, where Chee was part owner of a trading post. By the time he gained the chairmanship he was a wealthy man and experienced in the ways of the Navajo and Anglo world. Not surprisingly, he looked to the well-being of all Navajos, even given his strong ties to the southern Navajo country. Surely his elevation to the chairmanship must have pleased him greatly, both for the honor to himself and as a symbol of the coming together of his people.[42]

In a sense, then, the meeting of the council marked the end of one era and the beginning of another. The formal establishment of the council meant the official end of Navajo isolation. Even if the council at first could be little more than a paper organization, now that it had been formed there could be no turning back. At first the people in the more distant reaches of Navajo country could afford not to pay much attention to this fledgling enterprise. Yet sooner than they could have known the council and The People as a whole would be swept unwillingly into the tumultuous period of livestock reduction. Then the council, to say nothing of Washington, would take on a new significance.

THE STOCK
REDUCTION ERA

2

Sam Ahkeah, Navajo Tribal Council chairman from 1946 to 1954, termed livestock reduction "the most devastating experience in Navaho history since the imprisonment at Fort Sumner from 1864 to 1868."[1] Years later, Navajo Community College Press would issue a volume of Navajo remembrances of the era and entitle it "Navajo Livestock Reduction: A National Disgrace." Thus, to this day it is a period remembered with bitterness and anger among the Navajos. While the stock reduction program took place, it affected everything on the reservation: not only the daily lives of the people, but the tribal government and the other programs of the federal government as well.

While today one inevitably associates the stock reduction scheme with one man, Commissioner of Indian Affairs John Collier, in fact the idea for the reduction preceded the commissioner. As has been noted, observers on the Navajo scene remarked upon the problems of soil erosion and overgrazing even before the turn of the century. During the 1920s the Indian Service made important additions to Navajo water sources as it began to attack the problem of overgrazing. It finished 166 deep wells with pump, windmill, and storage tanks, developed 269 springs, and built twenty-one reservoirs. Nonetheless, the program was but a minimal effort in the context of an overwhelming need. Voluntary stock reduction marked this period, along with attempts at sheep scabies eradication, elimination of wild horses, and controlled breeding of Navajo sheep with supposedly superior stock. Scabies eradication proved by far the most successful of the three programs. Horse reduction and selective breeding encountered widespread resistance.[2]

23

There is a striking similarity between the tactics employed by the Indian Service during the 1920s and the strategies tried again during the Collier years. Attempts at stock reduction carried out in later years were of course more widespread, and the results more seriously threatened Navajo social and cultural integrity. Yet, for example, the efforts of the Indian Service to reduce the number of horses in the pre-Collier days involved the same carrot-and-stick approach used again in the 1930s; Navajos learned that if they were to have any chance at all of gaining additional grazing land through the approval of Congress of boundary extensions, they would have to go along with the horse reduction plan. Not surprisingly, Navajos living in the area most in need of additional land proved the most cooperative.[3]

The Indian Service began serious consideration of stock reduction in 1928. At a meeting in Leupp, Arizona, Assistant Commissioner of Indian Affairs E. B. Meritt told assembled Navajo councilmen about "eventually limiting the number of sheep, horse, goats and cattle for any Indian so that benefits of the range may be more equitably distributed among all Navajo Indians." That year Meritt and District Superintendent Chester E. Faris broached the matter of grazing practices to the Tribal Council. These gentlemen suggested that any Navajo who owned more than 1,000 sheep should pay a fee of fifteen cents per head for each sheep over that total. But Councilman Little Silversmith noted in return that his 2,000 sheep were not really his: they had to be divided among his wife, seven children, and three grandchildren. He actually had about 300 head of sheep; would he have to pay a tax? Meritt said he would not. Little Silversmith and subsequent speakers remarked that if such were the case the entire tribe would be exempt. The council wound up on a seven-to-five vote placing a tax of eleven cents a head on sheep in excess of 1,000 per family.[4]

Such a solution was no solution at all and the council knew it. Even given the innocuous nature of the resolution, the seven-to-five vote is indicative of the division that would appear later when strong measures were proposed. Given the Navajo approach to consensus decision making, a close council vote was and is a rarity. Almost always, a vote is not taken until some degree of agreement is felt among most members. Meritt and Faris must have worked hard to get a vote taken at all; federal government officials would have to work harder in the years to come.

In 1930 Indian Service forester William Zeh surveyed Navajo range conditions. He reported that the Navajo range was "deteriorating rather steadily and more rapidly each year." According to Zeh, the "primary factor contributing to the overgrazed condition" was "unquestionably the lack of sufficient water for stock." Sheep and goats would travel long distances for water and in the process trample the range. Zeh also believed "the type of stock used and the composition of their herds" contributed to overgrazing. Rodent control, elimination of excess horses, and development of water, Zeh predicted, would "produce results in a comparative short time"; over the long run, old Navajos should be educated in new methods of handling stock, and young Navajos should be instructed in principles of range management and stockraising.[5]

Clearly something had to be done. By 1931 the idea of serious reduction of the Navajo livestock had gained currency among top Indian Service administrators of the Navajo region. These administrators met on February 19-20, 1931, under the direction of Special Commissioner Hagerman. William S. Post, the new direction of irrigation for the Indian Service, stated bluntly at the conference's outset that the Navajos had three times the proper amount of sheep and additional water sources would not help. Perhaps some of the Navajo livestock could be relocated on other reservations. Hagerman praised Post's "very instructive ideas," which coordinated, he said, with Zeh's earlier report. Post contended that the Indian Service should not put in any more water holes until the Navajos modified their stockraising methods. Zeh, in attendance, was even more blunt. He argued that you "have to eliminate large numbers of stock or you will not get the range back in condition." Superintendent C. L. Walker of the Western Navajo jurisdiction added, "With the present number of sheep on the range, the range will grow worse. It can't stand still. A gradual reduction will just enable us to hold the range where it is. The thing to do is to have a big and sudden cut." Post expected there would be no problem in addition in resettling some of the Navajo elsewhere, such as on the Pima reservation. But, he queried at the end of the session, would there be "a reaction when they know they will have only half the number of animals as a matter of income?" The superintendents replied confidently the Navajos in their areas would see the necessity of carrying out such a program.[6]

Hearings conducted in Navajo country in April and May by a Senate subcommittee, however, did not reflect fully these predictions. The hearings explored the possibilities of adding to the Navajo land base, in addition to reviewing the general situation in the Navajo area. Some of the senators clearly did not approve of extending the Navajo boundary or thought it politically unlikely. Arizona Senators Ashurst and Hayden noted that Arizona had only 13 percent public land and had to resist extension of Indian reservations. Hayden said that if the Navajos were having trouble they "must do just like the white farmers have done in all the history of this country. When the farms will not support them they must move to town. They must engage in industry and they must learn other occupations." Senator Burton K. Wheeler of Montana stated it would "be very difficult, if not impossible, to get more land for these Indians." Therefore, he concluded, "the one thing they have to strive for is to improve the stock the Indians already have. All of the surplus scrub goats should be done away with; they should cut down the surplus horses they have."[7]

Off-reservation interests also responded sharply to the prospect of additional Navajo land. The president of the New Mexico Wool Growers Association, Floyd W. Lee, who ran a huge ranch in northwestern New Mexico near Navajo land, said the Navajos did not need more land. Rather they needed to fence the land they had, develop their water sources, and reduce their livestock:

We believe that this country can be made to produce twice what it is doing now. We do not believe that an increase of land is a cure for overgrazing or overstocking. . . . We believe it is being attacked from a wrong angle and should be attacked from a different viewpoint at this time.

Wheeler responded, "I agree with you; much more can be done if they would properly protect the flocks which they have rather than buy more land."[8]

The leaders of the New Mexico Wool Growers Association helped spearhead the successful move by New Mexicans in the 1930s to block additions to the Navajo land base within the state. The wool growers found "no fault with the policy of liberal treatment toward the Indian" and commended "the policy of extending substantial helpfulness toward self-support and industrial independence and prosperity of the Indians, but we object to the burden being imposed on our State taxpayers." Indian lands, they argued, "limited to an embarrassing extent the ability of the State to raise necessary revenue essential to the general purposes of Government." They thus viewed "as a menace to the future welfare of the State the extravagant disposal of the public lands for other than actual bonafide needed, beneficial productive use and settlement and recommend a cessation of such grants to Indians."[9]

Liberal reformer John Collier pursued the twin goals of Navajo live-stock reduction and Navajo land expansion. He succeeded partially with both but fully in neither. Collier and his cohorts vigorously advocated stock reduction. Some of the important reasons for their doing so had little to do with the Navajos' welfare and illustrate the declining insularity of Navajo society. For example, silt runoff from eroded Navajo soil reduced Boulder Dam's efficiency soon after its construction. South-westerners who would benefit from the dam had a stake in reducing or eliminating this complication. The Depression meant lower and lower prices for wool, goat meat, and mutton; Indian Service personnel be-lieved Navajos should depend less upon livestock in these troubled times. In the days of the Dust Bowl, federal employees looked to the checking of erosion in the Navajo area as a symbolic victory needed to impress the fruits of soil conservation upon the entire country. Thus the first United States Soil Conservation Service demonstration project was started at Mexican Springs on the Navajo reservation.[10]

Those like Collier who in fact valued Navajo culture and wished to have it endure looked to stock reduction as a means to preserve Navajo society. No one knew how long the Depression would last. The Navajos would have to make critical changes or they might not survive. Super-intendent E. R. Fryer believed, as did many in the Indian Service, "The future of the Navajo is in our hands. His very economy is dependent upon our successful solution of his land problems." And, Fryer concluded, in livestock reduction "we believe that we have found that solution."[11]

The Navajos did not buy the diagnosis for their predicament; nor could they have been ready for the program to be impressed upon them. Most Navajos simply did not see their situation as such a dire emergency. The lack of sufficient water and the inadequate acreage on the reservation caused erosion rather than overgrazing. In time, the Diné believed, nature would provide. Eli Gorman, for example, later would call John Collier a liar for "telling people that it was the over-grazing that caused the situation. He was lying because it was evident that the lack of rainfall had caused the bad condition."[12]

The Navajos were not accustomed to programs affecting people at the grass-roots level throughout the Navajo reservation. The Navajo tribal government and the federal government just did not disturb the daily pattern of life, and no program could have more basic cultural conse-quences than one providing that "the livestock load on the total range

should be cut in half without delay."[13] Most Navajos did not have large
herds and felt threatened for they did not feel they could spare any animals
at all. The People had grown up "in the midst of sheep herds"; stock reduction was self-destruction, likened graphically to cutting off one's
arms and legs and head. Not only would it be injurious economically,
it would cut at the heart of religious life. Good things do not come for
free. Sheep facilitated the entire ceremonial process; they were used to
pay the singers and feed the assembled people.[14]

So there would be resistance, widespread and unyielding. The attitudes
of prominent Indian Service officials did not hasten Navajo acceptance
of the new program. Fryer, for example, compared the difference in past
policies to the present with

an example in the raising of children. When formerly the parents placated
the children with a stick of candy when it cried, now the parents are
attempting to find the cause of the tears and to take such corrective measures as are necessary. . . . The youngster will not always understand a
dose of castor oil may sometimes be more efficacious than a stick of
candy.

A senior soil conservationist divided the opponents of stock reduction
into four groups: the wise guys, the ones who feared financial loss, the
mental cripples, and the enemies of the Navajo service. According to
W. G. McGinnies, there were "four different, distinct infirmities which
cause people to be opposed to stock reduction": "ignorance, blindness,
laziness and dishonesty." Convinced of the truth of their views and the
immediacy of the need to implement their policies, exorcists such as
Fryer and McGinnies saw opponents as possessed by a "stock reduction
complex." Their enemies were "creators of misunderstanding" and "im-
passioned demagogs" [sic] whose "irrational speeches" were "hidden
behind bombastic oratory as to appeal to the emotional and less intelli-
gent Indian."[15]

Because of the exigencies of the situation, as perceived by the government officials, the stock reduction program was implemented hastily
and without the kind of long-term educational efforts that would have
been necessary for the program to have any chance of success. Such an
effort was made but only in conjunction with the program and not pre-

ceding it. While it did encourage the development of a functional form of written Navajo, it did not reach all the people, and those it did reach it reached ineffectively. For the most part, Navajos simply did not accept the assumptions upon which stock reduction was based. The land would soon return to a more productive state. As Chischilly Yazzi would insist in 1936, "My land is not washed away. My land is all right." And no one could convince him to the contrary.[16]

If they did not agree that stock needed to be reduced, they were embittered as well by the way the program operated. Rather than reducing individual herds on a percentage basis, the initial version of stock reduction called for an across-the-board slashing of herds; large owners sacrificed their culls, but the small owners, who formed the vast majority, had the heart cut out of their meager holdings. This ill-advised operation, partially influenced by the political muscle of the wealthy Navajo stockmen, permanently crippled what finite chances the program had to succeed. Even Superintendent Fryer had to admit in 1937, "In all honesty the Navajos have every reason to fear and misunderstand land management. The previous adjustment program was certainly unfair to the smaller owners."[17]

Moreover, given the Depression economy, there was little market for livestock purchased by the government. Many of the stock simply were shot and left to rot on the ground; animals that were sold often brought only a dollar a head. This image, of seemingly purposeless slaughter of highly valued animals, became printed indelibly on the Navajo mind. One reads over and over again in the stories in *Navajo Livestock Reduction: A National Disgrace* of these butcherings and the anger and helplessness that accompanied them.[18]

John Collier quickly became (and still remains) the scapegoat for the stock reduction affair. At the end of the era, Hastin Nééz Kimble said, for example, "People place the blame entirely upon John Collier." One Navajo after another interviewed in recent years for the Doris Duke Oral History Project at the University of New Mexico expressed their strong feelings about the man who "took everything from the Navajo people." Ben Morris talked of riding all the way from near Crownpoint, New Mexico, to Tuba City, Arizona, to see Collier soon after he had taken over as commissioner. Morris was not impressed: "He was not a very handsome white man; he was kind of skinny, he was wearing black, he stepped out of a car like a big, black crow." At a later meeting in Crownpoint, police had to protect the commissioner; since Collier's mind could not be changed, the people said they were "going to beat him up and then they can produce their sheep."[19]

But even by 1936, Navajos had personalized Collier as the man to blame for their troubles. Navajos from the Northern Agency, home territory of Navajo political leader Jacob C. Morgan, flooded the 1936 congressional hearings on the proposed Navajo boundary extension in New Mexico with complaints about virtually every facet of the Collier program, and at the root of it all was stock reduction. The telegram sent from the councilmen and chapter officials at Shiprock said it all: "At present time we are in need, because we gave John Collier more than half of our sheep and all goats."[20]

What of those Navajos serving on the Tribal Council in Window Rock? How did they respond to livestock reduction? To what extent did they go along with it, and what kind of impact did stock reduction have on the tribal government? Thanks to such new studies as Donald Parman's *The Navajos and the New Deal* and Kenneth Philp's *John Collier's Crusade for Indian Reform*, we have both new perspectives on federal Indian policy as well as some insight into the Navajo response to that policy. Older studies, such as Spicer's "Sheepmen and Technicians" and the pertinent sections of Aberle's *Peyote Religion,* combined with Navajo historical sources and accounts help to complete the picture. While only a fairly brief summary is possible here, it is important to describe this era in some detail, for its effects reverberate to the present day.

Indeed, if the 1868 treaty reservation provided the foundation for the Navajo Nation, the livestock reduction era hastened the evolution of Navajo nationalism. The period represented the most serious disruption of Diné lives since the 1860s. The era estranged the tribe from the federal government. Relations between Washington and Window Rock would never be the same again. Not only did Collier's other programs suffer, but the Navajos began the long process of becoming a political unit. The tribal government mattered. The people could have boycotted it; they could have shunted it aside as nontraditional. Instead, most of them turned to it as a way of maintaining a separate, integral Navajo way of life. This is not to say that tribal council chairmen would be universally beloved or that council decisions would be always applauded, but the actions of the federal government, enforced and seemingly arbitrary, left the Navajos little choice. In paternalism's place, inevitably, would come the growth of the Navajo Nation.

Collier met promptly with the Navajo Tribal Council following his ascendancy to the commissionership. He was eager to achieve progress in the realm of the Navajo economy and had become convinced that live-stock reduction held the only answer. So in July 1933, at Fort Wingate, New Mexico, Collier introduced the issue of stock reduction. Noting the serious problems faced by the people and the land, he called a significant reduction of livestock absolutely essential. Again in October 1933 and March 1934, stock reduction headed up the council agenda. Under enormous pressure from Collier and other bureau officials, the council members agreed to institute and promote a reduction program on the reservation. By the 1934 session, however, they demanded relief for the families with small flocks, saying those with less than one hundred sheep or goats should be exempted from the scheme. Already, the initial, bungling attempts at reduction, featuring an across-the-board cut of Navajo stock holdings, had provoked an outcry.[21]

Given the massive unpopularity of livestock reduction, why would Navajo delegates go along with it under any circumstances? Spicer has argued that council members tended to be more acculturated, faced strong pressure from federal government officials, often became more convinced while in Window Rock of the need to reduce sheep, and had few real alternatives to stock reduction to consider. Younger delegates did play a vital role in the council. The Returned Students Association had sponsored candidates for the council and elected six of the seven they had backed, thus allowing them half the council seats, an impres-sively high percentage. The delegates as a whole were not a cross section of the Navajo populace. They also were split between "traditionalist" and "progressive" factions, as personified by Chee Dodge and J. C. Morgan, respectively, and by regional as opposed to national ties. But the more acculturated delegates tended to be the most critical of stock reduction and the most antagonistic toward Collier personally.[22]

As Philp has suggested, the Navajo response seems to boil down to two main points. First, they had very little choice; if they did not support stock reduction the government could impose it on them anyway. Second, if they did go along with it, albeit reluctantly, they stood to gain. And so, indeed, Collier told them. Given the difficult times—and the Navajos were willing to admit they were difficult—the federal government might help out with needed relief programs. More critically, from the Navajo vantage point, compliance with stock reduction meant the promise of additional land. If the council would support stock reduction, Collier guaranteed passage of a congressional bill extending the Navajo boundary in New Mexico.[23]

So, for example, the council voted unanimously on March 13, 1934, "that erosion and range control should be carried on as explained by the Commissioner and his staff; and further that stock reduction as explained by the Commissioner and his staff should take place." But they keyed this approval to two matters: "the understanding that the Council delegates will return to their people in order to explain the proposals so that the Navajo people may consider the matter" and "that it is imperative that the Boundary Bills be enacted at the earliest possible date." As the resolution so baldly reveals, the council members saw it as a tradeoff.

It was a tradeoff not to be realized. Navajos did gain some additional land in Arizona, but fierce opposition blocked the vitally important extensions in New Mexico. The Arizona Boundary Bill, passed by Congress and made law on June 14, 1934, contributed three parcels of land to the tribal estate. Most of the land was located along the southern boundary of the reservation and, given the steadily growing population which strained tribal resources, in itself represented a valuable acquisition. But the act served two other purposes. It strengthened the Navajo claim to the region that would become embroiled in the Navajo-Hopi land dispute, and, perhaps most significantly, the bill ensured that the land would be considered within the status of tribal trust. Much of the Navajo reservation in Arizona had been created through executive order. What the executive could create could be taken away, declared surplus, opened for non-Indian settlement. By limiting such potential withdrawal only to a specific act of Congress, the act therefore provided a stability for Navajo land in the state that it had heretofore not possessed.

New Mexico was another story. The 1931 congressional hearings had made clear that land additions in the state would be enormously difficult to achieve, Collier's promise notwithstanding. Newly appointed U.S. Senator Dennis Chavez took over the seat of the man who had defeated him the previous November, Bronson Cutting. Chavez believed Secretary of the Interior Ickes had backed his opponent in that election and wasted no time in getting back at "the old curmudgeon." Much to Collier's and Ickes's mutual consternation, Chavez strongly opposed the boundary extension proposal.

Chavez's opposition represented more than personal antagonism and support of the non-Indian ranchers in the land adjacent to Navajo country. Ickes contended in the 1936 hearings that many in New Mexico, from the governor and the land commissioner to local interests, favored the extension; only "a group of predatory interests that have no scruples at all about getting land or property from the Indians," Ickes charged, "and have been preying upon the Indians" and "want to continue to prey upon them" opposed the extension. But Chavez disagreed, claiming "the opposition to this bill in the State of New Mexico is universal." Not only did J. C. Morgan disapprove of the bill, he argued, but "the majority of the Navajos are not for the bill." He quoted resolutions passed by the Stock Growers Association, editorials from the Las Vegas *Daily Optic* in support of his view, claiming, as had Arizona representatives, that taxation was the key issue. As a newly minted, nonelected senator, Chavez knew what the proper political stance was on the issue. But, as one whose life had mirrored a Horatio Alger-like rise to prominence, Chavez surely differed philosophically with Collier's mystic vision of Indian life and the value of communalism. He disavowed the notion that any ethnic group should be entitled to special privileges and generally carried on a New Mexican political tradition not very sympathetic to Indian interests—as they so often conflicted with others in the state.[24]

The denial of the boundary extension in New Mexico not only marked "the worst blow the Navajo administration suffered in the New Deal," it also crystallized Navajo sentiment against Collier.[25] It was apparent by the time of the 1936 hearings that the boundary bill could not be passed; by 1938 Collier had dropped any pretense of continuing his fight for its approval. As they had earlier with the worst abuses on stock reduction, the Navajos angrily mounted a counteroffensive. Much as either man would have hated to admit it, John Collier made Jacob Morgan's political career. The articulate, combative Morgan probably would have become a central figure anyway in Navajo affairs, but the emergence of Collier and his programs assured his rise.

Morgan proved himself a force to be reckoned with in the Navajo vote on incorporating the tribal government under a constitution as provided for in the provisions of the Wheeler-Howard Act of 1934. Morgan's men clashed with men loyal to Chee Dodge, who supported the idea, not only in deference to the wishes of federal officials but also because it symbolized his own long-held dream of a unified Navajo government. The council split right down factional lines, with the seven Dodge men carrying the moment in favor of the constitution and the five Morgan delegates abstaining.[26] But in 1935 Morgan and his associates had their revenge. Under the provisions of the act, the Navajos as a people had to vote on whether or not to accept it. Morgan led the fight against it with help from such men as Howard Gorman. Gorman, who went on to play a leading role in Navajo political affairs to the 1970s and who later would part political company with Morgan, responded bitterly to Collier's personal last minute appearances in favor of the X, or yes, vote:

This thing, the thing you said that will make us strong, what do you mean by it? We have been told that not once but many times this same thing, and all it is is a bunch of lies. What are we to get in return for placing our votes in favor of this mark? What will become of the old treaties? You have not fulfilled those treaties yet . . . you're wasting your time coming here and talking to us.

Gorman was right. The X vote won over the 0 vote in four of the six jurisdictions, but the 0 vote gained the day. Voters in Leupp voted 701 to 74 in favor, and Keams Canyon voters also gave a clear stamp of approval by a 1,322 to 63 count. Western Navajo voters also said yes, 872 to 472, as did those from Chee Dodge country, the Southern, 3,276 to 2,291. But the eastern Navajos opposed it, 1,904 to 1,115 and the Shiprock area decisively defeated it, 2,773 to 536. The landslide vote from this area thus ensured defeat of the measure.[27] Animosity toward stock reduction obviously proved central to the results, but without Morgan's campaign the measure probably would have eked out a margin at the polls. In his annual report, Collier grudgingly noted the rejection:

Certain interests disseminated the most fantastic fictions in their effort to induce the 43,500 Navajos to reject the help the federal Government was offering them. . . . With the aid of these fictions, and by falsely connecting the referendum on the Reorganization Act with the unpopular but necessary stock reduction program, the propagandists succeeded.[28]

The war continued in the next year. Morgan and his followers employed the 1936 hearings to cast aspersions on every element of the Collier program. One matter that particularly incensed Morgan was the federal government's seeming change of rules after the game had been started on an irrigated farming project in Morgan's home area. According to Superintendent Fryer, the Fruitland project had first been proposed at a Senate hearing in Shiprock in 1931, with work beginning in 1933. At that time officials concluded "that about 20 acres was the smallest acreage that could be considered as a subsistence farm." Navajo families counting on 20 acres of irrigated farmland suddenly were confronted by a decision by Collier reducing the acreage per family to 10 acres. Collier applauded the move to encourage productive farming among the Navajo as part of the overall program to reduce dependence upon livestock. But he decided that 10 acres would open this agricultural avenue to twice as many families. The hearings provided Morgan with a perfect opportunity to embarrass Collier about this alteration.[29]

In Window Rock on August 19, 1936, Morgan confronted Collier and Fryer about Fruitland. When Collier implied that the 20 acre arrangement had never been considered final, Morgan quickly responded with various letters demonstrating that "a promise was made of 20 acres." Fryer admitted that Indians in the Fruitland area certainly had been led to believe they would get 20 acres, and it was only in April of 1936 that the decision had been made that 20 acres represented a commerical rather than subsistence level of farming and therefore a reduction to 10 acres would be advisable. Again, while we may sympathize, as Parman does for example, with the decision to reduce the acreage, politically if not morally the reduction could not be justified. From the Navajo viewpoint, Collier had not kept his word.[30]

Morgan also appeared at the center of the debate over tribal government reorganization. The movement came to a head in November 1936, when the council voted to try to reorganize itself. The delegates voted to approve a Collier-drafted resolution in favor of reorganization. Collier had been working for the goal of a representative, centralized Navajo government together with a more consolidated approach to federal services to the Navajo. He had achieved the latter goal in July 1935, when the six separate Navajo jurisdictions had been eliminated and one central agency headquarters was established at Window Rock. Predictably, this alteration met with mixed reviews from the Navajos, many of whom preferred closer contact with a government official in charge of their region.

Morgan and other Navajos fought consolidation for it meant less independence for their area. Morgan had argued earlier that, while the Navajos were one tribe, so "is the United States, so are the people in Mexico. They are one tribe, but they have several States, their own governors and officers, and so on, and I think they are doing all right."[31]

The council resolution of November 1936 created an executive committee empowered to call a constitutional convention. The committee members traveled all over the reservation talking to local groups and attempting to determine the "real" leaders of the tribe. Chee Dodge, Dashe Clash Cheschillege, and Henry Taliman were among the more prominent Navajos who transversed the high Navajo country in the midst of winter. Father Berard Haile of St. Michaels Mission accompanied the group and played an active role in their effort. Haile had lived on the reservation for over thirty years and was becoming the foremost non-Navajo authority on Navajo life. Fluent in the Navajo language, Haile had studied traditional Navajo culture sympathetically and with a genuine affection for traditional cultural patterns. He also was an old friend of Chee Dodge, the venerable Navajo leader who had been converted to Catholicism years before. Haile's affiliation with the committee was a damning association in the eyes of the Morgan group, who not only disliked Chee Dodge but tended toward anti-Catholicism in their personal views.[32]

The executive committee gathered the names of 250 local leaders and chose seventy of them for the constitutional assembly. It stipulated that the assembly could name itself the "Tribal Council." In March the committee set the meeting of the assembly for April 6, 1937. Morgan and his followers opposed the dissolution of the old council and argued that the tribe should vote on whether that body should have been dissolved. Perhaps fearing that Morgan would emerge victorious in an election, the federal government supported the idea that the assembly could become the de facto council without the benefit of an election.[33]

The assembly convened under these contested circumstances on April 9, 1937. The delegates predictably allocated the opening day for an extended discussion of the evils of stock reduction. Then they proceeded to name the assembly the new Tribal Council. The assembly attempted to move forward on the matter for which it ostensibly had been called to deliberate: a Navajo constitution. After Henry Taliman had been chosen chairman of the nominating committee, a resolution to permit Taliman to appoint a constitution writing committee prompted Morgan and his supporters to depart from the proceedings. Taliman retaliated by naming Morgan to head the committee. Morgan declined the honor. Attorney Thomas Dodge, a former council chairman and the son of Chee Dodge, then led the committee that drafted the constitution. By October 25, 1937, the group had forwarded the constitution and by-laws to Collier.[34]

Collier eventually rejected the constitution, probably in part because of the document itself, but he also may have been influenced by internal developments on the reservation during the tumultuous year of 1937. The suggested constitution actually mirrored those being put together by tribes under the Indian Reorganization Act. It established council membership, term of office, apportionment, and office holders and described the council's powers: control over use of tribal lands and property, authority over traders, acquisition of legal counsel, power to tax tribal members, and delineation of a code of laws. It also stipulated that "any resolution or ordinance adopted by the Navajo Council or Executive Committee shall take effect as soon as approved by the Secretary of the Interior," which took it a step beyond the IRA constitutions.[35] Collier was advised that if the tribe could vote on the constitution it might feel as though the council could have more power than it in fact could possess. Could enough people within the tribe understand a complex legal document? Given his experience with the tribal referendum on the IRA and the current chaotic situation on the reservation, Collier concluded that:

Any constitution submitted to the Navajo should be realistic . . . that it should consider the inchoate amorphous condition of the Navajo and that, in view of this inchoate condition, it should be short, concise, simple, limited to a few objectives and conferring initially a limited number of powers.

Collier likely still smarted from the IRA defeat and did not want to give the Navajos what they were not entitled to given their rejection of the IRA. He also knew all too well about various confrontations that had occurred on the reservation in conjunction with the ongoing stock reduction effort and Morgan's political organizing. Thus the commissioner turned down the constitution and finally substituted a simplified set of rules, which Secretary Ickes eventually issued in July 1938.[36]

While no substitution for a constitution, the rules did provide some significant changes in the form and method of Navajo tribal government. Seventy-four delegates from election communities replaced the twelve representatives. The commissioner of Indian affairs could no longer choose new delegates if the people would not elect them when a vacancy occurred. A secret ballot was instituted. The chairman could be reelected but once. The runner-up for the chairmanship became the vice chairman, as in the old system of designating the vice president in the United States and with similar liabilities, as the first election promptly showed.[37]

As expected, Jacob Morgan won the 1937 election for chairman, and Howard Gorman of Ganado, recipient of the second highest vote total, became vice chairman. At one time the two had gotten along tolerably well; they were, after all, as Gorman put it, "men of religion." But by 1938 Morgan and Gorman were as far apart as Jefferson and Burr. Gorman had incurred the wrath of Morgan and his supporters by serving as an interpreter for the Bureau of Indian Affairs. At the first session of the newly elected council, Morgan refused to recognize Gorman when the latter wished to speak, claiming Gorman was not a delegate and not entitled to the floor. Morgan's friend Charlie Damon stood up then and said, "Howard, the President's assistant in Washington usually takes a day off to go fishing during the conference; so why don't you go fishing? That's all you're good for." Gorman maintained years later that he still "managed to say a few words."[38]

While Morgan could indulge himself at Gorman's expense, in general his triumph proved more apparent than real. The new tribal council had become a reality and would not be undone. The central agency at Window Rock would remain. Collier and Fryer, for the time being, remained in their positions. And stock reduction did take place. Morgan had been remarkably effective on the outside as a critic. Now installed in the chairman's office, he perhaps gained a new perspective—so Fryer would later believe—or at least became more willing to meet Fryer and others part way. In many ways Morgan was more influential before he became chairman, or at least he had found that the role of critic and gadfly suited him well. His inauguration, as Parman has remarked, marked "the apex of his career as a Navajo leader."[39]

By Morgan's inauguration in November 1938 some partial accommodation could be achieved. It could only be partial, though, for if Fryer was willing to admit past errors on the part of the government he hardly was going to abandon stock reduction entirely. As we shall see in the next chapter, stock reduction continued as a government program throughout most of the 1940s. Ironically, Morgan received some criticism at the end of the 1930s for being too cooperative with the federal government. His acquiescence in the matter of horse reduction, for example, earned him some wrath in certain quarters. But there really was no one to take his place on the outside. Some Navajos turned away from political agitation to religious readjustment, as the Native American Church gained many new adherents on the reservation. As Aberle has shown in his magnificent study, the trauma of stock reduction provided the impetus for many Navajos to look to a new way of coping with their changed circumstances because established ways of accomodation were not proving wholly satisfactory. The Native American Church, or "peyote cult" as it sometimes has been termed, predictably met with severe criticism on the part of many traditional Navajo leaders as well as many Christian Navajos. Here Morgan, the Christian Reformed missionary worker, won a victory, as the Navajo Tribal Council passed a resolution drafted by Morgan outlawing the use of peyote on the reservation. But the council would have passed a resolution against the Native American Church regardless of Morgan's presence; only one council member, Hola Tso of Sawmill, himself a church member, defended the new faith. The resolution passed in June 1940 marked the beginning of official persecution of practicing Native American Church members but hardly the end of the church. The use of peyote continued as a political issue on the reservation until the contemporary period.[40]

EDUCATION

The beginnings of educational reform within the Bureau of Indian Affairs had begun with the publication of the Meriam Report in 1928. This study, called for by Secretary of the Interior Hubert Work and carried out by the Brookings Institute, castigated the bureau's educational program. The boarding schools came under direct attack as ineffective, costly, and damaging to the pupils. When Collier took over as commissioner, the stage had been set for a significant revision of the school program on the Navajo reservation.

Yet few could have expected the dramatic changes Collier attempted to fashion in the Navajo schools in such a short period of time. The pendulum swung rapidly toward an emphasis on a day school system. Designed to aid the preservation of Navajo culture, the day schools also served as centers for community education, including instruction in soil conservation and other matters relating to the livestock reduction program.

In January 1935, six day schools existed in the Navajo reservation area, but that autumn thirty-nine new day schools opened; eleven additional day schools built before the close of the decade completed a new Navajo educational network. John P. Harrington, Robert W. Young, and William Morgan (the last a recent graduate of the Charles Burke Indian School at Fort Wingate, New Mexico) from the Bureau of Indian Affairs developed a Navajo alphabet for use in the BIA Navajo literacy program. By 1940, bilingual readers had become available to Navajo children. At Fort Wingate, Stella Young and Nonabah Bryan worked together to encourage a renaissance in the use of native dyes in Navajo weaving. Navajo history and culture were to be encouraged, not discouraged. In short, the era saw a dramatic reversal of bureau educational philosophy.

The program represented in part a commitment to the progressive education movement. The first two Bureau directors of Indian education, W. Carson Ryan and Willard Beatty, also succeeded each other as presidents of the Progressive Education Association. Ryan had served on the commission that wrote the Meriam Report and served as head of BIA education from 1930 to 1936; Beatty held the post from 1936 until well after the Collier years. Neither Ryan nor Beatty had had experience in Indian schools or working with Indians. There is not much evidence for Ryan's strong concern for Native American cultures, and Beatty vacillated on the matter. Collier emerges as the central force behind Navajo educational change.[41]

Collier, in fact, not only believed in Indianizing Indian education, he had strong inclinations toward deschooling. He thought "all education" should "start from and end in the community group." "Indeed," he wrote in 1934, "if hopes are fulfilled there will be no formal schooling of the cloistrated [sic] or standardized order." Day schools would encourage Navajo culture as well as local parental participation and eventual control: "Indian schools should primarily be designed to discover Indian life and to discover to that Indian life its own unrealized needs and opportunities."[42]

Severe difficulties, however, were present from the beginnings of the new day school program and ultimately spelled defeat for the effort.

Teachers found themselves in extraordinarily isolated surroundings. Most of the teachers were single Anglo women who found life in their removed setting lonely and difficult; most did not stay long at their locations. Moreover, they were not prepared for what they were supposed to do. Not only could they not speak Navajo, they usually knew little about Navajo life and customs. Most did not remain long enough to learn enough to help them or to begin to be accepted by the community they were charged to serve. They certainly were not equipped to assist with instruction in land use management and the like.

Moreover, of course, the Navajo day school effort was launched in the midst of the socioeconomic disaster of stock reduction. That nearly meant defeat by definition because most Navajos applied a guilt-by-association principle to any facet of the Collier program. This is not to imply that Navajos entirely avoided the day school facilities. Beatty waxed enthusiastic at the 1936 hearings, for example, about the use being given to day school facilities by adult Navajos.[43] But they hardly attracted the numbers Collier assuredly envisioned.

Finally, many Navajos questioned the day schools as too great a departure from the form of schooling they had come to identify as education. Even at the boarding schools, such as Fort Wingate, they worried over alterations that might deprive them of the kind of education they assumed white children were receiving. When my grandfather, Paul Schmitt, attempted to institute a competency-based approach to school completion at Fort Wingate, he encountered the opposition of "traditionally minded school people" and "the conservative thinking Navajo themselves, who are rather inclined to believe that the subjects, classes and methods of older schools were best and that any departure from the beaten path is educational heresy."[44]

Given all of these problems, the schools had less impact on Navajo life than they might have had in less troubled times. Despite the tremendous opposition of such tribal leaders as Morgan and some of the more conservative missionaries, who were accustomed to having the Navajo educational field left largely to themselves, the educational program in retrospect clearly seems a worthwhile experiment. The Navajo experience in World War II would demonstrate vividly the need for greater exposure to formal schooling.[45] While the postwar era would witness a return to the emphasis on boarding schools, in the latter part of the 1960s the Navajos themselves would lead a movement toward greater Navajo control of Navajo education. Boarding schools would come under attack again, and many of Collier's ideas would be unearthed once more. This time, however, it would be a movement from within rather than without, and the chances for success would be greater. Nonetheless, Collier would be owed an intellectual debt that few Navajos of the contemporary era would remember, let alone acknowledge.

HEALTH CARE

The Meriam Report also scored the record of the Indian Service in Indian health. The Navajo reservation was no exception to the health problems afflicting Indians nationally. Trachoma and tuberculosis plagued the Navajos, and other diseases proved prevalent as well. Given the scattered locations of Navajo dwellings, the poor or nonexistent roads, the limited medical facilities, the shortage of trained medical personnel, and Navajo attitudes about Anglo medicine, it clearly would be difficult to make significant inroads in Navajo health care.

Just as Navajos and Anglos disagreed about Navajo educational philosophy and policy because of culturally determined values and perspectives, so, too, Navajos and Anglos differed over health care because of contrasting ideas about health and healing. In considering the cross-cultural problems involved in bringing the benefits of Anglo medicine to Navajos, one must realize the essential place of health—or more properly, harmony—within the Navajo life and the correspondingly high place Navajo singers or medicine men occupy within Navajo society. In the 1930s, the purveyors and recipients of Anglo medical care saw it as attempting to replace traditional Navajo forms of curing. Thus the institutionalization of Western European health care would be a long-term process lasting well beyond the confines of the 1930s.

The Navajos believed that the Holy People had instructed them to live within the four sacred mountains and had taught them the rituals by which they could maintain a harmonious relationship within themselves. Navajo religion, thus, was more than theology. Navajo religious ceremonies were to heal, and those who led the ceremonies, the singers, were individuals who united theology, law, and medicine.[46] One must consider the beliefs that form the foundation to the Navajo response to illness to appreciate why Navajos consulted a Navajo diagnostician first rather than an Anglo physician for the path to follow to ensure a cure.

A Navajo diagnostician, because of his or her gifts, would tell a person what caused the illness and what should be done to cure it. The cause for illness could be as immediate as a recent evil thought or as removed as contact years ago with a snake. The patient would be referred to one or a combination of specialists who would provide relief. As we shall see, in more recent times one might even be referred to an Anglo doctor, but in the 1930s this would have been highly unlikely.

The Navajo procedure for diagnosing illness and effecting its cure thus differed sharply from typical Anglo medical procedure. The differences tell us something about why Anglo medical aid was valued less highly by Navajos. Navajo diagnosticians told the patient what troubled him or her and why. From the Navajo viewpoint, Anglo physicians or nurses asked too many questions in taking a case history, asked the questions in a foreign language, and asked some questions that were none of their business. Anglo doctors offered symptomatic relief but not the total balance with the world that only the correct ceremony would bring. Anglo doctors provided services essentially free of charge. The Navajo singers' worth determined the price he would be paid; payment was deemed essential to the efficacy of the healing process.[47]

Other formidable obstacles made the Navajos slow to accept and use Anglo medical assistance. They found the atmosphere of the hospital alien and oppressive. Navajos frequently did not understand the purposes of the thermometer, for example, or the taking of a pulse, or the fact that isolation was necessary when one had tuberculosis. They did not believe the white man's idea about germs. They resented the physical examination being done by a stranger, and they were particularly anxious about being near where someone had died. This fear created a circular problem. Because preventive assistance was still in its initial phases among Navajos, the Diné who did come for medical attention did so often when critically ill. Thus medical staff frequently could do little and the patients died. The hospital then became known as the place to go to die or the place where one died.[48] Anglo medical personnel, of course, arrived ignorant of the land and the people. They did not speak Navajo, and they generally lived apart from the people. They often had less than positive images of Navajo singers and their Navajo patients. Accustomed to receiving the gratitude of patients who accepted their services eagerly and unquestioningly, Anglo doctors and nurses suddenly found themselves less understood and their services less appreciated. Many of the early doctors on the Navajo reservation were missionary physicians who staffed such hospitals as Rehoboth, just off the reservation near Gallup, or Sage Memorial Hospital, part of the Presbyterian missionary complex at Ganado. They believed fervently in assimilation and saw little value in traditional ways, in healing or elsewhere. The sign in front of the Ganado Mission read: "Tradition is the Enemy of Progress." Thus a medical missionary such as Dr. Richard H. Pousma of Rehoboth Hospital, run by the Christian Reformed Church, would lash out at Navajo ceremonies where, he believed, diseases were transmitted from one to another: "I think people who encourage the Indians in that work are idiotic, exceedingly stupid, and ignorant of conditions among the Indians."[49]

The Indian Service ran nine hospitals in the Navajo reservation area, at Chinle, Tuba City, Leupp, and Fort Defiance in Arizona, and Shiprock, Crownpoint, Tohatchi, Fort Wingate, and Toadlena in New Mexico. These tended to be poorly equipped and inadequately staffed. Collier hoped to improve Navajo medical facilities, increase the quality and quantity of Indian Service personnel, and, of course, make some progress in fighting such diseases as tuberculosis and trachoma. As in the field of education, the commissioner's hopes could only be partially realized.[50]

Some progress was made. Doctors achieved a major victory in the treatment of trachoma. New research had uncovered a better treatment, with sulfanilamide, for trachoma patients, and by the end of the decade widespread suffering among Navajos from that disease had definitely been reduced. In addition, the Indian Service opened a new central hospital at Fort Defiance in June of 1938. It served a vital need, providing the kind of facilities that had not existed before on the reservation, with the exception of Sage Memorial. Moreover, Dr. W. W. Peter, director of medical care for the Navajos, had singer Pete Price on hand at the inauguration of the hospital to perform a blessingway ceremony.[51] Symbolically at least, this ceremony marked the beginnings of slowly improving relations and understandings between the old ways and the new. With better physicians gradually being attracted to the Navajo area and the start of better communication between practitioners of Anglo and Navajo medicine, one could be hopeful by the late 1930s that better days would lie ahead. But it would be a very long-term proposition, one that even in the 1970s would still be fraught with difficulties.

Controversies over stock reduction, education, health care, and the Native American Church soon were overshadowed by the outbreak of

World War II. The war effectively curtailed many aspects of the Collier program on the Navajo reservation; the day schools, for example, were dealt a death blow. The war also evoked a new era for the Diné. For most of them it would be their first real association with the outside world, and that contact encouraged new perspectives and new values, which in turn would help usher in the modern period of Navajo life. Stock reduction would come to an end soon after the war's conclusion, but the Navajos would quickly face a host of new questions about their land and their future.

THE WAR AND AFTERWARD: GROWTH AND CHANGE IN THE 1940s AND 1950s

3

World War II changed Navajo life forever. In both small and large ways, the Diné found themselves in new situations—confronting new people, dealing with new problems, accepting new challenges, and in general becoming more a part of the world that surrounded their reservation. From the fabled Navajo Codetalkers to those who left home to find work in war-related industries, to all who remained but later heard, shared, and wondered about the wartime experiences, the war represented nothing less than a major turning point in Navajo history. Their world and the American world could never be the same.

Over three decades have passed since the conclusion of the war, but the Navajo Codetalkers in particular and Navajo servicemen who fought in the war in general remain honored men in Navajo society. The Codetalkers symbolized not only Navajo but American Indian commitment to the American war effort. Though the United States may have been a place where their rights often were denied—under state laws few Navajos could vote, for example, when the conflict erupted—they rallied in impressive numbers to defend it. Like other Americans, they had a variety of motives, but, as one put it:

I guess we decided to go to war and protect our people from other hardships . . . I would think, "I'm doing this for my people." I believed what we did was right, and it was worth it. We protected the many American people, also the unborn children, which would be the generation to come.[1]

They did not necessarily know precisely what kind of an ordeal lay ahead. Not only the danger of battle awaited them. Most of the Navajo servicemen had never been far from home, and the war represented their initial encounter with both foreign lands and American society.

Navajo service is particularly associated with the Pacific campaign, but nearly a year and a half before Pearl Harbor the Tribal Council passed a resolution recognizing "the crisis now facing the world in the threat of foreign invasion and the destruction of the great liberties and benefits which we enjoy on the reservation." The resolution noted that "there exists no purer concentration of Americanism than among the First Americans" and concluded "that the Navajo Indians stand ready as they did in 1918 to aid and defend our Government and its institutions against all subversive and armed conflict."[2] Navajos served in Europe, and some were captured eventually and became prisoners of war. Dan S. Benally, for example, became a German prisoner toward the end of the European campaign and "suffered from everything that I did over there. It was similar to an elderly man telling a story about the twins who visited their father, the Sun. I suffered from starvation and poverty."[3]

But it would be in the Pacific theater that the Navajo would carve out a special niche in the history of the war. Philip Johnston, son of a missionary who had worked for many years on the reservation, concocted the notion of utilizing the complex Navajo language as the heart of a code. Johnston was working in the Los Angeles area when the war began and took his idea to officers at Camp Elliott located outside of San Diego. By April of 1942, Marine Corps personnel had traveled to Navajo country to recruit volunteers for what would become the 382nd Platoon. The first twenty-nine men came from boarding schools at Fort Defiance, Fort Wingate, and Shiprock. Eventually 450 men would be recruited, and only thirty did not make it through the training program.[4]

Cozy Stanley Brown, one of the original Codetalkers, recalled the formulation of the code: "We named the airplanes 'dive bombers' for ginitsoh (sparrow hawk), because the sparrowhawk is like an airplane— it charges downward at a very fast pace. We called the enemy ana'i, just like the old saying of the Navajos."[5] The code proved impenetrable to the Japanese. It was used extensively in the Pacific campaign, and the Navajo Codetalkers emerged as well-publicized heroes in the aftermath of the conflict. Many of its members have gone on to become prominent members of the Navajo social and political community, including the two men elected in 1970 as chairman and vice chairman of the Navajo Nation: Peter MacDonald and Wilson Skeet. Today the Codetalkers still hold reunions, march in such events as the Rose Parade, and relive those memorable days of more than a generation ago.

The Navajo contribution to the war effort did not end with men fighting in Europe and the Pacific. Many others served, including Navajo women in the service and men and women who migrated off the reservation to employment in war-related industries. At least 500 Navajos, for example, worked at the Navajo Ordnance Depot in Bellemont, Arizona, just west of Flagstaff. Perhaps 10,000 Navajos gained employment during the war. They picked cotton in Texas and lettuce in Arizona. They toiled in the sugar beet fields in Colorado and Utah. Many worked for the railroads. Not all would return to the reservation once the war had been concluded.[6]

The war clearly brought both benefits and problems to the Navajos. It provided an invaluable experience for many in terms of pride and a feeling of accomplishment. For many others it brought the first wage-earning job. Many were freed to seek new careers and discover more of the world in which they lived. Financially, the war meant new sources of income for many families and a prosperity unknown during the 1930s. It is easy, however, to overemphasize the degree to which the war economy marked a departure from the Navajo pattern. Robert A. Young has documented recently in his dissertation that "there was strong market integration through the institution of the trading post" by the time war came and that many Navajos had in fact been employed in the 1930s through "temporary employment created by school and road construction, water supply and erosion control projects and by jobs at the local trading posts." In part because of the ravages of stock reduction, most families "were dependent upon income from multiple sources rather than just one particular sector"; wage employment, herding, and crop cultivation were all important. Nonetheless Young concludes that "World War II provided job opportunities on a scale never seen before by Navajos." With 3,600 Navajos in the service and 10,000 to 12,000 employed in industry, over half of the Navajo population nineteen years or older was gainfully employed.[7]

But there were liabilities one associates with the war years. Many Navajos who wished to serve in the armed forces could not do so because of physical ailments or limited knowledge of the English language. Others confronted discrimination as they left the reservation. Others had trouble

with alcoholism. Many Navajos had their hopes raised by employment
during the war years and returned home to an economy that had little
place for their training experience or their aspirations. The states of
Arizona and New Mexico discouraged them from voting. Stockraising
disappeared as an alternative for the families that had forfeited their
grazing permits by their departure during wartime.[8] By 1947 new reports
reverberated around the country echoing a plea for assistance; hunger was
widespread once more. What could be done?

The response by the Navajos and by state and federal governments
comprised a variety of programs that would alter the face of the reservation and the situation faced by the people living within and near its
boundaries. These included programs in education and economic development, highlighted by the Navajo-Hopi Long Range Rehabilitation program.
The departure of John Collier from the commissionership of Indian affairs
assured a departure from previous practices on the part of the Bureau of
Indian Affairs. Creation of the Indian Claims Commission by Congress in
turn encouraged the tribe to acquire legal counsel. All of these developments helped to transform Navajo life by the end of the 1950s.

In 1946 Republicans won control of Congress, bringing with them a
rise in the "termination" philosophy, always at least latent in U.S. Indian
policy but temporarily thwarted during the Collier years. The budget-
conscious Republicans predictably feared that too many federal dollars
were being lavished on the Indians. Senator Arthur Watkins of Utah would
lead the crusade to "free" the Indian from governmental control and in
the process, of course, free the government from undue expenditure.
Watkins and his cohorts found ready allies in the executive branch. With
Collier's departure, the Bureau of Indian Affairs lacked strong leadership
for several years. After several individuals came and went, Dillon Myer
was appointed to the top post in 1950. Myer had gained his experience
in minority affairs through administrative responsibility in the War Relocation Authority. In the eyes of his critics, he would bring the same
kind of sensitivity to his new job. Myer proved more than eager to cooperate with Congress. He laid the groundwork for the termination program of the Eisenhower years presided over by his successor, Gallup
banker Glenn Emmons. Congress, in turn, passed House Concurrent
Resolution No. 108 and Public Law No. 280 stressing the need to make
Native Americans "subject to the same laws and entitled to the same
privileges and responsibilities as are applicable to other citizens of the

United States, to end their status as wards of the United States, and to grant them all the rights and prerogatives pertaining to American citizenship."[9]

The Navajos thus faced a critical choice. If federal control were to be lessened and federal services reduced, then what party would take on new responsibilities? Could the Navajos turn to the states of Arizona, New Mexico, and Utah? Perhaps. But given the states' record it seemed an unlikely option since they had shown little interest in assisting the tribe in education, highway construction, and other areas. Public opinion in the region hardly favored cultural pluralism, let alone the maintenance of the kind of ethnic boundary endorsed by the Diné. If the states were to help, then with the aid would come the kind of regulations and demands definitely not desired.

So the Navajos chose to assume as much of the financial burden for reservation services as they could. They were blessed, of course, by the great oil finds which by the end of the 1950s had brought in huge sums to the tribal treasury. This development made it possible for the Navajo government to serve the people in a way almost completely different from before. This trend, inaugurated in this decade, would continue to the present, with a constant growth in the number of tribal employees, tribal programs, and tribal dollars being allotted.

It was thus an era of changing perspectives on the part of both the federal government and the Navajos. Navajo tribal officials symbolized this transition. Chee Dodge and Sam Ahkeah gained the chairmanship and vice chairmanship of the Tribal Council in 1942, replacing Jacob Morgan and Howard Gorman. They were reelected in 1946, but Dodge contracted pneumonia that winter and died on January 7, 1947. Ahkeah then assumed the chairmanship. Dodge was eighty-seven at the time of his death. He had been to Fort Sumner as a boy and by the time of stock reduction had already assumed the mantle of elder statesmen for the Navajo. Ahkeah might well be called the first of the modern Navajo chairmen.

Born in 1896, Sam Ahkeah grew up in the Rock Point area of Navajo country hearing the old stories and herding sheep. In 1904 a bureau official encouraged his family to send him to school. He went to Fort Lewis, Colorado, where the school superintendent altered the Navajo word for boy, "ashkii," to Ahkeah," with "Sam" thrown in for good measure as a first name. Ahkeah survived the remarkable new world re-

quired of him and by 1908 was attending the boarding school at Shiprock.
Eventually tuberculosis drove him from the school to ranch work near
Alamosa, Colorado, and then to work as a foreman of other Navajos
working in the Telluride mines. From there he built up his own ranch
fifteen miles north of Shiprock and worked for fourteen years as a foreman of a maintenance crew at Mesa Verde. The tumultuous stock reduction years ruined his ranching business and brought him to the fore in
Navajo politics as a thoughtful and serious critic of government policy.[10]

Ahkeah served as chairman for eight years, until Paul Jones gained the
post in the 1954 election. He presided over the impressive changes taking
place within Navajo country. The Tribal Council now met one hundred
days a year rather than four; the tribal chairman assumed new stature.
The new oil money would make possible an old hope of Ahkeah's: the
creation of a tribal college scholarship fund. In a time when Bureau of
Indian Affairs officials were preaching that the reservation represented
an economic dead end, Ahkeah saw the fund as a means of eventually
bringing to his people trained Navajo professionals, who were sorely
needed in this new age:

We must encourage our young people to go on in education. They are our
future. We need thousands of young lawyers, doctors, dentists, accountants,
nurses and secretaries. We need young men and women who have majored
in business administration. We don't want them to get an education and
take jobs off the reservation. We need them here! We older ones will do
all we can, with the little education we've had, but it is up to the young
ones of the tribe to step in, as we step out, and do a much better job than
we've done.[11]

Ahkeah spoke out for Navajo rights within the Southwest. In 1950,
for example, he and Howard Gorman presented the Secretary of the
Interior with the Navajo claim that the San Juan River belonged to the
Diné and that it was wrong to be "making plans to develop for various
purposes that water, without the knowledge of and without including
the Navajo people."[12] In addition, Ahkeah hired Norman Littell in 1947
as the tribe's first attorney. This proved to be a fundamental step in
Navajo political development.

Littell's selection came in the wake of the creation of the Indian Claims
Commission. Congress approved the Indian Claims Act in August of 1946.

The commission would allow Indians to sue the federal government for losses and other grievances sustained during the history of the United States. In order to press their claims effectively tribes would need the benefit of legal counsel. The act permitted tribes to obtain such counsel, and the Navajos wasted no time in doing so.[13]

The Tribal Council initially authorized a ten-year contract for Littell, but he would serve as general counsel for nearly twice that length of time. While assisted by other attorneys of his selection, Littell became *the* Navajo attorney and through his ability and personality became a vital figure in the everyday proceedings of Navajo government and the movement toward Navajo nationalism. Initially hired "to act as General Counsel for the Navajo Tribe, and to investigate, formulate and prosecute claims," Littell's influence spread throughout the workings of Navajo life.[14]

Like most attorneys hired for claims work by Native American tribes, Littell had had no previous experience in the field of Native American law. A Rhodes scholar, Littell graduated from Wabash College and took his law degree from the University of Washington Law School. After five years as an associate in the Seattle law firm of Bogle, Bogle and Gates, he became a partner in the Seattle firm of Evans, McLaren and Littell in 1934, and in the following year became an assistant solicitor in the Department of the Interior and special assistant to the U.S. attorney general. Littell had charge of the Lands Division, Department of Justice, from 1939 to 1944, with responsibility for condemnation and litigation of land and natural resource matters in the public domain. In 1944 he established his own practice in Washington, which he continued after assuming his duties as general counsel to the Navajo tribe.[15]

Littell's arrival on the Navajo reservation coincided with a critical juncture in Navajo history. The war, the resignation of John Collier at its end, the growth of congressional sentiment for terminating federal trust responsibilities for Native Americans, and the passage of such measures as the Navajo-Hopi Long Range Rehabilitation Act all combined to create a situation ideally suited to the energies and talents of a lawyer like Littell to help fashion great changes in Navajo government.

In reviewing his accomplishments during the first ten years of his tenure as legal counsel, Littell saw them as helping to achieve three goals:

to dissolve the mists of power which lay like a miasmic fog over the reservation . . . [to guide] the Navajo leaders squarely to the legal posi-

tions on which they are entitled to stand as free American citizens . . .
to throw a bridge across from an isolated society heretofore maintained
deliberately as a matter of erroneous policy, as a museum piece, to the
broader life of American citizens in the world beyond their reservation—
to which they are rightfully entitled and to which they are rapidly attain-
ing as full-fledged participants in the rich endowments of our free way
of life.[16]

Littell's attempt to promote Navajo involvement in American life found
a receptive audience from many Diné who had been involved in the
World War II effort and who took great pride in the Navajo contribution.
In fixing the blame for the contemporary Navajo situation squarely on
John Collier and what Littell termed the Collier cult, the new general
counsel also gained immediate disciples.

Littell's strong critique of Collier's philosophy and particularly the
stock reduction program helped the attorney to solidify his position of
strength as an advisor to the Navajo government. Not only did he label
stock reduction "a hot branding iron which seared the soul of the Navajo,"
he quickly succeeded in aiding the Navajos in bringing the program to a
formal conclusion.[17] At Littell's urgings, Secretary of the Interior Julius
Krug dispatched an assistant, Lee Muck, to review Navajo range resources.
While agreeing that "a serious state of maladjustment exists between the
Navajo people and their environment" and noting that "the grazing resources will not support the large human population," Muck recommended
that the reduction be halted because soil erosion had not been greatly
diminished and in any event the program could not proceed without the
active cooperation of the people concerned.[18]

Stock reduction on the Navajo reservation had occurred; the number
of livestock had sharply declined. From 1933 to 1947, goats were reduced from 173,000 to about 56,000, horses from about 44,000 to about
35,000, cattle from 21,000 to about 11,000, and sheep from 570,000
to about 358,600. Total wool production, on the other hand, had dipped
only slightly, from about 2,089,121 pounds in 1933, to 2,046,597
pounds in 1945-47. The average weight of wool per sheep thus had increased by 50 percent in the fifteen-year period, and the weight per lamb
had increased by about ten pounds.[19] If in that sense stock reduction had
succeeded, it also had critically damaged other vital programs in education, health care, and tribal government reform. It had driven a wedge be-

tween the tribe and the federal government and encouraged Navajo nationalism. The larger questions of range use, moreover, had not been resolved. Stock reduction did not change a majority of Navajo's attitudes about grazing limitations so that, even if they wanted to, future political candidates could not feel fully free to face the dilemma of soil erosion. Resistance on the part of Navajos to stock reduction thus blunted the ultimate goals of the entire soil conservation program on the reservation.

The bitterness engendered by stock reduction altered the Navajo attitude toward the Bureau of Indian Affairs and, in the words of one close observer of Navajo politics, "drove the Navajos into Littell's arms"; in the 1950s Littell became "the sparkplug of tribal political development."[20] He and his associates helped the Navajo government make the first significant regulations of trader activities on the reservation. Now traders had to pay 1.25 percent rental on gross business, had to sign a definite lease which could be terminated for cause, and had to account for their earnings on sales and on pawn transactions.[21] With Littell's aid the council obtained higher royalties from mineral leases.

In addition to gaining more funds for government operation, Littell's activities promoted far greater Navajo control over the operation itself and limited potential state intervention in tribal affairs. In the 1950s Littell and his associates won two significant cases, *Williams* v. *Lee,* which reserved the right for Navajos to regulate their own affairs free from state interference, and *Native American Church* v. *Navajo Tribal Council,* in which the Tenth Circuit Court of Appeals ruled the tribe could enforce its ban against the use of peyote since the tribe's status must be viewed as separate and higher than the states, the states being bound by the First Amendment to preserve freedom of religion.[22] The Navajo general counsel as well helped Sam Ahkeah achieve a long held goal: to permit the Navajo government to allocate its own funds. This major turning point came in conjunction with the passage of the Long Range Rehabilitation Act, whose benefits the Navajos could obtain without accepting state jurisdiction. Finally, Littell and his associates often drafted resolutions for council consideration, and the scope and sheer number of these resolutions expanded remarkably during his tenure. From 1947 to 1957, for example, the council passed 2,300 resolutions, where in the previous twenty-five years it had passed but 266.[23]

Passage of the Long Range Rehabilitation Act in 1950 came about in the wake of Navajo economic difficulties and termination sentiment within Congress. The Navajo economic situation was sufficiently desperate in the late 1940s, and the growth of feeling in Washington for a retreat from federal trust responsibilities for Indian affairs was accelerating; the act might bail out both sides. Had the congressmen and senators realized what the full ramifications of the act were, perhaps they might have had second thoughts. The bill coupled with such developments as the great oil strikes of the 1950s would not only reinvigorate the Navajo economy but would also bring about the birth of Navajo nationalism.

The postwar economic situation for the Navajos had deteriorated rapidly. The war had meant jobs within the service and in industrial jobs off the reservation. Now most of those jobs had disappeared. Fewer than 1,000 Navajos had full-time jobs, but 7,800 received some form of welfare.[24] A terrible blizzard in 1947-48 worsened an already difficult picture. Though the winter worked an enormous hardship on the people, it also generated national publicity about the Navajo condition. Donations poured in from all over the country. Public outcry encouraged Congress to ask Secretary Krug to propose a long-range program for the Navajos and the Hopis.

Krug's recommendations, "The Navajo . . . A Long Range Program for Navajo Rehabilitation," were released in March 1948. The Navajo-Hopi Long Range Rehabilitation Act (Public Law 81-474) passed Congress in 1950. It provided $88 million in the following decade. The act allocated major amounts for roads and school construction and over $1 million for six other areas: development of industrial and business enterprises, irrigation projects, hospital and health facilities, resettlement on the Colorado River irrigation project, revolving loan fund, and water projects (see Table 1).[25] The Colorado River resettlement indicated congressional representatives' belief that the Navajo reservation could only support a fraction of its population, yet the total sum provided for the Navajos would ultimately mean quite the opposite. A growing number of Navajo children would be able to attend school in their home areas, and Navajos would be able to stay within the boundaries in greater numbers than anticipated.

Road construction dramatically altered the face of the reservation during the decade. It significantly improved tourist and industrial development potential in addition to ameliorating the daily lives of the average Navajo. Before 1950, three main paved highways skirted the reservation: U.S. 66 to the south, U.S. 89 north from Flagstaff to the west, and U.S.

TABLE 1

Summary of Funds Allocated Through the Navajo-Hopi
Long Range Rehabilitation Act (P.L. 81-474)

Project	Amount Allocated
School construction	$24,997,295
Hospital and health facilities	4,750,000
Agency, institutional, and domestic water	1,356,670
Irrigation projects	6,616,775
Roads and trails	38,237,680*
Soil and moisture conservation, range improvement	7,097,175
Development of industrial and business enterprises	238,000
Resettlement on Colorado River irrigation project	3,449,750
Surveys and studies of timber, coal, and minerals	436,895
Off-reservation placement and relocation	194,600
Telephone and radio communications systems	250,000
Revolving loan fund	1,800,000
Housing and necessary facilities and equipment	26,300
Common service facilities	495,100
Total	89,946,240

*P.L. 81-474 was amended in 1958 to authorize an additional $20 million to complete Routes 1 and 3.
Source: Robert W. Young, ed., *The Navajo Yearbook*, vol. 8 (Window Rock, Ariz.: Bureau of Indian Affairs, 1961), p. 5.

666 from Gallup to Shiprock to the east. Most reservation roads should have been labeled trails; a good rainfall or snowfall promptly rendered them nearly or completely impassable. By the end of fiscal year 1961, 291 miles of bituminous-surfaced highway and 360 miles of gravel-surfaced road had been added. One could now drive on paved road west from Window Rock through Ganado to Tuba City and northeast from Tuba City nearly to Kayenta; one could go from Burnside's Corner, six miles west of Ganado, north through Chinle and almost to Round Rock, and east from Red Mesa—in Arizona, almost on the Utah border—through Teec Nos Pos to Shiprock (see map 2).[26]

The act also greatly alleviated the pressing need for adequate school facilities. All of the old bureau school facilities from the early part of the century had been closed by 1960, with the exception of Toadlena, Crownpoint, and Shiprock, and these closed down early in the 1960s as new buildings became ready. Enrollment in BIA reservation area boarding schools increased from 6,009 in 1950-51, to 9,850 in 1960-61, while

MAP 2   Navajo Road Construction, 1950

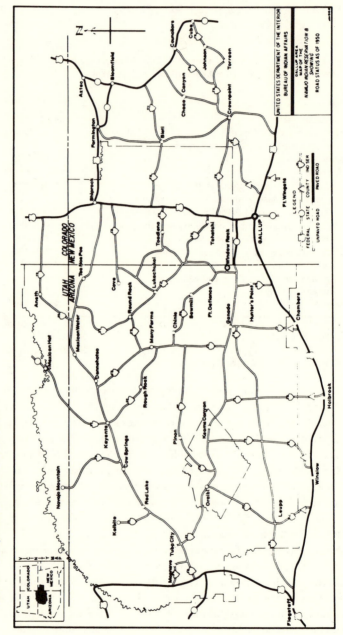

Navajo Road Construction, 1961

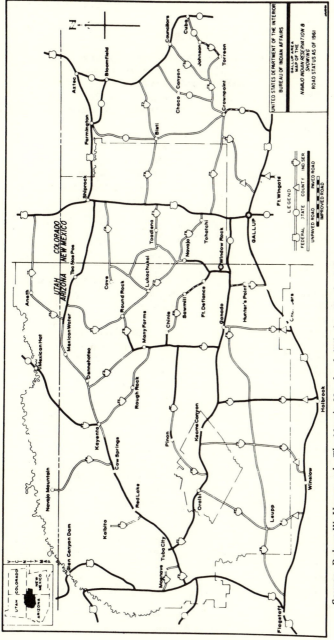

Source: Robert W. Young, ed., *The Navajo Yearbook* (Window Rock, Ariz.: Bureau of Indian Affairs, 1961), pp. 140-41.

TABLE 2

**New Schools and Additions to Existing Facilities
Made Possible Through the Navajo-Hopi Long
Range Rehabilitation Act**

School	*Enrollment (Expansion)*	
BOARDING SCHOOLS		
Chinle	800	
Cheechilgeetho	85	
Greasewood	180	(7 day students)
Hunters Point	90	(conversion to boarding)
Kaibeto	188	(8 day students)
Kayenta	450	
Kinlichee	256	
Leupp	600	
Nazlini	180	
Pine Springs	64	
Piñon	310	(enlargement, 20 day students)
Seba Dalkai	128	
Shiprock	1,000	
Standing Rock	64	
Steamboat	158	(conversion)
Thoreau	150	(conversion)
Teec Nos Pos	64	
Tuba City	600	
Wide Ruins	96	
Wingate	820	(expansion)
BOARDING DAY SCHOOLS		
Canoncito	64	boarding, 64 day students
Lukachukai	256,	(64 expansion)
Mariano Lake	90,	(30)
Crystal	145,	(20 conversion to boarding)
Round Rock	45,	(45)
Sanostee	140,	(60)
DAY SCHOOLS		
Beclabito	60	(expansion)
Blue Gap	30	
Borrego Pass	120	
Bread Springs	90	
Chilchinbeto	50	
Coalmine	25	
Cottonwood	75	
Cove	120	

TABLE 2—Continued

Del Muerto	25	
Dilcon	25	
Dinnebito Dam	50	
Hatch's Store	25	
Indian Wells	25	
Inscription House	50	
Jeddito	25	
Jones Ranch	90	
Kimbeto	50	
Ojo Encino	50	
Red Lake	110	(conversion)
Salina Springs	30	
Smoke Signal	30	
Tahchee	25	(expansion)
Whippoorwill	25	
White Cone	90	

Source: Robert W. Young, ed., *The Navajo Yearbook*, vol. 8 (Window Rock, Ariz.: Bureau of Indian Affairs, 1961), pp. 21-24.

BIA day school enrollment fell from 705 students at thirteen schools in 1950, to 545 students at eleven schools in 1960. An additional thirty-six trailer schools opened in the 1950s to serve slightly more than 1,000 students on a day basis in extremely isolated areas. Through an agreement concluded with various border town public school systems, the Bureau constructed boarding facilities for the use of Navajo high school students in Gallup, Albuquerque, Holbrook, Winslow, Flagstaff, Richfield, Snowflake, and Aztec. The BIA also enlarged existing dormitory facilities at Crownpoint, Huerfano, Magdalena, and Ramah.[27] The impact of the long-range act on Navajo education is summarized in Table 2.[28]

All of this construction of course would have had little importance were it not for the change in Navajo attitudes toward education in the aftermath of their wartime experiences. As more and more parents encouraged their children to attend school, a tremendous impetus developed to improve the capacities of existing institutions. In 1946 members of Navajo delegations in Washington, D.C., stressed the importance of education to the Navajo future and the critical shortage of schools. Tribal Chairman Chee Dodge said that the Diné sought the fulfillment of the 1868 treaty agreement providing a teacher for every thirty schoolchildren.

Dodge, Vice Chairman Sam Ahkeah, Scott Preston, Joe Duncan, and
Billy Norton all called for more boarding schools. Ahkeah claimed, "We
got used to the boarding schools just about the time they took them
away from us." Preston added that Navajos felt handicapped when war
came:

We started thinking it was something lacking that we should have and we
said it was education. If we were educated we would be doing the things
the other people were doing to win this war. That started us to think
about it. We have to change and we have to be educated.[29]

In other hearings before the House Committee on Indian Affairs that
spring, Dodge, Ahkeah, Frank Bradley, Sam Gorman, and Herbert Becenti
all emphasized increased educational opportunities as the key to improving
Navajo well-being.[30]

While educational opportunities increased, Navajo students still had to
depend to a great extent on off-reservation boarding high schools for
post-elementary education. A large percentage of the high school-age
students spoke little or no English, had little previous formal education,
and had not been away from home. Given the prevailing assumption of
the time, which some Navajos shared, that the Navajo Nation could not
provide a living for most of these people, a special program had to be
developed to meet the group's needs. Under the Special Five Year Navajo
Educational Program, Navajo students received instruction in English,
training in vocational skills, and preparation for the Anglo world they
would enter. The newly established Intermountain School in Brigham
City, Utah, enrolled the most Navajo students, but the other Bureau high
schools, such as Sherman, where the program began in 1946, Chemawa,
Chilocco, and Phoenix, also had large numbers of Navajo students. By
1950 enrollment in the program had reached 3,431 and increased to a
peak of 6,560 by 1957, though by this time the program had been modified as Navajo enrollees became more similar to other high school students
with the addition of more elementary education opportunities.[31] The
five-year program as well as the trailer school program became unnecessary
in the 1960s. Elements of the five-year program remained in some Bureau
schools, though, with a heavy emphasis on vocational training and a continuing assumption that Navajo students should assimilate into the general
American population.

While large numbers of Navajo high school students continued to leave the Navajo Nation for their high school education, passage of federal legislation in the 1950s made possible the creation of a public school network on the reservation which permitted an increasing percentage of Navajo high school students to attend on a day basis. The Johnson-O'Malley Act passed by Congress on April 16, 1934, had allowed the Secretary of the Interior to contract with the states for provision of educational and other social services, but this law had had relatively little impact within the Navajo Nation. Border town school systems had used the act to obtain additional funds—not always, in fact, to benefit Navajo students. But the states showed little interest in supporting a public school system for the Navajos, who did not pay state taxes. The passage of Public Law 874 and Public Law 815, however, removed this obstacle. Public Law 874 and Public Law 815 as initially considered supplied funds for "federally impacted" areas which maintained military installations. Amended in 1953 to assist school districts with Native American pupils, Public Law 874 yielded funds for operating expenses, and Public Law 815 contributed money for school construction.[32] Large public school facilities at Fort Defiance-Window Rock and Ganado became the first of many schools to be constructed and financed from this new source. Within the Navajo Nation between 1950 and 1960, public elementary schools were built as well at Chinle, Crownpoint, Kayenta, Shiprock, Tohatchi, and Tuba City, and public junior high schools or high schools built at Chinle, Shiprock, Tuba City, and Window Rock. Border communities, such as Gallup, Bloomfield, Cuba, Kirtland and Thoreau in New Mexico, and Page, Arizona, also received substantial assistance.[33]

The impact of this assistance to the public school system within the Navajo Nation is reflected in the steadily rising enrollment figures for the public schools. A comparison of the different school systems indicates the shift (see Table 3).[34] By 1960-61, the public school enrollment on the reservation nearly equalled that of the bureau reservation school system. The BIA reservation network did not include any schools at the secondary level, while its off-reservation system consisted almost entirely of boarding high schools. Two hundred ninety-two Navajos still attended Keams Canyon School on the Hopi reservation, while the remaining students who attended off-reservation institutions went to such schools as the all-Navajo Intermountain (1,994 students) and multitribal schools like Sherman (744 Navajo students), Chemawa (583), Albuquerque (558),

TABLE 3

Growth of Public School Attendance in
the Navajo Nation

Type of School	Actual Enrollment		
	1939	1952-53	1960-61
Bureau of Indian Affairs		9,659	15,759
Boarding total	2,401		
Reservation		7,342	10,001
Nonreservation		2,317	5,758
Day total	2,262	698	1,472
Trailer day		117	541
Public	98	2,385	10,564
Peripheral dorms			3,134
Mission and other	359	1,190	1,379

Source: Robert W. Young, ed., *The Navajo Yearbook*, vol. 8 (Window Rock, Ariz.:
Bureau of Indian Affairs, 1961), p. 65.

and Chilocco (479). While enrolling a steadily smaller percentage of the
Navajo school population, the mission schools provided an education for
many Navajos who would later assume leadership positions. The four
most important schools, which enrolled nearly two-thirds of the students
attending mission schools, all had been established around 1900: Navajo
Methodist Mission School (Farmington), Ganado (Presbyterian) Mission
School, St. Michaels (Catholic) Indian School, and Rehoboth (Christian
Reformed) Mission School (at Rehoboth, near Gallup).[35]

The 1950s, finally, witnessed the formal involvement in Navajo education by the Navajo national government. While tribal leaders had previously been interested in promoting more educational opportunities for
Diné, this decade marked the establishment, for example, of the Tribal
Council's education committee under the leadership of the youngest
council delegate, Dillon Platero of Canoncito. Platero helped organize
annual conferences on Navajo education and greater participation by
Navajos in their children's education. The Navajos, Howard Gorman said,
"began to realize that Navajo education belonged to the Navajo and not
to people in Washington or Phoenix or Santa Fe."[36]

The culmination of the trend toward greater Navajo involvement in
Navajo education may be seen in the joint educational policy statement
issued on August 29, 1961, by the Navajo Tribal Council and the BIA

and adopted by the council as the tribe's official educational policy. The "ultimate educational objective," according to the document, was "educational competency for all Navajo people so that they may participate in the local community, state and national life equally with other citizens." To achieve this basic aim, five policy objectives had to be reached: providing schooling for Navajo children through grade twelve on the Navajo Nation so that "all children may be near their parents," developing public schools for Navajo children at all grade levels, using existing off-reservation schools for Navajos as long as needed, providing educational opportunities for the mentally and physically handicapped, encouraging Navajo high school graduates to utilize fully further educational or training opportunities, and providing adult education. To implement the objective of having Navajo children attend school close to home, boarding schools should be used only for the remaining students unable to attend a public or bureau day school; these boarding schools should be gradually converted to day facilities as roads and transportation systems improved.[37]

Health care among the Navajo also evidenced dramatic change during the 1950s. Prior to that decade the Navajos were plagued by a number of significant health problems, including tuberculosis. In 1947, the tuberculosis rate for the Navajos was fourteen times the national average, yet only one tuberculosis sanitarium existed on the reservation. Pneumonia and diarrheal diseases also plagued the Diné, but five reservation area hospitals had closed since 1941, and of the six remaining five had only one physician. Of Navajo deaths, over half occurred among children under five years of age.[38]

Again, the long-range act had a clear effect. Funds now became available for construction of new hospitals at Shiprock and Gallup and new clinics at Chinle, Kayenta, and Tohatchi. In addition, when the Public Health Service assumed responsibility for Indian health care in 1955 (taking over from the Bureau of Indian Affairs), more physicians were assigned to the Navajo area. From sixteen physicians serving the Navajos in 1950, the federal doctors increased in number to twenty-three in 1955, and to forty-three in 1960. Additional physicians would be employed at the new Gallup PHS hospital when it opened in June 1961.[39] The inauguration of the doctor draft aided the increase but also altered the character of the physicians serving within PHS. Many of the new, younger physicians were trained in psychiatry and the social sciences, giving them greater insight into the Navajo perspective on health.[40]

In time, these physicians not only came to possess greater appreciation for and sensitivity to Navajo ways—there were of course exceptions—but also demonstrated in a relatively short period the power of their cures for tuberculosis and the other diseases that had afflicted the Navajo so seriously. Their work made an even greater impact upon the Navajo consciousness because of the untiring efforts in community education carried on by such tribal leaders as Annie Wauneka. By 1955, Scott Preston, both a singer and Navajo Tribal Council vice chairman, could say:

As I see it, all the diseases which hurt the Navajo people may be divided into three kinds. There are those diseases that we medicine men have given up on. We know that you white doctors have better cures than we do. One of the diseases of that sort is tuberculosis. Then there is sickness which comes from getting too close to where lightning struck. Right now there are probably some patients in this hospital who are sick from that illness and you doctors have no way of even finding out what is wrong with them—but we medicine men can, and we are able to cure such cases. A third type of illness is snake bite. You can cure that, and we Navajo also have our own medicines for that.[41]

Ever pragmatic, the Navajos gradually increased their patronage of Anglo medical facilities. In 1960 46 percent more Navajo women delivered their babies in hospitals than in 1955. The number of general patients admitted to hospitals increased during the same period from 6,458 to 10,300. Outpatient visits more than doubled, to a total of 138,210. The infant mortality rate dropped nearly 50 percent from 1954 to 1959, while the tuberculosis rate declined almost 60 percent between 1952 and 1960.[42]

In the Many Farms-Rough Rock area, a special medical demonstration project carried out by Cornell University, funded principally by PHS, and supported by the tribe, took place between 1955 and 1962. Not only did the program benefit the people from the immediate area, but its personnel were able "to define the proper concerns of a health program among the Navajo people and to attempt to develop practical means for the delivery of the necessary health services in a form acceptable to the people."[43] In their analysis of the Many Farms experiment, Adair and Deuschle concluded that "the respect the medical team showed towards the Navajo and their religion, with its central concern for the health of the individual, was of the utmost importance in the success of the project."[44] The medical team involved Navajos in administration of the clinic and frequent consultation with tribal leaders on policy matters, gave careful individual attention to each patient, and emphasized accurate medical interpretation in order to establish that respect. While established as a demonstration with a limited life span, the lessons from it would remain applicable to the delivery of health care services to the Diné.

The scope of Navajo governmental activity widened during the era. The degree of change in the responsibilities and ambitions of the Navajo Tribal Council may be ascertained in part through a comparison of salaries, length of time spent in the Navajo capital of Window Rock, and size of the tribal budget. In 1940 the chairman earned $200 per month; in 1950 he received $5,000 a year. In 1952 his salary increased to $7,800, and in 1956 a rising salary rate took effect, starting his salary at $9,000 and then increasing it to $10,000, $12,000, and $13,000 for the final year of his first term. A reelected chairman would receive $15,000 annually. The vice chairman's salary increased as well, to $7,000, with $1,000 added each additional year in office. By 1961, a reelected chairman received $20,000 during his seventh year of office, and a reelected vice chairman received $13,000. Delegates earned $3 a day and no salary, but by 1960 they earned $24 in salary and $16 per diem for each day the council convened.

The number of council meeting days increased, too, from about four to one hundred days annually.[45] The tribal budgets for fiscal years 1954 and 1957 showed a dramatic increase in available funds (see Table 4).[46] In the following fiscal year, 1958, the council approved a $12-million

TABLE 4

Navajo Tribal Budgets for Fiscal Years 1954 and 1957

Sector	1954	1957
Administration	$251,539	$373,698
Law and Order	189,546	586,762
Community Services	154,734	834,014
Resources	426,828	983,715
Carry Over	—	476,136
Total	$1,022,647	$3,254,325

Source: *Adahooniligii*, August-September 1953, June-July 1956.

budget, including $5 million for a college scholarship fund for Navajo students, $1 million for land purchases, and $0.5 million each for a new tribal office building, chapter house, and community center construction and for clothing for schoolchildren. The four categories listed in Table 4 all received sizable increases, with additional amounts devoted to industrial development and water resources development.[47]

Some Navajos refer to the 1950s as the period when the Navajo Nation was born. The era certainly represents a time when Navajo government leaders were engaged in broadening the scope and ambition of tribal government programs and reorganizing the structure of Navajo government in order to carry out these programs. The existence of newly found revenue encouraged these leaders to involve the tribal government in unprecedented fashion in a full-scale effort to improve the quality of Navajo life. Significant revision of the government's organization included revival of the chapter system and the expansion of the responsibilities of the legislative, executive, and judicial branches.

The Navajo Tribal Council instituted important reforms in 1950 and 1951. Election procedures were altered and a tribal court system established. The reservation had been parceled into four districts for elections, with a major community serving as headquarters within each. Nominating conventions held in these locations, while theoretically open to all, in fact limited participation. As the Navajo road system had yet to be adequately developed, many individuals could not attend the conventions and thus could not take part in selecting candidates for chairman and vice chairman of the council. The amendment permitted people of election communities to choose a delegate to these conventions. In addition, the Navajos started formal voter registration and inaugurated the use of paper ballots. Voters also elected court judges for the first time. Previously the Commissioner of Indian Affairs had appointed judges to be on the Court of Indian Offenses. While the council had confirmed these appointees, now the people participated more directly.

Because of its utilization of money generated by oil discoveries, the Navajo tribal government became a strong force throughout the Navajo Nation during the administration of Tribal Chairman Paul Jones. The Aneth, Utah, oil strike of 1956 yielded $34.5 million in royalties for the tribe's coffers in that year alone. Jones and the council delegates wisely resisted the temptation to divide up the money among the Navajo people, many of whom desperately needed additional financial assistance. Given the steadily growing population, per capita distribution of the wealth would have meant a mere $425 per person: a nice dividend, to be sure, but a transitory one. Instead, the Tribal Council members moved to establish the tribal scholarship fund, to build chapter houses, to finance other local improvements (including the expansion of electrical services through the newly created Navajo Tribal Utility Authority), to try to diversify the tribal economy, and to sponsor a massive tribal works program.[48] In general, the government representatives could set their sights realistically on a comprehensive reservation development program, one designed to provide both immediate relief and long-term benefits to Diné. Many of the projects and ideas initially funded with the oil money have continued and expanded with passing years to meet the needs of the growing Navajo Nation.

The chapter house building program helped to revive the whole chapter system, which had experienced a decline during the stock reduction era. In the first years of stock reduction, federal personnel used the chapters as a way of informing local Navajos about the new program. As reduction was put into effect more widely, the chapters emerged as centers of resistance to the program, and the Bureau of Indian Affairs withdrew support from them. However, chapter meetings had become stigmatized as places to consider stock reduction, and popular interest dwindled as well.[49] Lacking community support and an adequate meeting place, most chapters remained inactive until the early 1950s. By that time, chapter officials were petitioning the council for financial assistance and recognition.[50]

In June 1955, the council recognized that "for more than twenty years the chapter system on the Navajo reservation has met an urgent need of Navajo communities in providing a medium of the dissemination of information, a center for local planning and discussion, and a ready agency for the mediation of local disputes," and thus gave "official recognition and status to the local chapters . . . to continue the valuable functions . . . and to constitute a 'grass-roots' foundation for the Navajo Tribal Government." The tribal government in subsequent resolutions provided for the paying of chapter officers, the certification of individual chapters, and the requirement that the chapter meet at least once a month.[51]

Thanks to the oil revenue, the tribal government could well afford its massive building program of chapter houses in the late 1950s. Support for such a construction program had been voiced for some time in the council, but the lack of money had kept the council from embarking upon the project. More than half the chapters had a new chapter house constructed by 1962, and today nearly all chapters now meet in buildings that have modern conveniences and equipment and serve as general community centers. According to Williams, for many Navajos the chapter houses "stand as symbols of tribal unity, optimism, and prosperity."[52] Once formally blessed through a blessingway ceremony, or a portion thereof, the chapter house is ready to serve as intended, as a forum for community issues, problems, grievances, and development: for example, land use, livestock, water, tribal public works, and emergency relief programs. About one hundred chapters exist today, including four formed in the 1960s: Crownpoint (1965), Low Mountain (1967), Red Mesa (1967), and Rough Rock (1968).[53] Local people have continued also to build new chapter houses; the people of the Teesto (Arizona) chapter completed construction of their chapter house in July 1973.

As the chapter system revived at the local level, the Navajo government at the national level grew more complex as its tasks increased during the 1950s. Hearings in Washington in 1947 on the proposed Long Range Rehabilitation Act prompted the creation by the Tribal Council of a nine-person ad hoc committee to testify on the Navajos' behalf. During the next four years this committee received more responsibilities, until the newly elected Tribal Council of 1951 formed a nine-person committee representing the various reservation regions to become, in effect, the council's executive committee. This committee, which became known as the Advisory Committee, could meet when the full council was not in session and was empowered to act for the council. Shepardson has contended properly that the institutionalization of the Tribal Council "dates from the establishment of this continuing committee."[54]

The Navajo Tribal Council added many significant committees to oversee its growing responsibility. The Codification of Laws Committee reviewed, considered, revised, and approved codes of law for submission to the Advisory Committee and the council. The Education Committee expanded to include representatives from each subagency on the reservation. At the request of the council members, Tribal Chairman Jones appointed a permanent Committee on Elections to plan for the conducting of state and federal elections on the reservation. Jones also appointed a Judiciary Committee to determine the qualifications for Navajo judges and to screen potential candidates for these positions. A Utility Committee took charge of "general policy guidance in utility matters" and served as the council's watchdog on the Navajo Tribal Utility Authority.[55]

The executive branch equally reflected growing Navajo interest in administering Navajo affairs. The council chairman emerged as a Navajo national figure and a representative of the people to the Southwest and to the United States. Sam Ahkeah, chairman from 1947 until 1955, and Paul Jones, Chairman from 1955 to 1963, both helped to extend the duties of their office and made the executive branch a more powerful part of Navajo tribal government.

The changes in Navajo life during the late 1940s and early 1950s may have been instrumental in Jones's political ascendancy. The Navajo voters who elected him over the incumbent, Ahkeah, chose a man with more formal education and facility with the English language and wider experience in the world beyond the reservation with which the Diné increasingly came into contact. Paul Jones was born Tl'aashchi'i Biye, October 20, 1895, near Naschitti, New Mexico. In the early twentieth century, upon his arrival at the Tohatchi BIA board school, the principal named him Paul Jones. Jones finished the eighth grade at Tohatchi. Then, at age seventeen, he accompanied the Christian Reformed Church missionary from Tohatchi, Dr. Lee Huizenga, on a trip to the East. They traveled to Grand Rapids, Michigan, and then to New York City. Jones went to high school in Englewood, New Jersey, for one year, residing with the Huizenga family, and then returned to Grand Rapids to enter the high school program at Calvin College. Drafted into the army before he could finish high school, Jones served overseas during World War I, survived a gassing of his unit, and returned home. Jones worked briefly in Navajo country and then went back to McLaughlin's Business College in Grand Rapids. Following his training there, he went to Chicago, where he worked for nearly a decade, mostly for the National Tea Company, before going home for good in 1933.[56] Jones gained a job with the Emergency Conservation Work program at Fort Defiance and then went to work for the BIA as a district supervisor in the Pinon area. By 1951 he had become established in Window Rock as a full-time interpreter. Gradually he emerged as a well-known figure in the Navajo capital and increasingly had the opportunity to travel to Washington and elsewhere. Articulate in both Navajo and English, he seemed like the kind of man the Navajos needed for this new era they were rapidly entering. Jones chose Scott Preston as his running mate. The medicine man from the western Navajo country nicely complemented the more progressive Jones from the eastern area.

Sam Ahkeah had been in office for eight years, and the Navajo voters
appeared in a mood for a change. They elected Jones and Preston handily
by a vote of 10,211 to 6,700 over Sam Ahkeah and Adolph Maloney.
The vote, if it signified anything, wrote Mary Shepardson, was a vote "for
modernization and acculturation."[57]

Jones worked closely with the Tribal Council to institute the benefits
brought by the Long Range Rehabilitation Act funds and by the tribal
oil money and with federal officials stationed in Window Rock as well as
in Washington. He also helped shape the reorganization of the executive
branch of Navajo government, which the Tribal Council approved in an
August 6, 1959, resolution.[58]

Illustration 3 will illustrate the changes in the executive branch of
Navajo tribal government. As shown, four departments became directly
responsible to the chairman: Land Investigations, Legal, Public Relations
and Information, and Research and Planning. While the latter three departments' responsibilities are evident by their titles, the first department's duties merits clarification. Land Investigations' functions have
had clear importance for all Navajos, given the complex status of Navajo
lands and land usage. The Land Investigations Department is in charge
of "preparation of studies and reports on land problems, human land use,
and occupancy, and the settlement of boundary and other land use disputes" and responsible for "the gathering of data and the preparation of
reports and appraisals for negotiation of land exchanges, land acquisition,
land disposition and leases on and off the Reservation."[59]

Another innovation of the Jones years—critical during his tenure—
came with the addition of the executive secretary's position to the
executive branch of Navajo tribal government.[60] It is difficult to describe
the duties of the position without considering the personality and character of J. Maurice McCabe, who held the post from its inception. McCabe
(who died unexpectedly in 1974) was a complicated man, highly capable,
and apparently a first-rate administrator. As McCabe developed the position, the executive secretary became a more important figure than the
vice chairman, who had served primarily as a stand-in for the chairman.
The executive secretary coordinated the workings of the public services,
resources, and administration divisions and the various departments within
each. He could hire and fire in the absence of the chairman and the vice
chairman, and he supervised preparation of the budget.[61]

3 Organization of the Executive Branch of the Navajo Tribe, 1959

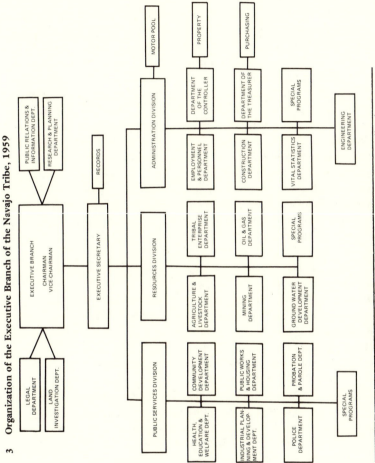

Source: Aubrey Williams, *Navajo Political Process*, Smithsonian Contributions to Anthropology, no. 9 (Washington, D.C., 1970). p. 27.

As executive secretary, McCabe, in the words of Peter MacDonald, "created and implemented the first real administrative organization of the Tribe." As such, MacDonald added, "In many ways he is looked upon as the architect of the Navajo Tribal Government . . . the foundation he built for the Tribe will serve as a solid basis on which we will continue to build a better Navajo Nation." McCabe had a strong business background, a remarkable memory, and a penchant for details.[62] His willingness to wield authority, combined with the newness of his position, contributed to frequent confusion and occasional hostility. On the other hand, the position as middle man and executive manager seemed appropriate and necessary for a developing nation. McCabe's position and the position of an executive secretary generally, however, ultimately rested on his relations with the chairman to whom he reported and to the council with which he had to deal. While Paul Jones remained as chairman, McCabe could be assured of maintaining his authority, but the election of Raymond Nakai in 1963 altered McCabe's status. Nakai promised during the campaign to neutralize McCabe's power and eventually succeeded in achieving that objective.[63] Since that time, while still included in the 1969 edition of the Navajo Tribal Code, the position of executive secretary is not diagrammed as part of the new organizational structure of Navajo tribal government.

A final addition to the Navajo government structure in the 1950s was the establishment of a judicial branch in 1959. Under the new system, the council approved individuals selected by the chairman to serve as justices in the Navajo courts. The development of accepted tribal court procedures allowed The People to institute a method of hearing cases and adjudicating them in a manner that balanced traditional ways and the demands of the American legal process. The clear separation of powers among the executive, legislative, and judicial branches marked, as Young put it, the "formalization" of Navajo tribal government.[64] A review of council debate and discussion on Navajo court system reform reveals the sweeping changes voted by the council to be influenced both by the Navajo desire to promote a more effective, efficient, and encompassing system and by the concern that the states neighboring the Navajo Nation would make inroads into Navajo jurisdiction if prompt action were not taken. The passage of Public Law 280 by Congress threatened the Navajos with the clear prospect of Arizona, New Mexico, and Utah attempting to eliminate the Navajo court system and substitute state jurisdiction in its place. Given the termination atmosphere of the 1950s and the general powers granted through Public Law 280 to the states to assume jurisdiction over reservations, the Navajos and their counsel believed it incumbent to be able to show the tribe instituting and operating a competent judicial system.[65] This movement, again, would be part of a general assumption by the Navajos of greater responsibility over their own affairs. As the Navajo Tribal Council began to consider reorganizing the judicial system in October 1958, counsel Lawrence Davis reminded it of potential state intervention and the problems such intervention would cause:

As this Council is well aware, under Public Law 280 the State Legislature in any state can sweep away the Navajo Court System and substitute the State Courts. You have had no experience in litigation in State Courts, and a juror has to speak, read, and write English so the Navajos for the most part are banned from jury duty in Arizona. You also know that for the most part the Arizona Judges know nothing of your way of life. Now, if you don't have an effective court system in the Reservation, you are going to get State jurisdiction sure as shooting. If you get State jurisdiction you are not going to get justice for the judges don't know your way of life and don't understand your language and you are not going to have your own people to serve as jurors. . . . The State is going to do just that if the Tribal Courts are not capable of administering justice and I am afraid at the present time they aren't.[66]

Davis mentioned as a case in point the problem of debt collection: if Navajos wanted to avoid being sued in the state courts by traders for debts, then the tribal courts had to be the place where civil actions such as debt collection could be handled inexpensively and justly. He warned if merchants could not collect in such a manner through the tribal court system they would not give credit to Navajos: "That means a Navajo who has some money but not enough to buy what he needs will spend it on liquor because nobody is going to give him credit if there is no way to collect the debt."[67]

In addition to debating points within the proposed revisions about such matters as salary and age, Navajo delegates expressed concern about the liabilities of the present system through which judges gained their positions by election. Chairman Paul Jones said, "Because of their elected condition you have no authority over them, you have no regulations governing them." Councilman Dillon Platero of Canoncito added, "It is very important that politics not play a part in our judicial system or in any way influence them to make decisions whereby maybe a Councilman in trouble or something like that, just because he is a Councilman, might get a little lighter sentence than another person."[68]

After several days of debate, the Navajo Tribal Council approved as amended the newly established judicial branch of the Navajo government. The judicial branch consisted of the Trial Court of seven judges appointed by the chairman and the Court of Appeals of three judges, the chief justice, and two judges of the Trial Court called by the chief justice to serve on particular cases. The chairman could select any Navajo over thirty years of age as a judge; appointees were subject to a probationary period of two years and were required to undergo a course of training. The Trial Court had original jurisdiction over violations of the Law and Order Code committed by Native Americans within the Navajo Nation, Native American civil actions within the Navajo Nation, and all cases involving domestic relations. Jury trials were to be provided in civil and criminal cases if requested by the defendant. Subject to three challenges, the judge would select six local citizens over twenty-one years of age to serve on the jury. Judges could be impeached for cause by a two-thirds vote of the Navajo Tribal Council. The courts would follow present procedures until changed by a majority of the judges, with review by the tribal attorney and approval of the chief justice.[69]

The adoption of the modern Navajo court system came as an integral part of the Navajo effort to administer law and order within the Navajo Nation. Thus, in January 1959, the Navajo Nation adopted as tribal law the law and order regulations of the Department of the Interior. For the 1959 fiscal year, the Bureau of Indian Affairs had contributed only 6.5 percent to the cost of the law enforcement program within the Navajo Nation ($85,000); the Navajo national government had contributed 93.5 percent ($1,313,766). Since they already had been paying for nearly all the cost of law enforcement, the Navajos believed it proper for them to take charge of it as well. The tribe said it did not intend "to usurp or interfere with enforcement of the Eleven Major Crimes law or any applicable Federal law," but from 1950 on it would be responsible for the enforcement of tribal regulations and would cooperate with federal authorities when necessary in the enforcement of federal regulations.[70]

Thus the Navajo government established its own police department, and the chairman appointed the police superintendent, with the advice and consent of the Tribal Council. The police superintendent held office at the pleasure of the chairman. The council established basic qualifications for police department personnel and specific guidelines for police procedure, including search and seizure, warrants, arrests, and detention. These procedures have remained basically the same as delineated in 1958 and 1959 resolutions, though alterations have been made as needed; for example, defendants are now allowed to post cash bonds for bail purposes if the defendants are deemed eligible for bail.[71]

The growth of the Navajo economy fueled the development and strengthening of the tribal government. In particularly the Navajos attempted to make more productive use of their land resources. Certainly income increased remarkably from sources such as oil and timber. In this takeoff period of the tribal economy, certain choices were made or perhaps dictated by the needs of outside interests and forced by the relative Navajo inexperience in economic matters. Navajos in the 1970s would look back upon some of these decisions with mixed emotions. In retrospect it can be said that there were clear successes as well as failures. It should be added that the context for decision making would be altered greatly within the next two decades.

The impact of the presence of vast quantities of oil underlying Navajo lands upon the creation and growth of the Navajo tribal government cannot be denied. The desire to exploit Navajo oil inspired formation of the Tribal Council in 1923 to approve leasing arrangements; widespread use of Navajo oil reserves created a new, much more powerful and comprehensive role for the council in the 1950s with the addition of vast revenues to the tribal treasury through royalties and other benefits.

New discoveries and exploitation between 1955 and 1959, especially in the Aneth, Utah, area, proved dramatic, indeed. Table 5 shows increases in production and royalties to the tribal treasury from 1955 to 1959. Even given—or perhaps because of—this remarkable increase in wealth, the Secretary of the Interior did not feel sufficiently confident to entrust the Navajos with a greater degree of control over these resources. A classic illustration of this attitude came in 1955 and 1956.[72]

Determined to gain a higher rate of return than the allowable 12.5 percent royalty and $1.25 per acre year rental, Navajo Tribal Council

TABLE 5

Oil Production and Oil Royalties,
Navajo Nation, 1955-1959

Fiscal Year	Barrels	Oil Royalties (Excluding Bonuses)
1955	174,000.52	$ 49,964
1956	387,467.83	114,008
1957	1,303,947.36	257,797
1958	5,599,477.28	800,000
1959	29,814,234.59	$ 9,752,317

Source: Robert W. Young, ed., *The Navajo Yearbook*, vol. 8 (Window Rock, Ariz.: Bureau of Indian Affairs, 1961), pp. 267, 269.

delegates became interested in creating a partnership with an oil company. They called a moratorium on leasing and then accepted a proposal the following year from Delhi-Taylor Oil Company granting the company sole exploration and drilling rights to 5.1 million acres. After a deduction of expenses, the company and the tribe were to split the profits. The scheme was risky in that lease-bonus payments which the tribe had received previously would be lost if little oil and gas were found. The plan died because of Interior Department and congressional disapproval, ironically during a period when "termination" was a popular catchall in American Indian affairs.[73] In fairness it should be added that the Navajos would later receive millions of dollars in lease bonuses for exploration rights. Much of the land, in fact, produced little or no oil so one could argue that the secretary was right. Still the Navajos had not been able to make their own decision.

Oil was not the only mineral to be exploited more fully in Navajo country during the 1950s. Uranium had gained national significance and value following World War II, and discovery of its availability on Navajo land quickly led to mining of the mineral by outside concerns. Tribal income from uranium increased from $65,755 in 1950 to over $650,000 just four years later.[74]

A Tribal Council resolution passed unanimously on October 14, 1949, instructed the Advisory Committee "to study and actively consider such changes in procedures as are necessary for positive results in securing greater development" of uranium and urged individual Navajo initiative in mining the mineral with "not less than 10 percent of the net proceeds from the sale of vanadium and uranium-bearing ores" being reserved to the tribe. Two resolutions approved by the council in 1951 called for the Advisory Committee to draft new mining regulations and for the chairman in consultation with the tribal attorney to obtain "a competent person to investigate the manner and method used in determining ore contents, manner of payments, etc. . . . and to determine whether the Tribe and individual members of the Tribe are receiving payments of royalties to which entitled."[75] These actions are typical of the concern paid by the national Navajo government during the critical early years of uranium development on Navajo land.

Since 1960, the Navajo Tribal Council has sought to increase royalty money from uranium. An Advisory Committee resolution, ACO-144-61, passed on October 16, 1961, adopted a new royalty schedule for uranium. This schedule included both a sliding royalty percentage of mine value per dry ton (up to 20 percent on a dry ton with a mine value of $100.01 or more) and another sliding scale for royalties "when crude ore from the mine is upgraded in an upgrading plant before shipment to the mill." The Advisory Committee, through authority of a 1951 council resolution, enacted six different royalty schedules between 1951 and 1968.[76]

The existence of rich coal deposits in the Navajo area, of course, had long been known. But the full impact of coal mining would not be felt on the Navajo reservation until the 1960s. The 1950s, however, marked the period when the importance of these deposits became realized. On November 27, 1943, the Tribal Council passed a unanimous resolution noting that coal resources were not being developed and that "the income of the Tribe would be materially increased through the proper development of such resources." The council urged the general superintendent of the Navajo Service and the council chairman to "investigate and make recommendations for the proper development of coal resources of the Reservation and report their findings at the next Council."[77] Income from coal remained minimal through the 1950s, while other mineral royalties increased greatly. From 1950 to 1958, the largest amount earned from these sources totaled a mere $3,450.19 in 1953; 1959 and 1960 showed only slightly higher sums ($13,210.00 in 1960).[78]

The mushrooming energy demands of the Southwestern states suddenly changed this picture. Arizona Public Service Company, in conjunction with over twenty other Southwestern power concerns, decided to build a huge generating plant, the Four Corners Power Plant, six miles east of

Fruitland, New Mexico, between Shiprock and Farmington. Utah Construction Company leased approximately 25,000 acres of reservation land to mine coal for use at the plant. In 1961 in the *Navajo Yearbook* Robert W. Young predicted "at full load, the furnaces will consume 4,200 tons of coal per day," and "the strip mining of Reservation coal deposits will become a thriving industry in the 1960s." Young also noted:

Some of the power produced by this development will be made available at wholesale to the Navajo Tribe for industrial and domestic use on the Reservation, and a number of Navajos will find employment in construction phases, as well as in the production and transportation of coal."[79]

The lumber industry also expanded in Navajo country during this era. We associate Navajo land with the desert and yet 5 percent of that land is forest. Most of the wooded territory is included in a vast stand of ponderosa pine, spruce, and fir covering the Fort Defiance plateau and extending northward through the Lukachukai and Carrizo mountain areas. For years, Navajo families have journeyed many miles to the region to gather wood for home use. Sawmill operations actually have a lengthy history here, and the quality of the timber stand combined with planning, management, and investment have made Navajo Forest Products Industries the Navajo Nation's most successful tribal enterprise.

The Bureau of Indian Affairs constructed the first Navajo sawmill in 1880. Initially the sawmill provided boards for constructing Fort Defiance Agency buildings and later provided lumber to any buyer. Other sawmills, including one for the Shiprock Agency built near Toadlena, served bureau purposes during the early twentieth century. These efforts basically fulfilled a local need, were on a small, inefficient scale, and usually excluded Navajos from the direction of their operation.

Tribal interest in the main sawmill, which had come to be located centrally a few miles north and west of Fort Defiance at a place known simply as Sawmill, was rekindled in the late 1930s. By this time the existing mill, in the words of the agency forester, was in a "dilapidated condition" and "continued operation was impossible." He recommended that "the mill be liquidated, the indebtedness paid off and the worn-out equipment junked."[80]

Thus on May 18, 1939, the Tribal Council passed Resolution No. CM-10-39 to obtain a loan of $50,000 from the federal government "for the purpose of supplementing present funds for the purchase of material, equipment, construction of a sawmill" and to waive a debt of $15,253.20 owed by the BIA to the Navajos for stumpage logging. Once the debt had been paid, the council stipulated that "the profits accruing from the operation can be used for establishing other tribal projects, providing the proposed projects are for the purpose of giving employment to the Navajo people and the development of Navajo resources." The federal government granted the loan, and nearly three years later the council passed another resolution "to promote Navajo tribal lumber industry" by appropriating $165,000 for expanding existing facilities, increasing employment, and thus more fully utilize the lumber resources and potentially increase the return on the investment to the tribe.[81]

The modern period of Navajo forestry began with the hiring of the first nongovernment employee as superintendent of lumber operations in April 1944. Frank L. Carter moved the Sawmill plant toward more progressive operating procedures, and the industry joined the Western Pine Association. Carter held his post until 1960, and during that era the Navajo enterprise changed enormously in scope and direction.

The Navajo government's officials took a significant step in the early 1950s by formulating a master plan for Navajo timber management. It included the best hard data yet available on the timber resources of the reservation: "547,638 acres of timber with 458,457 acres merchantable and nearly 2.1 billion board feet, net merchantable volume, with 98 percent of it ponderosa pine." The plan called for cutting to go ahead at 28 million board feet a year, taking 35 percent of the forest volume, with the forest gone over by 1978, at which time a second cut of 24 million board feet per year could begin. The Tribal Council and the Advisory Committee quickly attempted to put the plan into effect. They hired two specialized consulting firms to recommend how this process should take place, and in 1956 these consultants produced a five-volume report, "Forest Development and Utilization Studies for the Navajo Timber Lands." This analysis revealed a larger timber stand that would allow for the processing of 38 million board feet per year.[82]

From this report, the tribe concluded that it should take on the lumbering industry as a tribal enterprise. Moreover, it decided a new modern center was needed to replace the antiquated Sawmill facilities. A new community, named Navajo, was started from the ground up along Red Lake, thirteen miles north of Fort Defiance. The next step in the development of this tribal enterprise was taken on May 1, 1960, when the Navajo Forest Products Industries' Management Board took over the sawmill's operation.

The management board combined outside expertise with Navajo direction. Four prominent Navajo administrators, Maurice McCabe, Ned Hatathli, Leigh Hubbard, and Sam Day III, were joined by Charles Wheeler, Louis Gervais, and Jan Oostermeyer, all retired lumber and industrial executives, and Herbert Jensen, a consulting forester,[83] a blend of administration that proved singularly successful. Navajos came to view Navajo Forest Products Industries as a Navajo enterprise, and Navajo personnel took increasingly central places in the day-to-day operations. Retired executives recruited from the outside provided necessary experience and the technical know-how essential for a multimillion-dollar business.

By the end of the 1950s, Navajo life had changed significantly. The Long Range Rehabilitation Act had altered the reservation markedly. Schools had been constructed and roads built. Royalties had poured in from development of oil reserves, and other minerals promised vastly increased tribal revenues and individual jobs in the next decade. While the economic picture for the Navajos had improved, unemployment remained a serious dilemma that would influence Navajo political leaders in the years to come.

Despite continuing economic questions, there could be no question that on balance these years had evidenced remarkable progress. In an era of termination—when Bureau of Indian Affairs officials labeled reservations socioeconomic cul-de-sacs—the Navajos showed their future might well be characterized by greater control of their own destiny. Their economic picture had brightened. Moreover, their political system clearly had matured. The tribal government had been reorganized, the chapter system reinvigorated, and the court system developed. The 1950s had indeed witnessed the birth of the Navajo Nation. The 1960s would reveal its gradual maturation.

YEARS OF STRIVING AND STRIFE: THE 1960s

4

The election of Raymond Nakai as Navajo tribal chairman in 1963 ushered in a new era in Navajo politics and Navajo life. Nakai's election proved that a virtual outsider to the Navajo Tribal Council could go to the Navajo people and gain the Navajo Nation's highest office. Nakai would be reelected in 1966 before being defeated in 1970 by Peter MacDonald. His two administrations were characterized by both striving and strife. For the Navajos, important changes took place in the areas of legal representation, economics, and education. The presence of new forces and new sources of power sometimes riddled the decade with factional disputes.

The era showed the Diné attempting to prove that their reservation could be a viable place to live, not only socially but economically. That deep desire influenced Navajo representatives to make a series of vital decisions, some of which in retrospect appear advisable and others ill-advised. Given these decisions and the changes that swept across Navajo country, strong disagreements inevitably emerged. These were, to say the least, interesting times.

Nakai hailed from Lukachukai, Arizona. Born in October 1921, the fourth child of Mr. and Mrs. John Nakai ("Nakai" in Navajo means Mexican, attesting to the varied strains that contribute to the Navajo heritage), enrolled in school at eight years of age. He attended Lukachukai Day School and Fort Wingate Boarding School and graduated from high school in Shiprock in 1942. Nakai then joined the navy and, like many other Navajos, served in the South Pacific campaign during World War II.

Following the war, he worked for the Navajo Ordnance Depot at Bellemont, near Flagstaff. He stayed there until his election in 1963. Nakai
gained general public attention through his campaigns for the chairmanship in 1955 and 1959, and through his radio program over KCLS in
Flagstaff.

Too young perhaps by Navajo standards to be elected in the 1950s,
Nakai compelled attention not only by his persistence but by his articulacy,
particularly in the Navajo language. He presented a sharp contrast to
chairman Paul Jones, just as Jones had appeared a fresh alternative to
Sam Ahkeah. While Jones swept the 1959 campaign, Nakai did sufficiently
well to establish him as a political figure of note. In 1963 he earned a
plurality of the votes cast, gaining 11,190 votes, to 9,296 for Jones and
7,422 for Sam Billison. All three candidates in the 1963 election were
well educated (Billison had a college degree) and had lived off the reservation. Nakai won in the end because of his ability to capitalize on widespread feelings on several vital issues.[1]

Most important, Nakai pledged he would not subject members of the
Native American Church to the harrassment and disruption they had
known under the Jones administration. Second, he promised to fire
Norman Littell, general counsel to the Navajo Tribe since 1947; Nakai
charged Littell with dominating council affairs. Third, Nakai implied he
would not enforce existing grazing regulations, thereby allowing Navajo
families dependent solely on stockraising for subsistence to increase the
size of their herds.

The Tribal Council had prohibited peyote use on the reservation as
early as 1940, but arrests of Native American Church members had increased sharply during the late 1950s and early 1960s. Although a Catholic
and not a Native American Church member, Nakai endorsed the idea of
a referendum on the matter and explained that his concept of freedom
of religion would mean legalization of peyote use for religious purposes.
By 1963, many Navajos had joined the Native American Church; in the
1963 election most of them voted for Raymond Nakai.[2]

Upon assuming office Nakai confronted a Tribal Council dominated
by delegates affiliated with the previous administration who soon became
labeled the Old Guard (or Old Guards) and who seemed determined to
challenge him at every turn. Both sides had formidable weapons at their
disposal. Nakai could cite his election by all the people and could interpret
his election as a mandate for his views. He also had the support of the

Navajo Rights Association, an organized group of people who lobbied readily on his behalf. On the other hand, the council could rely on its traditional power and on resolute and prominent delegates like Annie Wauneka of Klagetoh and Howard Gorman of Ganado. Only on the issue of stockraising could there be some kind of tacit understanding between Nakai and his supporters and the Old Guard: essentially a hands-off, laissez faire approach to enforcement of the number of sheep units (land necessary for each sheep) possessed.

Thus throughout the first term of the Nakai administration a running battle ensued: charges and countercharges echoed between Nakai and Littell, Nakai and the Old Guard, Nakai followers and the Tribal Council and eventually the Secretary of the Interior, Stewart Udall, and all of the other parties. Tribal government business often came to a standstill, and many of Nakai's proposals were rejected out of hand. His first term was replete with extraordinary happenings, including the forced opening of J. Maurice McCabe's safe as directed by an attorney for the Secretary of the Interior, declining tribal revenues, occasional shouting matches in the Tribal Council chambers, and generally the presence of the most divisive factionalism perhaps in all of Navajo political history.

Littell really had become a divisive figure in Navajo politics by the late 1950s. Sam Ahkeah had raised two central questions about Littell's performance when Ahkeah sought to unseat incumbent Paul Jones. Ahkeah had charged Littell with controlling the Tribal Council and with accomplishing nothing in the Navajos' case before the Indian Claims Commission; the Navajos had claimed 23 million acres as properly theirs by right of aboriginal occupation and the tribe had invested sizable sums in the research and legal representation necessary in advancing their case.

Nakai capitalized on these contentions, then, in his successful campaign, and his unyielding opposition to Littell became steadily more popular among the Navajo people. The young Navajo editor of the *Navajo Times,* Marshall Tome, blasted Littell for the delay in passage of the Navajo tribal budget in an editorial entitled, "Mr. Littell . . . Where Have You Been?"[3] The decision brought by the special three-judge panel in *Healing* v. *Jones,* which ruled that Hopis had equal rights to the disputed land within the joint use area, disappointed many Navajos and, of course, created anxiety among those Navajos residing in the area itself. The lengthening delay before a definitive claims ruling also bothered Navajos and clearly did not aid Littell's general standing.

The standoff between Navajo Tribal Council Chairman Raymond Nakai and the Old Guard majority on the Navajo Tribal Council continued throughout Nakai's first term. Littell criticized Nakai, privately referring to him as a stooge and puppet of Secretary of the Interior Udall. Nakai tried to terminate Littell's contract, but the council blocked the attempt. Acting upon a Navajo Advisory Committee resolution asking him to "investigate, audit, and terminate" Littell's contract, Udall fired the Navajo general counsel. Littell, of course, took Udall to court and succeeded in gaining an injunction from U.S. District Court Judge John J. Sirica on May 9, 1965, which kept Udall's action from taking effect. The U.S. Court of Appeals reversed Sirica's order in September 1966, contending Littell's "admitted unauthorized use of tribal staff attorneys on claims cases constituted adequate grounds for canceling his contract as general counsel" and defending Udall's "broad authority vested by Congress . . . to oversee Indian affairs, particularly in light of the long history of concern over tribal relations with attorneys, includes the power to cancel contracts between a tribe and its attorneys for cause."[4]

As Littell appealed Circuit Court Judge Burger's opinion to the United States Supreme Court, the internal debate within the Navajo Nation raged on, fueled by the November 1966 tribal elections. One of the leading members of the Old Guard, Annie Wauneka, said the Burger ruling "if followed through all the way would put us back to the days of Fort Sumner where the Secretary and the Indian Agent told us what to do and we had no voice in the matter." Two other attorneys associated with the tribe's legal department, William Lavell and Jerry Haggard, claimed Udall had been "considering the possibility of taking over the administration of the Navajo Tribal Government for some time if he deemed it necessary." Despite such voiced concerns, Navajos reelected Raymond Nakai and voted in a Tribal Council more sympathetic to him. Nakai sympathizers on the new council gave the chairman power to appoint the Advisory Committee, and so another bastion of Littell support toppled.[5]

The November 1966 tribal election may have amounted to a referendum on Raymond Nakai's views and actions. If so, then the chairman won a vote of confidence, albeit a narrow one. The council as a whole would be more in accord with his perspective. In the balloting for chairman and vice chairman, Nakai and Vice Chairman Nelson Damon defeated the team of Sam Billison and Paul Jones by 1,560 votes, 13,941 to 12,381. The election returns appeared to reveal that Nakai benefited substantially from the easing of the peyote issue. Although the use of peyote remained illegal, enforcement of the regulation had been much less strict in Nakai's administration. Nakai received his strongest vote in the 1966 election in the Shiprock Agency (defeating Billison 3,559 to 1,366), where the Native American Church had its strongest following. His margin of victory was the widest in the precincts where peyote influence had been important for many years: Shiprock (925 votes for Nakai, 255 votes for Billison), Aneth (267 to 79), Rock Point (255 to 14), Sweetwater (265 to 6), Teec Nos Pos (345 to 54), Mexican Water (344 to 13), and Red Rock (343 to 136). These seven precincts gave Nakai an advantage of 2,197 votes, more than his winning margin. The other three communities listed by David Aberle in *The Peyote Religion Among the Navaho* as having large Native American Church memberships also gave Nakai large majorities; in Lukachukai, Nakai won by 213 to 120, and he won as well in Many Farms (306 to 100) and (Lower) Greasewood (244 to 119). While Aberle's data dates from the early 1950s and thus is only suggestive, he found that peyotism was growing in strength in the northern part of district four and the region immediately west of the Rock Point-Mexican Water area, where Nakai ran strongly.[6]

These voting patterns are indeed intriguing, but Nakai's reelection in 1966 cannot be explained by one issue. He clearly did not make it a one-issue campaign, and other factors must be weighed. Nakai also protested strongly against the Tribal Council, blamed Littell and the BIA for many of his administration's problems, and spoke out firmly on livestock grazing, the issue that most affected the average voter.[7] These stands may all have aided the chairman's chances.

It is difficult to evaluate Billison's candidacy and the Navajo response to it. Billison's campaign focused on what he considered to be the negative aspects of Nakai's term; as challengers to incumbents so often must, he seemed to run more against his opponent's record than on his own. He strongly criticized what he saw as administrative errors and the atmosphere of "great misunderstanding and chaos" that he felt had prevailed. By adding Paul Jones to the ticket, he attempted to appeal to the broadest possible spectrum of the electorate. Billison pledged to carry out the objectives of unity, progress, and democratic government "with our hearts in tune with our traditions, and we shall never disrupt the harmonious pattern of our Navajo life and religion in order merely to introduce the white man's ways between the sacred mountains." However, Billison and

the Old Guard generally stopped short of questioning the form of
economic development, industrial promotion, advocated by members of
the Nakai administration.[8]

Following the 1966 election, Nakai moved quickly to consolidate his
position. Council delegates voted to give the chairman the power to
appoint members of the Advisory Committee. They also soon approved
the use of peyote in religious ceremonies. General Counsel Norman
Littell resigned, following the refusal of the United States Supreme Court
to hear an appeal of *Udall* v. *Littell,* which would have permitted Udall
to remove Littell from his position for violation of his contract.

The February 1967 decision by the United States Supreme Court not
to hear Littell's appeal had indeed removed the general counsel's final
hope of remaining in his position. Littell resigned in late February, and
an era of nearly twenty years came to an end. In his resignation statement,
Littell urged the two existing factions by all means not to each hire an
attorney ("This is contrary to all governmental and corporate experience") but for the council to unite to select someone that a majority
could support. The *Navajo Times* editorialized: "The man to head this
department must be able to represent his clients, the Navajos, to the
exclusion of other interests. He should represent all Navajos . . . not a
particular faction."[9] The new counsel, hereafter, indeed would have to
enjoy both the council's and the chairman's confidence, would have to
assume a lower profile, and would have to devote an increasing percentage
of time strictly to Navajo concerns.

The concern and uncertainty that the new Navajo Tribal Council and
its chairman felt about the new general counsel could be seen in the five
months taken to select its new head attorney and in the divided vote of
39 to 28 that confirmed the choice. The selection of Harold Mott on
July 20, 1967, reflected the Nakai majority on the council, while the
minority Old Guard delegates questioned Mott's degree of experience in
Native American law. A Georgetown Law School graduate, Mott worked
for the Federal Communications Commission from 1940 to 1942, and
then entered private practice in Washington, D.C., in 1946. The council
selected Mott over the Washington firm of Wilkinson, Cragun and Barker,
which had been preferred by Navajo Area Director Graham Holmes, a
member of the screening committee, because of a stronger background in
Native American law.[10] With the $100,000 flat fee granted by the council

to Mott for salary and expenses, the new general counsel hired two attorneys, Edmund D. Kahn and William T. MacPherson, and a law clerk, Lynn W. Mitton, to assist him.

Mott served as legal counsel for slightly more than three years, resigning his position after Peter MacDonald defeated Raymond Nakai for Navajo Tribal Council chairman in November 1970. He claimed after his first year that his office's work load had increased "at least two or three times" that of the previous general counsel. Mott became a close advisor to Chairman Nakai and assisted him in promoting Navajo industrial development and attempting to discover new employers for the rapidly expanding Navajo work force.[11] Perhaps the most significant legal decision reached during his tenure came with the long-awaited Indian Claims Commission decision in June 1970, stating that the Tribe must be reimbursed for the value of 12.33 million acres of aboriginal territory taken from it in 1868. While the acreage represented only slightly more than half of the approximately 23 million acres claimed by the Navajo Nation, the commission's decision meant the eventual addition of a sizable sum to the Navajo treasury and the reaffirmation of The People's historical roots.

Harold Mott contended that greater cooperation with other departments of the tribe and the Bureau of Indian Affairs had been made possible "by establishing a hard and fixed rule that the attorneys of the Legal Department shall not engage in tribal politics and shall render assistance to all members of the tribe, regardless of their political outlook."[12] It was one thing to make the assertion, but the assertion could not always be equated with reality. By definition, the counsel became the chairman's man and inevitably would be entangled in political controversies.

THE OFFICE OF NAVAJO ECONOMIC OPPORTUNITY

Toward the end of Nakai's first term, a new agency emerged which became powerful and influential within the Navajo Nation: the Office of Navajo Economic Opportunity. The ONEO represented a sharp contrast to the prevailing philosophy in the post-Collier era; the reservation could be seen as potentially viable rather than an economic dead end. The ONEO would use the money available through the Office of Economic Opportunity in Washington, D.C., to revitalize Navajo life at the local level. The

Navajos themselves could run this internally directed, locally centered program. BIA officials first intended to be in charge. However, prompt Navajo protest permitted the tribe to gain approval to design it, and in the four weeks allotted them, tribal representatives Peter MacDonald—then serving as tribal director of management, methods, and procedures—and Joe Watson, Jr. drafted a plan. On September 8, 1964, the Navajo Tribal Council passed a resolution by a 48-1 vote authorizing participation in the Community Action Program under Title II of the Economic Opportunity Act. Meetings in the autumn of 1965 at various chapters and interviews with Navajos across the reservation led to the writing of specific proposals for preschool, recreation and physical fitness, and manpower training programs. The funding proposal also requested money for leadership training study and a survey to consider locating a community college within the Navajo Nation.[13]

The Office of Economic Opportunity informed the Navajo Tribe in January 1965, that its first funding request for $920,000 had been approved, and the tribe embarked on an intensive effort to take full advantage of the money. On April 7 the Advisory Committee voted to establish a separate Office of Navajo Economic Opportunity and to approve the plan of operation for the ONEO. That month members of the nine-person ONEO Executive Board began to consider how to proceed and whom to select as ONEO executive director. A month later, in May 1965, Peter MacDonald became ONEO executive director, a position he held until resigning in 1970 to seek the chairmanship of the Navajo Tribal Council. By the end of 1965, ONEO had established a far-flung preschool program, a small business development center, a Neighborhood Youth Corps summer program involving 3,500 Navajo young people, a "reservation-wide" recreation and physical fitness program, and a local community development program. The ONEO directors had investigated the possibility of starting a community college, begun planning for several other projects, and supervised the first of the waves of VISTA volunteers arriving on the reservation.[14]

During 1966 and 1967 ONEO programs expanded into many new fields and had an impact on literally almost everyone living in the Navajo Nation. By its own estimate, ONEO directly served 23,382 people and indirectly an additional 78,188 by the end of 1967 through the following programs: Home Improvement Training, Navajo Culture Center, Neighborhood Youth Corps, Local Community Development, Alcoholism, Head Start,

Migrant and Agricultural Placement, Recreation and Physical Fitness, and Operation Medicare Alert. The most successful programs proved to be those with the most local input and the most relevance to community people's lives.[15]

ONEO worked because it had money, because it involved bread-and-butter issues, because it encouraged local involvement, and because it had Navajo administrators. It came to be in the affluent days of the War on Poverty, and, unlike so many government programs designed to aid Native Americans, it had generous funding, which the Navajo tribe supplemented. From fiscal year 1965 through fiscal year 1968, for example, the ONEO received slightly over $20 million in federal grants. Programs such as Home Improvement Training, Local Community Development, and the Neighborhood Youth Corps were especially tangible: individual communities could see, participate in, and be affected. These three programs alone received about three-fourths of the ONEO's appropriations during the same period. These programs provided jobs, training, and materials which could be put to direct use in the immediate community rather than in Albuquerque or Phoenix, as had been the thrust of the relocation effort of the 1950s. As of December 31, 1967, ONEO employed Navajos in thirty-four of forty administrative positions, thus helping to ensure Diné control. Only forty-six of the 2,720 persons employed by ONEO at that time were non-Indian, primarily serving as preschool teachers (twenty-six) and DNA (Dinébiina Nahiilna Be Agaditahe) attorneys (seven). Finally, in Peter MacDonald, the ONEO employed an individual who gave the program continuity by remaining in his position for five years and more critically, was trained leadership.[16]

DINÉBEIINA NAHIILNA BE AGADITAHE

The DNA program actually had been discussed in one form or another for years. Certainly the need for legal assistance to individual Navajos long predated the establishment of legal service programs for them. Harry A. Sellery, Jr. of the tribe's Legal Department wrote to Navajo Area Director Allan G. Harper in February 1954, to complain that attorneys hired by the tribe to do work for the tribe faced a "steadily increasing volume of requests by individual Navajos" for legal assistance. He recommended soliciting cooperation of state bar associations to provide off-reservation

legal aid for Navajos unable to pay for it, while employing an attorney
to advise on-reservation Navajos. However, Sellery felt such an attorney
could not represent the individual Navajo in court for three principal
reasons: time, legal ethics, and the need for Navajos to pay for such
services whenever possible.[17]

While Sellery termed the employ of an attorney and the provision of
off-reservation aid the "solution to the problem," these measures acknowledged the dilemma but did not solve it. Navajos continued to have
significant legal difficulties off the reservation, and one attorney could
not begin to solve the various legal problems of Navajos, many of whom
could not get to Window Rock to seek help. This one attorney, nonetheless, made a start at advising individual Navajos on legal matters as a
result of Tribal Council and Advisory Committee resolutions authorizing
his employment in 1953 and 1954.[18]

In August 1958, the council moved to provide more substantial legal
aid service to individual Navajos. It asked for Norman Littell's recommendations on how to provide this service and endorsed Lawrence Huerta
of the general counsel staff to serve as chief legal aid officer.[19] The council
adopted Littell's suggestions for operation of the Navajo Legal Aid Service
in an October 9, 1958, resolution, which called for the employment of
"not less than two attorneys" with one full-time interpreter and secretarial assistance in Window Rock for legal problems that other established
agencies could not handle. Nonetheless, the record of council discussion
at this time revealed an awareness of the limitations of the approach being
taken, despite Huerta's willingness to travel to other areas of the reservation and despite the aid that might be forthcoming from other attorneys
far removed from the reservation. Norman Littell summed up the problem:

Suppose the Government hadn't let the contract for the Glen Canyon Dam
but put two men out there with two shovels and said, "Get to work," and
then would come back and ask, "What the hell is the matter with you?
You haven't made any progress here!" You can't move an immense volume
of earth with a couple of guys with a couple of shovels. And you have got
a Glen Canyon Dam with 83,000 Navajos wanting legal assistance.[20]

Thus, when the Office of Economic Opportunity offered the Navajo
Nation the opportunity of funding an extensive legal services program,
the ONEO responded favorably, organizing the operation and initially

calling it the Office of Navajo Economic Opportunity Legal Aid and
Defender Society. Navajo chapters elected agency committees who in
turn elected a board of directors, thus ensuring grass-roots representation
and a proper distribution of Navajos from all over the Navajo Nation. On
December 27, 1966, the ONEO Executive Board unanimously selected
Theodore R. Mitchell as the first director of the program; Mitchell said
he would start work in mid-January. Byron Tsingine of Tuba City
seemed to summarize the feelings of many Navajos in saying, "This program will be of great benefit to the people. We need it badly. I am happy
that we can now get it started."[21]

From the outset, however, Dinébeiina Nahiilna Be Agaditahe (DNA,
as it quickly became known), Incorporated, appeared destined for controversy.[22] Sam Billison, Benjamin Hogue (Burnham councilman), and Annie
Wauneka protested to the OEO in Washington about Ted Mitchell's application even before the ONEO hired him. Since Annie Wauneka signed this
letter and would later be involved in a dispute with Mitchell that would
culminate in his temporary exclusion from the Navajo Nation, it is worth
noting this initial protest in some detail. Mitchell had graduated from
Harvard Law School in 1964, and had worked for Navajo Tribal Legal
Aid Service from January 1965 to March 1966, before becoming regional
legal services director of the OEO Southwest Region Office in Austin,
Texas. Billison, Hogue, and Wauneka claimed Mitchell left Navajo Legal
Aid under circumstances that made him "unwelcome" on the reservation.
They also argued that Mitchell's employment with OEO and application
to head the ONEO legal aid program represented a conflict of interest
and said other candidates had applied for the post with more experience
and better qualifications. Finally, and ironically given Nakai's eventual
opposition to DNA, they said that the ONEO Executive Board headed
by Raymond Nakai refused to meet with the Advisory Committee to discuss the applicants for the positions; therefore, they charged the OEO
program with not working with local government. In sum:

We feel that his [Mitchell] being considered is a purely political maneuver
involving tribal politics, and for that reason is against all the precepts of
the War on Poverty program. We want an OEO sponsored legal aid program
for the Navajo people and we want it to be run for the benefit for the
Navajo people as a professional program, and not as some form of political
boondoggle."[23]

In the months and years to follow, essentially the same charges would continue to be leveled against DNA.

Still, the initial response to advertisements for attorneys, counselors, interpreters, and secretarial staff far exceeded some observers' expectations: over fifty attorneys applied and more than thirty people applied for each of the remaining types of positions. Mitchell announced that staff offices would be established in the agency towns of Shiprock, Crownpoint, Tuba City, Chinle, and Window Rock, with two attorneys, two counselors, and two interpreter-investigators at each office. By September 1968, DNA employed even more lawyers, eighteen in all, most of them recent graduates from top law schools.[24]

From April 3, 1967, through July 31, 1968, DNA attorneys, counselors, and investigators served nearly 8,000 clients, as shown in Table 6.[25] These clients represented those who could not afford to employ their own legal assistance and who probably would not have had any without DNA. DNA also embarked upon an ambitious community education program, reaching by their estimate within this time period 15,281 people at chapter, community, and school meetings through oral presentations

TABLE 6

DNA Case Load, April 1967 to August 1968

Problem Area	Number of Clients
Consumer and employment (sales contracts, garnishment, wage claims, bankruptcy, etc.)	1,230
Administrative (state and local welfare, social security, workmen's compensation, veterans administration, unemployment, insurance, etc.)	535
Housing (private landlord and tenant, housing code violations, public housing, etc.)	31
Family (divorce and annulment, separation, nonsupport, custody and guardianship, paternity, adoption, etc.)	1,949
Miscellaneous (tort juvenile school cases, misdemeanors, other criminal commitment procedures, etc.)	4,164
Total	7,909

Source: *Law in Action* 1, no. 1 (August 27, 1968).

in Navajo and English concerning legal services, preventive law, and consumer and community education, all basic thrusts of the DNA program. In addition, DNA filed suit in special cases on matters with applicability to large numbers of Navajos, including extradition, welfare regulations, and state income tax.[26]

DNA thus stepped into a void which had been readily acknowledged for years: the absence of generally available legal assistance for Navajos with incomes of less than $3,500 a year. Through an energetic program with some tangible and immediate results, DNA became a formidable power within the Navajo Nation. Just as the popular reaction to ONEO programs had worried members of Navajo government unaccustomed to having their power and influence challenged, so DNA's success in attracting widespread support concerned not only members of the Navajo Tribal Council and its chairman but ONEO leaders as well. In retrospect, it is often difficult to distinguish opposition to DNA during its first years from personal animosity toward Ted Mitchell, who symbolized the independent nature of the legal services operation. At one time or another leading Navajo political figures took potshots at the fledgling program and its director. By July 1968, Raymond Nakai had called for Mitchell's dismissal, Sam Billison had protested the initial Mitchell appointment (though he eventually supported DNA), and Peter MacDonald had squabbled with Mitchell and DNA over funding. Moreover, the *Navajo Times* under the editorship of Dick Hardwick frequently criticized DNA.[27] Annie Wauneka's personal conflict with Mitchell, however, produced an incident that ignited a public and legal battle over whether or not DNA would continue.

The Advisory Committee on which Wauneka served voted twelve to three in August 1968 to exclude Ted Mitchell from the Navajo Nation. Its action followed Wauneka's reaction to Mitchell's "silly, dirty laugh," which she believed directed "all the action of the tribal chairman, the Tribal Council, and members of this Advisory Committee." Mitchell had laughed during an Advisory Committee meeting during which the provisions of the 1968 Civil Rights Act were being explained to the committee by Acting Associate Solicitor on Indian Affairs Duard Barnes. Barnes, when queried about the tribe's ability to exclude people from the reservation being affected by the act, replied to Wauneka, "I would have to know who you have in mind." Wauneka said, "I do not have anyone in particular in mind." Mitchell, who was observing the proceedings, then laughed because "everybody in the room knew she was talking about me when she asked that question to Barnes. There was a ripple of laughter that went around the room from everyone in the room, not just myself." The next day, Wauneka met Mitchell, slapped him on the face and told him to leave the room. Mitchell left. The Advisory Committee resolution to exclude him from the Navajo Nation quickly followed.[28]

Once Nakai and BIA Navajo Area Director Graham Holmes concurred with the Advisory Committee action, the Navajo police escorted Mitchell over the reservation line.[29] Mitchell's attorney, Jeremy Butler of Phoenix, tried to negotiate with the Navajo government for several weeks but eventually filed suit for DNA in September. Three plaintiffs and three defendants became involved in *Dodge* v. *Nakai*. "A class of indigent Navajo Indians" receiving legal aid from DNA, DNA through its eight Navajo directors, and Ted Mitchell jointly brought the action against Nakai, Holmes, and V. Allen Adams, Navajo police superintendent. Nakai and Adams had enforced the Mitchell exclusion with Holmes concurrence; thus DNA sued the three individuals rather than the tribe itself, a distinction often overlooked in the controversy that naturally followed the suit. The main basis for the suit lay in the recently enacted Civil Rights Act, especially Title II, which provided in part:

No Indian tribe in exercising powers of self-government shall make or enforce any law prohibiting the free exercise of religion, or abridging the freedom of speech, or of the press, or the right of the people to peaceably assemble and to petition for a redress of grievances . . . [or] to deny to any person within its jurisdiction the equal protection of its laws or deprive any persons of liberty or property without due process of law.

While the defendants argued that "any person" should be applied only to "any American Indian," the court ruled that it had no "justifiable reason for so restricting the plain language of the statute."[30] Mitchell thus could not be excluded from the Navajo Nation.

Justice Craig's ruling, however, while permitting Mitchell's return, gave hope to Mitchell's adversaries by stating that "the tribal government through ONEO is entitled to negotiate for provisions in the ONEO-DNA contract that may curtail DNA's activities or subject that organization to closer supervision by ONEO." Craig added:

The demands by the Advisory Committee that Mitchell be removed as director of DNA do not constitute unlawful activities. Just as members of the Advisory Committee are subject to criticism for the manner in which they perform their functions, the Director of DNA may be sub- ject to charges of incompetence and unsuitability for the position that he occupies.

The Advisory Committee therefore voted twelve to one in March 1969 to direct Chairman Nakai not to release funds for the DNA for the 1969 fiscal year—funds which Peter MacDonald as ONEO executive director had been allocating all along on the assumption they would eventually be released—and to seek a new legal services organization, to be composed of one-third tribal-elected representatives, one-third at-large Navajo repre- sentatives, and one-third members of groups in the Navajo community, such as the Public Health Service, the Bureau of Indian Affairs, and others.[31]

Though an emergency grant from the ONEO and a direct funding grant from the OEO in Washington saved the DNA from financial fore- closure, it faced one confrontation after another with the Navajo govern- ment during the remainder of Ted Mitchell's tenure as director (until the end of February 1970) and afterward until the Navajo tribal elections in November 1970. In late April 1969, the Tribal Council voted thirty-eight to sixteen with four abstentions to remove Mitchell as DNA director and to fund DNA through the Tribal Council. Given the independent sta- tus of DNA, though, the vote remained as an expression of council sentiment without affecting the legal services program; the DNA board voted twelve to three to retain Mitchell, with three Navajo members on the board—Loncie Brown, Jimmie Yazzie, and John Dodge—voting to fire him. A week before, the Navajo DNA board members had voted five to two to fire Mitchell, but Bessie Yazzie and Anson Damon reversed their votes the next week. Despite Tribal Council protests in the autumn of 1969, the OEO continued to fund DNA directly. Ted Mitchell offered to resign at this time, but the DNA board refused to accept his resignation. The Tribal Council then added members to the DNA board in a new effort to influence its direction. Mitchell resigned his directorship in February 1970, staying on for the remainder of the year as director of DNA's litigation and law reform unit before accepting, in December

1970, the directorship of an OEO legal services program in Micronesia.[32]

With the resignation of Ted Mitchell from the directorship of DNA and the assumption of that position by Leo Haven, a Navajo who had formerly served as deputy director of the program, the debate over DNA entered a new stage. Although Mitchell remained with the program, DNA still stood less to be criticized as being dominated by an outsider now that Haven headed the operation. Two of the three leading candidates for the chairmanship of the Navajo Tribal Council, Sam Billison and Peter MacDonald, expressed support of DNA in the summer of 1970. Chairman Nakai, however, remained resolute in his opposition. One of his floor leaders in the council, delegate Frank Luther from Inscription House, led another foray against DNA in June 1970. Luther utilized Monroe Price's "Lawyers on the Reservation: Some Implications for the Legal Profession" to bolster his argument that DNA represented a political force that encouraged less reliance on existing political struc- tures, such as the tribal government. Leo Haven tartly replied that "this one white man's philosophy will not affect the fate of Indian culture."[33] The council turned aside a DNA proposal for council endorsement of direct DNA funding from the OEO, referring the resolution to a review committee composed of Nakai, Vice Chairman Nelson Damon, General Counsel Harold Mott, and Director of Administration Edward McCabe, which came back with a completely revised resolution calling for a legal services program other than DNA to be funded and placed under council control. This resolution passed, with thirty-three delegates voting yes, twenty-six no, four abstaining, and eleven absent.[34] However, the OEO continued to fund DNA independently of the council. Peter MacDonald's election to the chairmanship of the Navajo Tribal Council in November 1970, together with the election of a clear majority of council delegates sympathetic to his ideas, meant new life for the em- battled legal services program.

The years 1969 and 1970 involved more for DNA than its troubles with the Nakai administration and its supporters on the Navajo Tribal Council. In 1970, for example, DNA accepted almost 12,000 cases brought to it by individual Navajos. These cases are summarized in Table 7.[35] In addition, DNA attorneys engaged in other activities both within and outside of the Navajo Nation. They helped to alter Gallup, New Mexico, policies toward Navajos charged with intoxication.[36] They

TABLE 7

DNA Cases Handled During 1970

Problem Area	Number of Cases
Consumer and employment	1,593
Sales contracts	812
Garnishment and attachment	12
Wage claims	79
Bankruptcy	5
Other	685
Administrative	1,633
State and local welfare	968
Social Security	133
Workman's Compensation	56
Veterans Administration	47
Unemployment insurance	46
Other	383
Housing	45
Private landlord and tenant	8
Housing code violations	0
Public housing	11
Other	26
Family	2,671
Divorce and annulment	640
Separation	30
Nonsupport	311
Custody and guardianship	239
Paternity	408
Adoption	125
Other	918
Miscellaneous	6,008
Torts	440
Juvenile (Tribal)	54
School cases	48
Misdemeanors	2,456
Other criminal	75
Commitment procedures	6
Other (land disputes, pawn, grazing rights)	2,929
Total	11,950

Source: *Law in Action* 4, no. 6 (March 29, 1971).

worked to alter existing pawn regulations and continued to appeal the McClanahan case concerning the states' right to collect state income tax from Navajo wages earned within the Navajo Nation. In *State of Arizona v. Turtle*, they affirmed the right of the Navajo Nation to refuse to extradite Indian citizens to a state if it so chose.[37]

DNA counsel also affected the perspective and goals of Navajos about the legal profession, the possibilities of achieving change, and the roles they could play in bringing about desired changes. Despite the attention usually given to the actions of DNA directors and attorneys, the central importance of DNA counselors and interpreters at the local level should not be underemphasized, as they affected the tribal court system's operation and underwent a kind of leadership training program for Navajos who have since been active in community concerns.

INDUSTRIAL DEVELOPMENT

If industrial development did not emerge as a central issue in the Jones-Nakai campaign of 1963, perhaps it should have. The Nakai years marked a clearly different approach to economic development, particularly in the realm of industrial promotion.

A March 3, 1964 Tribal Council resolution thus "invites and encourages investment by private capital to develop the extensive natural and human resources of the Navajo Reservation." While the tribal government affirmed that it favored full investment by private sources, it suggested it would share investment costs in projects that promised "to provide employment for Navajo individuals in substantial numbers." Given the absence of available industrial buildings, furthermore, the tribe declared that it might construct or have constructed industrial buildings that could be rented to industry wishing to locate in the Navajo Nation.

Though the council noted that Diné preferred to participate in the economic development of the Navajo Nation "by using its land instead of its money," it left the door open to substantial aid to any industry willing to open a plant on Navajo land.[38] By autumn of 1966, the Tribal Council had appropriated $1 million for industrial development, and several industries had been assisted by the use of these funds.

In Nakai's words, he and the council "adopted as the goal the bringing in of industry and job opportunities to the Reservation." In the first years

of his two terms in office, a number of industries did locate on the Navajo
Nation, including Fairchild Semiconductor of Shiprock, but also several
smaller concerns, such as Cardinal Plastics and Navajo Concrete. The key
to this industrial expansion, as Nakai saw it, was to make sure there were
sufficient inducements for industry: "Industrial plants like people grow
in places where they feel wanted and needed. They know when they are
wanted and needed by the sacrifices made to help them be born." He concluded:

One of the primary problems in bringing industry onto the Reservation
is the lack of community facilities to support industries. Houses are needed
for workers, the company must have a permanent building. The company
buildings and the workers' houses must have water, electricity, fuel, and
a sewer system, child-care services are needed for working parents. Workers
need a place to shop for food and clothes. Recreational facilities are
needed for leisure time. These problems industry does not normally have
to face, they simply locate in towns and cities that already have these
facilities. If we are to get additional industries on the Reservation, we
must provide communities that will support such industries.[39]

This enthusiastic clasp of industry led the tribe to take on some questionable clients. The two most outstanding debacles were provided by
the Armex Corporation of New Jersey and the Westward Coach Corporation. Armex began a short-lived operation manufacturing tennis shoes at
Mexican Springs, New Mexico, while Westward Coach located at Mexican
Hat, Utah, to manufacture trailers, accessories, and campers. Both concerns
came to the reservation during 1970, the final year of the Nakai administration, and initially were lauded as "outstanding accomplishments."[40] All
too soon, as discussed in Chapter 5, it would become evident that the
tribe had been swindled by both corporations.

The two most highly publicized industrial plants to be located in this
era on the Navajo reservation were Fairchild Camera and Instrument
Corporation and General Dynamics Corporation. While notable additions
to the Navajo economy, they must be viewed analytically. Fairchild
chose its Shiprock location primarily because of a resource the Navajos
themselves advertised strenuously: of cheap labor. General Dynamics, in
turn, selected its Fort Defiance site on the basis of the Fairchild
experience.[41]

Both Fairchild and General Dynamics received generous assistance from the tribe and the federal government in preparing the plant site, construction, lease arrangements, and salaries for workers. At Shiprock, Fairchild leased an industrial site built to Fairchild's specifications. The Navajo Nation constructed the plant, using the tribal treasury for one-third of the costs and obtaining the remaining two-thirds from an Economic Development Administration loan. Fairchild provided the working capital, machinery, and technical expertise to run the plant. The tribe built and leased the plant for General Dynamics. Under the lease General Dynamics paid back three-fourths of the building costs in five years; Fairchild was to pay back a similar percentage in twelve years. Both General Dynamics and Fairchild received government assistance to train Navajo workers.[42]

Though Fairchild and General Dynamics have employed many Navajos, their defense-related contracts had suffered by 1970 with the decline in some areas of defense spending and the downturn in the national economy. General Dynamics began to lay off some of its original staff, as did Fairchild. This trend toward reduction of the Navajo labor force at the two plants would raise questions about the companies' motives and the advisability of supporting such economic development.

Lorraine Turner Ruffing's analysis of the costs involved in establishing plants for Fairchild and General Dynamics is persuasive. Ruffing argued that the rate of return to the tribe and to the Economic Development Administration (for whom she prepared the study) has been far less than generally understood. Her summary of the cost of setting up the General Dynamics operation in Fort Defiance and the Fairchild operation in Shiprock is shown in Tables 8 and 9.[43]

What then, did it cost to create jobs for Navajo workers at these two plants? The job creation cost for the ninety-five Navajo employees (of 106) at the General Dynamics plant has been $10,136 per person. At Fairchild, the job creation cost for the 724 Navajo employees (of 750) has been $4,571 per person, plus on-the-job subsidy costs of $1,101 per person. Once Economic Development Administration interest charges were deducted, the tribe's rate of return on its investment as of 1971 was 14 percent for the General Dynamics operation but only 1 percent for Fairchild.[44]

Given the limited capital that the Navajos (let alone the EDA) have to utilize, there may be more profitable and efficacious ways for them to

TABLE 8

General Dynamics Costs

Investor	Amount	Type of Fund	Interest	Rental
Fort Defiance park				
EDA	$101,000	Grant	—[a]	—
Tribe	25,000	EDA loan	$611	—
Tribe	17,000	Own funds	—	—
G.D. building				
Tribe	600,000	Own funds	—	b
G.D. equipment				
Tribe	200,000	Own funds	—	b

a Zero

b Withheld by request of the Navajo Tribe

Source: Lorraine Turner Ruffing, "Economic Development and Navajo Social Structure" (unpublished, prepared for the Economic Development Administration, 1973), p. 91.

TABLE 9

Fairchild Costs

Investor	Amount	Type of Fund	Interest	Rental
Shiprock park				
EDA	$122,400	Grant	—[a]	—
Tribe	30,000	Loan	$ 785	
Shiprock water				
EDA	1,000,000	Grant	—	—
Tribe	650,000	Loans	27,930	—
Fairchild facility				
Tribe	462,800	Loans	28,476[b]	c
Tribe	22,000	Loans	11,664[b]	c
Tribe	366,000			
Total	$3,331,800		$68,775	

a Zero

b Estimate.

c Withheld by request of Navajo Tribe

Source: Ruffing, "Economic Development and Navajo Social Structure," p. 91.

invest their money. The solution Ruffing provided, to which a growing
number of Navajos would subscribe, is to use Navajo capital to create
industries truly controlled by Diné. However, as Ruffing pointed out,
the general approach to economic development taken thus far by the
tribe is to use the vast majority of development funds for infrastructure.
Such an investment, she contended, is necessary but not sufficient:
it provides the potential for growth but not growth itself.

Ruffing believed that future Navajo economic development should be
tied to existing strengths in the Navajo social order. Diné economic
planners should make use of existing cooperative behavior at the local
and community level. The traditional stockraising economy could be
made much more profitable without radical reeducation of rural Navajos,
she argued.[45]

While Ruffing's field experience in the isolated Shonto (Arizona)
region may have made her overly optimistic about the vitality of the
traditional economy and its potential for contributing to the overall
amelioration of the Navajo economy, her perceptions revealed a basic
truth too often overlooked by outside analysts clucking their tongues
about the supposedly abominable living conditions in which Navajos
live.[46] While one cannot deny the widespread existence of poverty within
the Navajo Nation or ignore the very human problems yet to be solved,
it would be quite misleading to base one's estimation of Navajo well-being
solely on unemployment figures or per capita income statistics. There is,
in fact, much that is desirable about the traditional way, much in it that
urban, seemingly acculturated Navajos continue to find attractive and
important. Traditional economic pursuits would continue to be a vital
element in the economic strategy planned by the Navajo national
government.

NAVAJO MINERAL RESOURCES

As noted in the previous chapter, by the final years of Paul Jones'
administration, Navajo coal had assumed increased importance. Growing
Southwestern power demands coupled with the availability of not only
Navajo coal but Navajo water as well had altered the picture. Coal-fueled
power plants in the region could utilize Navajo coal and, in most instances,
water to which Navajos had some claim. For the Mohave plant, in Clark

County, Nevada, coal could be slurried in an eighteen-inch steel pipeline from Black Mesa, Arizona, over a distance of 273.6 miles. The Navajo power plant at Page, Arizona, would receive its needed coal by a specially built railroad stretching eighty miles from Black Mesa to Page.[47]

Since the mid-1960s national publicity has been given to the vast coal resources of the Western states. Power-producing interests have placed a high priority on using these reserves. It is essential to remember that when the Navajo Nation signed leasing agreements for its coal resources with Utah Mining and Manufacturing for the Four Corners plant in 1961, and with Peabody Coal Company for Black Mesa in 1964 and 1966, coal's importance was portrayed in a far different manner. The Navajos believed their coal could be of value only in the immediate future; nuclear power facilities would make the Navajo coal practically obsolete for energy-producing purposes. If Diné were to benefit at all from their coal, they had to make an agreement for its utilization promptly. Graham Holmes put it the most precisely: "The Navajos were told fossil fuel wouldn't be worth a tinker's damn."[48]

In addition to fearing their coal reserves would soon be irrelevant, why else did The People make agreements to participate in and have their resources used for electrical power production? Financial incentives surely influenced these decisions. From the strip mining operation at Black Mesa, for example, the Navajos will receive over $2 million per year in royalties for thirty-five years. Mining operations and power plant construction also promised many jobs for Navajo workers. Navajo Tribal Council Chairman Raymond Nakai had been persuaded of the importance and value of bringing in such industrial projects. Officials from South-western states, industrial concerns, and the Bureau of Indian Affairs as well as Navajo tribal technical advisors, advised Diné that they should proceed. Graham Holmes, for example, recalled Navajo tribal lawyer Norman Littell, who negotiated the Peabody contract, "walking up the Council aisle, waving papers for the Council to approve, like the Saviour had returned."[49]

These positive reasons for making such agreements represented only part of the picture. Many Navajo representatives did not foresee the environmental difficulties that coal strip mining and coal-fired power plants would cause. They misjudged the public controversy these operations would bring and overestimated the financial benefits Navajos would receive. Most delegates did not expect the awesome pollution that the

Four Corners power plant emits. Astronauts high over the earth's surface would report later that they could view but one man-made creation: the particulate matter spewing forth from Four Corners. Council members generally did not anticipate the vision of the strip-mined land, nor could they have predicted the intensity of the Navajo and non-Navajo opposition. One critic labeled Black Mesa strip mining "like tearing down St. Peter's to get at the marble." The ability of these opponents to rally public sentiment must have been underestimated. Such organizations as Dinébeiina Nahiilna Be Agaditahe (DNA), the legal services group, which figured prominently in the dispute, had not yet been created. Finally, the number of jobs created for Navajos and the duration of much of this employment doubtless became inflated in the hopeful atmosphere surrounding the project's beginnings.

The Black Mesa controversy illustrated the importance of providing complete information and allowing for full debate prior to the signing of a lease or any other agreement by the Navajo Nation. Councilman Keith Smith later admitted of the Peabody contract: "It was done without adequate deliberation; the Council never had a good discussion on it." Of particular significance is the informing of local people most directly affected by such an operation. Again and again, residents of Black Mesa claimed they were not informed; Many Mules' Daughter's complaint is typical: "Where they are mining now is my land. My father is buried there. His grave was torn up in the strip mining. I never approved of anything in the agreement to mine this area. I don't know of anybody who agreed to the contract."[50]

The Black Mesa power plant affair also showed that the Navajo were still getting insufficient technical advice. Navajos had to rely on the expertise of economists, lawyers, geologists, engineers, and others; many Navajos have cited Black Mesa as a case in point for the need for more trained Navajo professionals, who would be in the best position to advise the Tribal Council as to the most proper course to follow.

The Black Mesa power plant controversy finally provided a classic example of the way outside pressures can affect the use of resources owned by another group of people. Whether viewed from a colonial, metropolis-satellite, or other model, the situation represents the dilemma faced by Native American peoples across the country: how to best utilize their resources in the face of external pressure and internal needs. Many Navajos came to perceive what they saw as a highly complex series of interrelationships and dependencies, ranging from the Navajo shepherd displaced by the mining operation to the fellow in Albuquerque with an electric toothbrush.[51]

NAVAJO WATER RIGHTS AND WATER USAGE

Navajo water rights and water usage are nearly synonymous. Given the importance of prior appropriation of this rare Southwestern resource, we may say that Navajos must use water resources almost before they can claim the right to do so. The Navajo Nation exists in a region where the availability of water is unusual, and the right to use those limited quantities is highly contested. Thus water is a key not only to Navajo national economic development but to the growth of the entire Southwest. The picture is complicated by many factors, including the special status of Native Americans and Native American water rights. The Bureau of Reclamation, for example, the chief competitor for Navajo water, co-exists with the Bureau of Indian Affairs in the Department of the Interior. Thus Bureau of Reclamation projects requiring Indian land and thus, ultimately, Interior Department approval may have a built-in conflict with Indian interests. Such conflicts have had important repercussions for the Navajos.

We must develop some understanding of Navajo water rights before considering the contemporary struggle for water usage. The demands of the Navajo for fair appropriation of available water in the Colorado River basin are usually couched in terms of applicability of the Winters doctrine. This doctrine refers to an early twentieth-century United States Supreme Court decision that profoundly affected Native American water rights. In *Winters* v. *U.S.*, 207 U.S. 564 (1908), the court ruled in favor of the Fort Belknap Indians of Montana, who claimed water rights on the Milk River also claimed by non-Indians. The justices' decision held that the federal government must reserve water needed for agricultural production on an Indian reservation. Applied to the Navajos, this ruling should reserve for agricultural purposes sufficient amounts of water from the Colorado River and its tributaries, the Little Colorado and its tributaries, and the San Juan River and its tributaries.[52]

But what is sufficient? How do Navajo rights mesh with the rights of the Southwestern states? These and other questions have yet to be fully resolved by the courts, although court rulings subsequent to the Winters decision have often related to the Navajo situation. As is frequently the case, proponents on one position may use one decision while opponents use another to buttress their various contentions.

The issue of reservation of Navajo water rights provides a good example of conflicting interpretations. Did the Navajos through the Treaty of 1868 reserve water rights for themselves? Those who so believe cite *U.S. v. Winans*, 198 U.S. 371 (1905), which contends Indian water rights stem from time immemorial; those who do not may refer to *Arizona v. California*, 376 U.S. 340 (1963), which supports the theory that the government specifically reserves water from the public domain for Native Americans. University of New Mexico student Nancy Hilding noted:

Winters rights must be given a priority date that places them within the state's prior appropriation time-line. In all court cases thus far, the Winters priority dates have been held to be the dates of the federal action that created the reservation. This is accepted law but it might be changed, if someone were to argue a Winans interpretation in court. If Indians reserved their own "time immemorially" owned rights then the priority date would be time immemorial.[53]

Attorney Robert Dellwo called *Arizona v. California* "perhaps the most important water rights decision in history" for it contained "in uniform sequences, a series of holdings affirming the priority of the Indians' water rights." This ruling granted Lower Colorado River rights for five small tribes of 895,496 annual acre feet but specifically exempted Navajo rights to this water from consideration at that time. The decision, nonetheless, according to Dellwo's interpretation, would hold great significance for the Navajos. Dellwo summarized the findings:

1. The doctrine of equitable apportionment for the allocation of waters between states is not binding on Indian tribes;
2. The U.S. did have authority to make implied or express reservations of water for the benefit of Indian reservations in navigable water either by executive order or by statute before and after statehood;
3. The Court made short shrift of the date of the decision of any distinction between the Indian reserved water rights on true reservations and those set apart by Executive Order;

4. The Court unqualifiedly approved as applicable to the Colorado River watershed, the Winters Doctrine of implied reservation of water for the Indians; and

5. The Court rejected the contention of the State of Arizona that the reservation of water for Indians should be on a per capita rather than per acre basis and held that the amount allocated should be measured by the amount of irrigable acreage.[54]

Despite these important contentions, Navajos and other tribes must act to support these rights. Until very recently, few Navajos possessed substantial knowledge of these rights. While tribal attorneys lobbied in court for rights to Colorado River water, they did so without great success and apparently without the full awareness of the Tribal Council, let alone The People themselves. Thus the Diné not only fell victim to the old Western water adage, "use it or lose it," but the Tribal Council eventually made some agreements with outside interests that severely limited the extent to which Navajos could press their rights.

Navajo land is mostly high, arid desert country. Yet, according to DNA attorney Robert Hilgendorf, at least 2 million of the 16 million acres of reservation land are irrigable and would require 12 million acre feet of water per year, whereas the Navajos now are using only 13,500 acre feet per year.[55] Given the fifth point summarized by Dellwo above of *Arizona v. California,* surely the Navajos would be entitled to a larger share than they are presently receiving of the Colorado River water available to them. Moreover, it would seem wise for the Navajos to explore carefully all available sources of water on the reservation and to use these fully for Navajo purposes.

Unfortunately for the sake of Navajo self-sufficiency, both existing and potential Navajo water resources became part of the bargaining in the efforts to increase electrical power production in the Southwest. Moreover, water projects of the Southwestern states have generally gained a higher priority within the Department of the Interior; and thus Navajo projects like the long-awaited Navajo Indian Irrigation Project near Shiprock have been subjected to continual delays.

Environmentalists' objections to Black Mesa and associated power plant development usually have focused on destruction to land and life style and air pollution. They have usually overlooked the question of water rights and usage. However, in the long run this issue may well be more significant to the cause of Navajo self-determination than any other effect of power production in the Navajo area. Equally, Navajo water is essential to the operation of the Mohave and Page power plants as well as the proposed coal gasification plants in the Burnham area. For example, the Mohave plant operation requires coal to be slurried 273.6 miles through an eighteen-inch pipeline from the Peabody mine on Black Mesa. Such an operation obviously requires a great deal of water, and in order to obtain it a series of five deep wells had to be drilled two miles apart. Approximately 2,310 gallons of water per minute may then be pumped from the Navajo sandstone level. This is an impressive amount of water, particularly in the Southwest, but even more so given the quality of this water and the fact that it cannot be reclaimed from ground level. It is a moot point whether Navajo tribal officials were misled about Black Mesa deep well water—some contend they were told it was brackish and not good for much—but, in any event, all now acknowledge it is excellent, perhaps the best the Navajos have.[56] It could be put to other and more profitable uses besides the slurrying of coal.

In all fairness to Peabody Coal officials, we may in all probability discount the fear that deep well pumping will affect the shallow wells area residents depend upon. The deep wells are sealed at the 2,000-foot level, below the Mancos shale area, and thus should not reduce the supply of water The People normally take. On the other hand, geological considerations also dictate that, if the Mancos shale provides a barrier in one direction, it also prevents recharging of the sandstone source from the Black Mesa surface. It is, therefore, as Bureau of Indian Affairs teacher Eugene Gade pointed out at hearings before a special Senate investigative body, "an essentially nonrenewable resource. Some recharge does occur but neither we nor our great, great, great grandchildren will live to see this recharge, because it takes thousands or even millions of years for water to percolate into such an aquifer in significant quantities."[57]

Navajo rights to the Colorado River are at stake in the utilization of Black Mesa coal. Arizona's newest railroad takes Black Mesa coal from the mine to the Navajo plant near Page. Page is not really a Navajo community. It is an island of nonreservation land created in 1957 by the construction of Glen Canyon Dam and the formation of Lake Powell. Navajos traded land here for land in the McCracken Mesa, Utah, area so that the dam could be built. Glen Canyon Dam came to be only after environmentalists' objections helped stop the damming of the Colorado River near the Grand Canyon. In the end, Glen Canyon, "the place no one knew," and the surrounding area were flooded and the area renamed Lake Powell.[58]

Lake Powell provided the water needed by the Navajo power plant, 34,000 acre feet, which must come out of Arizona's small appropriation of 50,000 acre feet of upper basin Colorado River water. On the basis of their Winters Doctrine rights, the Navajos had a potential claim to this water; given the Navajo reservation's location, in any case, the State of Arizona was not likely to try to use the source. In order for the Page power plant to function, Navajos had to be willing to relinquish these rights, and they did so through a Tribal Council resolution in 1968, which waived their Winters Doctrine rights for the life of the power plant and waived the leftover portion of the upper basin Colorado River water in exchange for having the plant built on reservation land near Page.[59] Moreover, the tribe declared that in the foreseeable future it would not need more than 17,000 acre feet of water for agricultural purposes, a highly conservative amount for significant agricultural development in the high desert.

Why did the Navajos make such an agreement? They did so apparently for much the same reasons for which they had approved other similar programs: the need for employment and additional revenues for the tribal treasury. Navajos gained preference for employment at the power plant and a buyer for their coal from the Black Mesa mines. Officials for the Page plant had to lease land for the power plant site, allow the Navajo Tribal Utility Authority to purchase electrical power from the plant, and grant $125,000 to Navajo Community College. DNA staff members suggested charitably that the college use the sum to endow a chair in water law. Diné also gained the assurance that, if additional water should happen to be transported into the upper basin area, Navajos would "share proportionately in that water." When this might happen and what proportion the tribe would receive remain altogether unknown. In addition, one must remember that the Navajo Tribal Council, in the words of Monroe Price and Gary Weatherford:

gained its information primarily from the Salt River Project, the Bureau of Reclamation, and the Upper Colorado River Commission—the entities that were negotiating with the tribe. Data on current water usage, irrigable acreage, future water use alternatives, and benefits to the tribe were primarily prepared by non-Navajo interests.[60]

As in the case of Black Mesa, the Navajo Tribal Council delegates doubtless were under great pressure to approve this development. Wayne Aspinall, head of the House Interior Committee and elected representative from southwestern Colorado, knew full well the threat posed to Colorado's substantial portion of the upper basin Colorado River water supply by the Navajos' Winters Doctrine rights. Aspinall apparently made it clear he would block Central Arizona Project funds unless the Navajos waived their water rights. The Department of the Interior certainly proved guilty of a conflict of interest. While the Bureau of Indian Affairs should have acted to safeguard Navajo interests, instead and as usual the Bureau of Reclamation gained the upper hand and its officials pressed for Navajo acquiescence.[61]

Arizona Congressman Sam Steiger, whose sprawling district included the Arizona portion of the Navajo reservation, provided additional evidence of this pressure by introducing H.R. 10534 on April 21, 1969. This bill transferred the Antelope Point area of 750 acres ceded by the Navajos back in the 1958 Glen Canyon land exchange to the tribe. In exchange, the Navajo Nation had only to grant 3,000 additional acre feet of its remaining upper basin Colorado River water for the use of Page and Glen Canyon Dam and limit its claim to 50,000 acre feet of upper basin water as allocated through the Colorado River Basin Compact, not only as long as the Page power plant was in operation but permanently. The Navajo Tribal Council, however, tabled a resolution supporting this arrangement. A later resolution would have accepted the Steiger plan in part but would not have waived Winters Doctrine rights permanently. At the present time, it is uncertain whether the Navajos may reclaim their waived rights. They have a chance of doing so only if they can prove they did not have the full knowledge necessary of the existence of their rights and all relevant facts. The fact that officers of the Department of the Interior and the Salt River Project drafted the resolution in question may not be sufficient.[62]

The Navajo Indian Irrigation Project must be included in any discussion of Navajo water rights and water usage. Recommendations for using San Juan River water to irrigate date back to the nineteenth century, the first field surveys being made in 1945. According to Young, the Navajo tribal government "played an active part in the drafting of a bill to authorize the Navajo Irrigation and San Juan-Chama Projects." New Mexico officials utilized Navajo desires, in fact, to put together the package deal of NIIP and the San Juan-Chama diversion project. Congress authorized both projects in 1962. The Navajo Indian Irrigation Project eventually would irrigate 110,630 acres of Navajo reservation land in the Shiprock area by taking 508,000 acre feet from the Navajo Dam on the San Juan River in northern New Mexico.[63]

The Navajo Nation has placed a high priority on completing the Navajo Indian Irrigation Project. In fact, so eager was it to have the project implemented that in 1957 the Tribal Council apparently waived Winters Doctrine rights to Navajo reservoir water created by Navajo Dam in exchange for the project—again at the behest of Congressman Aspinall. While former Interior Department solicitor Edward Weinberg contends this was a Navajo idea, Navajo administrator J. Maurice McCabe wrote Aspinall: "This concession was only agreed to by the Tribe in consideration of getting the Navajo Irrigation Project established in New Mexico." Senator Clinton Anderson of New Mexico concurred in a meeting of January 29, 1960, of the Congressional joint committee on Navajo-Hopi administration, "The actual fact is that the State of Colorado suggested that the Navajo irrigation project be held up until there was agreement with New Mexico as to how the bill could be amended to protect Colorado's interests what they regarded as adequately."[64]

It can be argued, nonetheless, that the wheeling and dealing that preceded the 1962 congressional authorization of the NIIP represented successful use of the Navajos' Winters rights. Because of the Navajos' potential claim, the tribe could get something—the NIIP—in exchange for relinquishing their special water rights. However, it is instructive to note that the two projects did not fare equally upon gaining approval. San Juan-Chama moved rapidly toward completion, whereas the Navajo irrigation project continually faced inadequate funding and support.[65]

In 1966, both Senator Clinton Anderson of New Mexico and Secretary of the Interior Stewart Udall asked that the NIIP be reevaluated. Anderson urged the projected 110,000 acres be reduced to 77,000. Udall wrote to Anderson that the project should be reconsidered in light of the heightened Navajo prospects for industrial development. Navajos threatened to withdraw their support of San Juan-Chama and Anderson backed off. Still, a Bureau of Reclamation task force noted alternative possibilities for Navajo water and accentuated the perhaps inevitable alteration being effected in the project's form—from small, family farms to tribal agribusiness. The project would continue, if in halting fashion.[66]

NAVAJO EDUCATION

The Navajo educational picture was characterized by seemingly conflicting developments during the Nakai years. On the one hand, the Bureau of Indian Affairs continued to play a significant role. In the last half of the 1960s the bureau constructed several large (600-1000 students) elementary boarding schools at Chuska, Toyei, and Many Farms and shut down some of the smaller and older boarding schools. Navajo students still attended Intermountain (Utah) School in large numbers, as well as Fort Wingate High School near Gallup, New Mexico, and the new Many Farms Boarding High School on the reservation.

The prominent position the Bureau occupied attracted wide criticism during this period. In the so-called Kennedy Report of 1969 and elsewhere, critics accused BIA teachers and administrators of being insensitive to cultural differences, providing poor instruction, overemphasizing vocational training at the expense of college preparatory work, and not trying hard enough to alter the boarding system. Taken in sum, the criticisms represented a serious indictment of an imposed, externally controlled system.[67]

Navajos often complained about their lack of control over Bureau schools. As the Bureau was under civil service guidelines, personnel based in Albuquerque hired staff. Navajos had no voice in teacher selection or placement. Thus, if they so chose, staff members could operate largely independently of the Navajo public. In her testimony before the Kennedy subcommittee in 1968, tribal council delegate Annie Wauneka provided an example of this lack of community control. She told of an incident at the Steamboat Boarding School, where the community wished to remove the top personnel because they "were unfair to the children, they were unfair to the employees, they were unfair to the community in certain ways." The Steamboat chapter members voted 171 to 0 asking for these people to be transferred, but Graham Holmes and other BIA officials responded that the civil service regulations would not permit it.[68]

One observer called the construction of large elementary boarding schools on the Navajo reservation in the late 1960s a shift toward the development of the noncommunity schools. The noncommunity school, this critic suggested, offered less real education because it isolated parents from the institutions, removed students from their home communities, and tended "to reduce classes to more or less manageable 'herds' of students with little real personal interaction with transient, non-Navajo teachers." The community school movement was a response to the short-comings of noncommunity schools.[69]

The community school effort began with a short-lived demonstration school project at Lukachukai, Arizona, followed by the establishment of Rough Rock Demonstration School in 1966. Residents of the Rock Point, Ramah, and Borrego Pass communities are also now served by their own schools. While the low income level of the residents in these communities prevents them from contributing substantial financial support to the schools at this time, local Navajos have participated in the community schools to a much greater extent than has been the case in Navajo education generally.

At the dedication of the Lukachukai project on April 30, 1965, Tribal Chairman Raymond Nakai said the experiment would "add to the existing academic program those things which make it possible for Navajo students to receive the best possible education based on new techniques and ideas," would "develop programs which will make the community and the parents a vital force in Navajo education," and would "make the Navajo children proud of who they are and knowledgable about their community, tribe and history." An adequate force of fully trained remedial teachers and language instructors, the presence of Navajo elders, and the availability of Navajos as Navajo language teachers would help in the effort to reach these goals.[70]

But despite these exciting and innovative approaches, the Lukachukai experiment proved a failure. The main problem seemed to be the addition of new staff and new ideas to the Bureau school operation, which had been present at Lukachukai for many years. In the end the graft did not take, although the demonstration had been blessed with significant funding from the Office of Economic Opportunity, support of leading Navajo advocates of Navajo control of Navajo education such as Raymond Nakai and Councilman Allen Yazzie, participation of experienced advisors such as Robert Roessel of Arizona State University, the backing of

Graham Holmes and other important bureau officials, and the direction
of Thomas Reno, a capable administrator. Ideally one should start anew,
with new facilities, a new staff, and children from the immediate community surrounding the school. It so happened that an opportunity for
such a school could be found at Rough Rock, a small community sixteen
miles west of Many Farms.

Situated at the geographical center of the Navajo Nation, in the shadow
of Black Mesa, the Rough Rock community represented the traditional
Navajo socioeconomic way. The people of Rough Rock raised sheep, did
their shopping for the most part at the local trading post, and spoke
Navajo. While Rough Rock was a typical rural Navajo community it was
equally a true challenge for those who advocated Navajo control of Navajo
education; the people had had little formal education and no previous
contact with a school in their community.

While Bureau personnel indicated their willingness to have the Rough
Rock school facility be utilized for demonstration purposes by OEO
officials, they could not contract with them directly so a prominent group
of Navajo leaders—Allen Yazzie, Ned Hatathli, and Guy Gorman—formed
a corporation to do so. The three men called the corporation Demonstration in Navajo Education (DINE). Robert Roessel was hired to be the
school's first director. Roessel engaged the school's first teaching staff,
and the school opened in September 1966. Meanwhile, the Rough Rock
community had elected five of its members to the school board. While
DINE served as the receiver of the OEO funds, the formal authority for
the operation and direction of Rough Rock School rested officially in
the school board.

During Roessel's tenure as director of Rough Rock School a controversy erupted over the actual exercise of control. Roessel left the school
in the autumn of 1968 to assume the presidency of Navajo Community
College; a Navajo, Dillon Platero, became the new director of Rough
Rock School. The dispute occurred early in the school's history and much
has happened at Rough Rock since Roessel's departure so one can overemphasize the importance of the disagreement. Yet since the controversy
is directly related to the problem of establishing genuine Navajo control
of Navajo education it deserves consideration.

As required by officials of the Office of Economic Opportunity,
Rough Rock School was evaluated by a team of outside educators led by
Donald Erickson, a professor of education at the University of Chicago.

While highly critical of the Rough Rock operation for not allowing the exercise of meaningful Navajo control, the evaluators did pay homage to the strengths of the school as they perceived them. They stated in the report that Rough Rock did represent a needed change from the mass, impersonal boarding school, a basic breakthrough in the instruction of Navajo history, culture, and language, and a much closer affiliation with the community than a typical Navajo school enjoyed.[71]

The basic disagreement, however, focused on the roles played at Rough Rock by the school board and the director. Roessel had contended consistently that the board provided the real direction for Rough Rock. He called the board the heart of the school and said Rough Rock had made it "clear that Indian people have the capacity and the interest to direct, lead and control their educational programs."[72] Broderick Johnson, now director of the Navajo Community College Press, wrote in *Navaho Education at Rough Rock,* a volume published by the Rough Rock School:

The board is not a rubber stamp for Roessel. In fact, it frequently disagrees with his proposals and recommendations. Even when it agrees, it generally goes into minute detail regarding the pros and cons of a matter and may give him a hard time before offering approval. And Roessel says, "That's exactly the way I want it. I want the Navaho people through this board to control the school. I want the board to prove that with sound judgment it can have the best and most efficient Indian school in the country—that the Indian can learn and adjust to both cultures and be a credit to his race—that we have here the beginning of the salvation of the Indian and his values, as well as an example for the nation and the world—and that this school holds great promise for the poor, uneducated people everywhere."[73]

In their investigation, however, Erickson and his associates found what they believed to be a remarkably different situation. Through an analysis of the school board minutes they were permitted to see, through community interviews, and through their own observations at the school, the evaluators concluded that while "important strides were made toward achieving community control at Rough Rock," "much distance remained to be covered." On the positive side, they noted that board members were "exceptionally well known in the community, were believed genuinely in control of the school and were viewed by at least half the parents as responsive to community opinion. The school was a remarkably focal community institution." Yet they found "the board's involvement in budgetary considerations and classroom and dormitory affairs was surprisingly limited." "With some exceptions," they added, "one could argue, its attention was wedded to functions not normally assumed by schools, such as community development and a rotating employment program for local people." While they concluded the board's "overall impact was no doubt very beneficial," they felt its structure "seriously needed revising" and was "not a model to be adopted elsewhere" for it did not have sufficient independence from the school administrator in part because the administrator paid the board's salaries through funds received from DINE.[74]

As project director, Erickson obtained the services of five consultants known for their sympathy to Native American control of Native American education and their personal commitment to the Rough Rock idea to discuss the early findings of the Rough Rock School evaluation. The five, including three anthropologists—Oswald Werner, Gary Witherspoon, and Sol Tax—a psychiatrist, Robert Bergman, and an attorney, Joseph Muskrat, strongly disagreed with what they saw as the direction of Erickson's interpretation. Before the final Erickson report actually had been published, they released a twenty-page mimeographed response "based entirely on the 'secret' preliminary findings," which contended that Erickson and his associates had been overcome by culture shock which had rendered them incapable of doing a proper study. They contested the evaluators' evaluative procedures (sampling techniques, translations, comparisons) and, more critically, their perceptions of the school board's control of Rough Rock. In short, they denied the evaluation's validity because of the evaluators' value judgments; evaluation, the five said, consisted of "research combined with value judgments."[75]

The point of this summary is not to take sides but to illustrate the problems of ascertaining educational progress and the natural sensitivity innovators in Navajo education have displayed. The Navajo school board members at Rough Rock issued a public statement in support of Roessel and his tenure at the school shortly after a brief summary of the Erickson evaluation appeared belatedly in late November in the *Navajo Times*. Erickson has received general support for his critique from a disinterested and respected analyst of Native American education, Murray Wax, and an articulate Navajo educator, Gloria Emerson.[76]

Rough Rock's curriculum center was one of several important continuing developments that merit inclusion in this consideration of community schools. The effort to utilize Navajo as a tool of instruction at the elementary level is dependent upon the production of written Navajo texts. With the exception of a few readers produced during the 1930s and early 1940s, these written texts simply did not exist before Rough Rock, Rock Point School, the University of New Mexico Navajo Reading Study Program, and other agents began to produce them. Written Navajo had been used by missionaries and ethnologists for their particular purposes, but school officials had not wanted to have anything to do with Navajo literacy. Thus the creation of stories and texts in Navajo by the curriculum center has been a vital and innovative task. With such available material the child's ability to learn to read and write is greatly enhanced. Navajo children can utilize their own phonological control of the Navajo language to acquire the central skill of literacy: alphabetic writing. Learning to read and write in Navajo first will not hinder the child's ability to read and write in English and may improve it because the principle has already been mastered.[77]

While Rough Rock has been utilized here as the example of a Navajo community school, in fact it was not the sole example of this kind of educational institution during the 1960s. Ramah Navajo High School, discussed in the following chapter, also came into being shortly before the decade's close. Rock Point School, while under the BIA, still evolved as a school wehre administrators and teachers were sensitive to the wants and needs of the local community. Indeed, under the leadership of principal Wayne Holm, Rock Point School emerged as a vital center for instruction in the Navajo language. Holm, like Roessel, was an Anglo married to a Navajo. He had a strong background in the Navajo language and became a promoter of Navajo literacy. Holm hired Elizabeth Willink following completion of her work at the University of Arizona in 1964 to head Rock Point's English as a Second Language program, when such programs were rare indeed on the Navajo reservation.

Holm's involvement with the Rock Point community apparently began soon after he arrived in 1958. At a community meeting, a Rock Point resident confronted him with the question of why the school had not expanded its facilities as promised. Holm suggested the community form a committee to work toward that objective. With his assistance, the community representatives successfully gained additional buildings at the school. The education committee continued to operate as a body representing the interests of the Rock Point community.[78]

Initially, Rock Point officials seemed to place less emphasis than Rough Rock staff members on a total bilingual approach to elementary education. Most of the Rock Point teachers were Anglo. Holm believed they should speak and instruct in their native language, English, while the Navajo teacher aides should speak and instruct in their native language, Navajo. Since that period Rock Point emerged as a center for Navajo literacy.

While far less publicized nationally than Rough Rock, Rock Point demonstrated equally the promise of the community school approach. These two schools foreshadowed the strong movement toward Navajo control of Navajo education, which would be a hallmark of the 1970s. At the post-high school level, a third educational institution had been established by 1969, representing an additional element in this movement. At Navajo Community College one could perceive the beginnings of a national Navajo approach to Navajo education. The college, ideally, stood to benefit the Diné as a whole and not merely one community.

As the Navajo Nation expanded its need for professional personnel increased. For Navajos to take over the functions of the BIA and other federal and state agencies, Navajos would require training beyond the high school level in large numbers. The Tribal Council decided to invest a large sum from the 1950s oil money into a college scholarship fund, and the availability of this assistance did encourage more Navajo students to attend college. Few students, however, could afford to leave the Navajo Nation for a prolonged period of time. Extended families depended upon their labor and earnings, and the ties of the Navajo homeland remained strong. Few Native American students attended college in the 1950s and 1960s, and most schools lacked Native American studies programs, Indian centers, proper counseling, and necessary tutoring facilities. While Navajos attended college in increasing numbers, few finished with a degree.

Many Navajos believed a college of their own would change the situation. Navajos could then stay near home, attend to family responsibilities, and enroll in a school that included personnel aware of their background and expectations. Raymond Nakai spoke of a Navajo college or academy in 1952. In 1959 Navajo Education Committee Chairman Dillon Platero advocated a feasibility study for the location of a college on the reservation. Two years later, Navajos asked Arizona State University to develop an extensive vocational training program on the Navajo Nation. A survey funded by OEO officials and carried out by Arizona State staff members demonstrated the reasons for starting a college within the Navajo Nation.[79]

Navajo Community College came into existence as a logical progression from the generally positive results achieved at Rough Rock Demonstration School. Many of the key people and critical funding sources present at Rough Rock emerged again at the new Navajo college. Bob Roessel moved from being director of Rough Rock to being president of the college. His replacement at Rough Rock, Dillon Platero, joined the college's board of regents. The DINE board of directors, Guy Gorman, Ned Hatathli, and Allen Yazzie, all assumed important positions at the new school. Gorman became chairman of the board of regents, Hatathli became executive vice president, and Yazzie became vice president for community services. Several teachers who had taught at Rough Rock joined the college's faculty. Broderick Johnson, who had assisted Rough Rock with its publications, directed the newly created Navajo Community College Press. OEO administrators contributed the principal amount of money needed to begin the college, just as they had at Rough Rock.

However, unlike Rough Rock and other community schools, Navajo Community College had as its fundamental community the Navajo Nation. The Board of Regents' membership reflected this constituency, with one representative from each of the five agencies. The Navajo tribe contributed $250,000 to the college and pledged continuing support, though it had not given any money to the community schools. Navajo Community College thus represented the first Navajo national educational venture. As it opened for classes, the *Navajo Times* called it "without question . . . the most exciting happening to come along on this reservation in a long time."[80]

In the months preceding the college's first semester, its Board of Regents and administrators considered what philosophy the school should follow and what programs it should offer. At a June 13, 1968 meeting of the regents, "key staff members" presented a proposed philosophy which the board unanimously approved. The philosophy's first two points encompassed central purposes for which the school would try to stand:

1. In order for any community or society to continue to grow and prosper, it must have its own means for educating its citizens. It is

essential that these educational systems be directed and controlled by the society it is intended to serve.

2. If a community or society is to continue to grow and prosper, then each member of that society must be provided with the opportunity to acquire a positive self-image and a clear sense of identity. This can be achieved only when each individual's capacities are developed and used to the fullest possible extent. It is absolutely necessary, also, for each individual to respect and understand his culture, its heritage and have faith in its future.[81]

The Board of Regents symbolized Navajo control of the college. The regents were well known and respected within the Navajo Nation; their willingness to serve on the board indicated the tribal government's full commitment to the new institution. Board members met regularly during the first years of the college and conscientiously and thoroughly considered basic issues confronting it. However, as people with many different responsibilites, removed from the day-to-day life of the school, they could not serve as initiators of policy. Rather they had to depend, as boards of trustees do, on the administration of the college to serve as initial policy makers responsible for the first-round decision making, while reserving the final and ultimate authority to themselves.[82]

As had been true at Rough Rock, though not for precisely the same reasons, the Navajo Community College Board of Regents thus relied heavily during the college's first year or two upon Bob Roessel and other top administrators such as Ned Hatathli and Allen Yazzie. It should be remembered that the regents, after all, had known Roessel, Hatathli, and Yazzie for years in their capacities as leaders in Navajo education. They had confidence in their abilities and their judgment. The regents' minutes for the first year of the college's existence thus show Roessel as the principal figure bringing issues to the board members for their consideration and presenting recommendations on personnel and other matters for the board members to ratify. While Roessel still attended regents' meetings when he stepped down from the presidency in the summer of 1969 to become chancellor of the college, the primary responsibility for representing the college fell properly to its new president, Ned Hatathli. The board had hired Hatathli upon Roessel's recommendation, but as executive vice president he had been the logical choice for the position and he did not take long to exert his authority.

Navajo Community College opened its doors in January 1969. At first it had to share facilities with the newly built Many Farms Boarding High School. While it began with much fanfare and promise, the college faced some difficult moments in the early days. The physical location was not the least of the problems. Many Farms was a very isolated spot and holding classes on a high school campus did not enhance NCC's image as a "real college." Many students had trouble handling the comparative freedom of college life; some quite frankly were there because it was free and it was something to do. Attendance and morale plummeted. Faculty and student turnover proved considerable. Yet, despite all the problems, Navajo Community College remained important in the 1960s. It was significant as the first Indian college on an Indian reservation and important as a symbol of Navajo education. If the initial results were sometimes disappointing, the college did have a great deal of potential. The 1970s would be a better test. Once the college moved to a permanent home and had had a chance to mature and become established, then one could better judge its lasting value.

As the 1960s concluded, Navajo Tribal Chairman Raymond Nakai undoubtedly could look back with some satisfaction on his two terms in office. While there had been some setbacks, in his view there surely had been advances, too, particularly in the economy and education. Nakai believed he had made a good beginning, yet felt his task was not finished. He decided to seek a third term as tribal chairman. Nakai knew, of course, that the odds could not be entirely in his favor. He had made enemies as well as friends. Some criticized his decisions, pointed to the remaining high unemployment rate, and argued that two terms were enough for any man. By 1970, not only had Nakai decided to seek reelection but his most formidable rival, Peter MacDonald, had just about concluded to challenge the incumbent. It would be a memorable campaign and clearly a centrally important election for its winner would lead the Navajos in the 1970s.

THE FIRST ADMINISTRATION OF PETER MacDONALD

5

In 1970, the Navajo people elected Peter MacDonald as their chairman. They followed tradition in rejecting a two-term incumbent's bid for a third term. But many Navajos voted not just against Raymond Nakai but for Peter MacDonald, who advocated greater Navajo control of Navajo resources and institutions. MacDonald's election ushered in a significant new era in Navajo life. His first term would be characterized by bold initiatives in a number of areas. Whether one termed it self-determination or Navajo nationalism, clearly the Navajos exerted major efforts to take charge of their social, political, and economic existence.

One man alone cannot achieve self-determination for a people. It would be simplistic to give all the credit or all the blame in various areas to Peter MacDonald. MacDonald had a lot of assistance, but he surely set a tone that marked a definite departure from the past. Not all Navajos would agree on his means, but most would subscribe to his ends, as stated in his inaugural address: protecting what is ours, claiming what is due us, replacing what we depend on from others with what we do ourselves, creating for ourselves what we desire but do not have. In the early 1970s the Navajos began to alter their social, political, and economic position in the American Southwest. MacDonald not only presided over this transformation but helped to effect it.

Peter MacDonald's life story delights advocates of the Operation Bootstrap school of socioeconomic advancement. He was born December 16, 1928, on the Navajo reservation in the small northern Arizona community of Teec Nos Pos, and his childhood was like that of most Navajo boys of his generation. He learned Navajo as his first language and learned traditional Navajo ways. He attended school. Before he entered high school World War II came, and the war changed his life.

MacDonald entered the United States Marine Corps in 1944. He served as a member of the Navajo Codetalkers and was honorably discharged as a corporal in 1946. In 1948 he enrolled in Bacone High School in Muskogee, Oklahoma. He graduated in one year as a dean's list student. By 1951 he had completed the Associate of Arts degree at Bacone Junior College, again making the dean's list. In 1957 he graduated from the University of Oklahoma with a B.S. degree in electrical engineering.

In the tradition of the termination era, MacDonald did not return home. Rather he moved to southern California, where he worked for six years as a project engineer and a member of the technical staff of the Hughes Aircraft Company. At Hughes Aircraft he thus gained a position of responsibility and useful experience in such areas as contract negotiation, budget preparation, and cost estimation. Finally, in 1963 the governor of New Mexico appointed him to be the first Indian member of the nine-person Economic Development Advisory Board. He returned to the Navajo reservation that year, assuming in June the directorship of the tribal Division of Management, Methods, and Procedures. In 1965 he took on the post that would catapult him to the center stage of Navajo political life: director of the ONEO (Office of Navajo Economic Opportunity).[1]

THE ELECTION OF 1970

The campaign began early to determine who would lead the emerging Navajo Nation in the 1970s. Sam Billison's home chapter of Kinlichee nominated him in April 1969, Chairman Nakai assuredly would seek a third term, and a growing number of Navajos expressed an interest in an alternative candidate. Nephie Cody of Kayenta wrote to the *Navajo Times* in February 1970:

Things have changed in the four years since the last election. For one thing, Mr. Billison has been away from the reservation all the time, and Mr. Nakai has more or less secluded himself in Window Rock, or at least has not been in contact with the local people. . . . Other activities, like DNA or ONEO have more impact on their [the people's] lives than the tribal activities. . . . The people, at least a good many of them, want a change. Many of these people supported either one of the two candidates in the last election. Either because they feel the incumbent has served his two terms or that Mr. Billison has had his chance to be chairman, they are looking for another man. In general, they want this new man to represent the local people and not be identified too much with either group that contested for power in the past. In the four years since the last election, particularly in the last two years, the number of individuals with this frame of mind has increased and is increasing.[2]

Cody's letter forecast not only Peter MacDonald's candidacy, soon to be announced, but many of the principal reasons for its success. MacDonald was unscarred by earlier political battles; he had never sought political office. His job as ONEO head had made him well known throughout the reservation, and the ONEO's programs generally had been well received. He combined a traditional reservation upbringing with a college education and significant off-reservation work experience. Moreover, the issues of this campaign promised to be different from 1966. For example, peyote would not be so important this time, but control of Navajo resources would be considered more thoroughly, and MacDonald would benefit from this change of focus. In addition, as a candidate from the northern part of the reservation, he could cut into the strong majorities that Nakai had forged there in the past.

While MacDonald did not announce his candidacy officially until June 1970, an endorsement by his home chapter of Teec Nos Pos on April 11 made it quite clear that he would run. As other chapters considered MacDonald's potential candidacy, pressure mounted from the Tribal Council and the Advisory Committee for MacDonald to resign his ONEO position, as tribal and BIA employees are required to do when seeking tribal office. He finally resigned under duress in early June, and the impression given to many people that he was being forced out of office perhaps boosted his chances for election. Within less than a week after his resignation became official, eleven chapters had endorsed MacDonald for chairman: Kayenta, Chilchinbeto, Teec Nos Pos, Piñon, Navajo Mountain, Coppermine, Gap, Sanostee, Jeddito, Low Mountain, and Hard Rocks. Seven of these chapters had voted for Nakai in the previous election, several of them overwhelmingly. Jeddito Councilman Ned Benally said MacDonald was the only candidate who had proven he could obtain financial assistance on a large scale from the federal government, and a

Hard Rocks chapter officer added that MacDonald differed from Nakai and Billison in that he had visited and worked with the community people during the last five years. Henry Zah of Low Mountain complained that Nakai had done nothing about ensuring Navajo claims to the Navajo-Hopi joint use area.[3] These three comments represented basic arguments which proved central to the effectiveness of the MacDonald candidacy.

In addition to Nakai, Billison, and MacDonald, three other people had announced their availability for the chairmanship by the end of June: Joe Watson, Jr., Donald Dodge, and Franklin Eriacho. Under the Navajo election procedures adopted in 1966, the two candidates with the most precinct support would be nominated formally at a central nominating convention to be held the fourth Monday in August. By mid-summer, it was apparent that not only Watson, Eriacho, and Dodge, but Billison, too, stood at best an outside chance of making the November ballot. Billison had spent most of his time since the last election pursuing doctoral studies in education at the University of Arizona. His absence and his previous unsuccessful campaigns limited his viability as a candidate in 1970.

While Billison remained the strongest of the four remaining candidates, Nakai and MacDonald maintained their support into August for the official precinct nominating meetings. The Shiprock central convention August 24 confirmed the results of these sessions, with MacDonald claiming forty precincts, Nakai twenty-six, Billison four, Watson one, Dodge one, and Eriacho none. The popular vote showed MacDonald with 4,879, Nakai 4,228, Billison 2,020, Dodge 354, Watson 82, and Eriacho six. This vote totaled only one-third the prospective November turnout so its significance seemed questionable, but the support for MacDonald by a majority of the precincts did appear important. Having received nearly 20 percent of the primary vote, Billison initially considered a write-in campaign but eventually gave his support to Nakai.[4]

During the campaign of the autumn of 1970, Nakai and MacDonald essentially repeated the main points the two men had stressed prior to the August convention. MacDonald selected Wilson Skeet of Bread Springs, New Mexico, as his running mate. MacDonald's choice made good political sense, for Skeet was well known and came from the area off the reservation, whose residents traditionally complained about underrepresentation in tribal affairs. During the remaining weeks prior to the election, MacDonald reemphasized his belief in local participation in tribal programs, his interest in eliminating factionalism, and his concern for preserving Navajo land resources, developing a private sector of the Navajo economy, and involving young people more fully in tribal affairs. He also reaffirmed that he would not interfere with the Native American Church: "It is up to the people how they use peyote. I will not turn the police on you. No one now has any quarrel with the use of peyote." Nakai countered MacDonald by underlining the achievements of the past eight years, which he said included new industry, "which pays good wages to our Navajo people," improved education (the establishment of Navajo-controlled schools), increases in tribal funds and assets ("to $67,231,615 in cash and over $200 million in total assets"), purchases of off-reservation land (over $1 million spent), and freedom of religion for the Native American Church. Sam Billison endorsed Nakai in the final week of the campaign because "it's silly to think you can replace eight years of experience and leadership with a candidate who is being investigated by the FBI." Billison was referring to an alleged review of MacDonald's handling of ONEO funds; MacDonald denied the charges.[5]

The Navajo electorate elected Peter MacDonald as its new chairman by a substantial majority, giving MacDonald 18,334 votes to 12,069 for Raymond Nakai. MacDonald carried fifty-two precincts to Nakai's twenty, with one precinct (Piñon) tied, and one not reporting (Rock Point). MacDonald carried all of Billison's precincts from 1966 except Alamo and carried them by larger margins, with the exception of Chinle, Kinlichee, Fort Defiance, and Burnham. MacDonald also narrowed Nakai's margin of victory in the precincts Nakai carried in all but three instances: Lukachukai, Steamboat, and Gap. Nakai carried only one agency, Shiprock, and that by less than 400 votes; MacDonald won by almost 4,000 votes in Crownpoint and by over 1,000 votes in Fort Defiance and Tuba City agencies.[6]

An analysis of the district voting totals reveals five of the twenty-one districts showing a striking move away from the support of Raymond Nakai between 1966 and the 1970 election. District 4 (Forest Lake, Hard Rocks, Piñon, and Blue Gap) is immediately to the north of the Hopi reservation, and District 5 (Bird Springs, Leupp, and Tolani) and District 7 (Dilkon, Indian Wells, Jeddito, and Teesto) are directly to the south. The growing friction over the Navajo-Hopi land use area during the last eight years adversely affected Nakai vote totals. The lessening of peyote as a political issue seems to have been reflected in the vote totals of District 7 but particularly in District 12, where MacDonald not only claimed

three precincts—Red Rock, Sanostee, and Two Grey Hills—but vastly
reduced the Nakai margin in the other two—Aneth, from 198 to 39, and
Shiprock from 670 to 189. It is not readily apparent why MacDonald
captured all of District 14—Coyote Canyon, Mexican Springs, Naschitti,
and Tohatchi—but the presence of Wilson Skeet on the ticket obviously
helped MacDonald throughout the southern half of the New Mexico portion of the Navajo Nation. Skeet's home precinct, for example, gave
MacDonald a vote of 1,035 to 224, and Mariano Lake reported a still
greater majority, 1182 to 165 (see Table 10).

TABLE 10

Precinct Shifts from 1966 to 1970

District	1966	1970
4	4 Nakai	2 MacDonald, 1 Nakai, 1 tie
5	3 Nakai	3 MacDonald
7	4 Nakai	4 MacDonald
12	5 Nakai	3 MacDonald, 2 Nakai
14	2 Nakai, 2 Billison	4 MacDonald

Source: Based on *Navajo Times*, December 1, 1966, and Gallup *Independent*,
November 14, 1970.

THE ADMINISTRATION OF PETER MAC DONALD

Peter MacDonald thus began his administration in January 1971 with
a solid mandate from the Navajo people. In his inaugural address Peter
MacDonald called for an end to "the ways of distrust, of recrimination,
of·acting in the dark, of counsel with oneself" and outlined the goals of
his administration:

First, what is rightfully ours, we must protect; what is rightfully due us
we must claim. Second, what we depend on from others, we must replace
with the labor of our own hands, and the skills of our own people. Third,
what we do not have, we must bring into being. We must create for ourselves.

In the first area, MacDonald pledged not to "barter away the Navajo birth-
right for quick profit that will cheat our children and their children after

them," promised to work to update the operation of the long-awaited San Juan irrigation project, and insisted his administration would act forcefully to claim funds due them as Navajos and as citizens. In the second category he contended that Navajos must cease "to depend on others to run our schools, build our roads, administer our health programs, construct our houses, manage our industries, sell us cars, cash our checks and operate our trading posts." MacDonald promised to work to alter this situation, to throw off "the bonds of forced dependency": "We must do better. We must do it in our own way. And we must do it now." In the third classification, MacDonald reminded Navajos they were fortunate in many respects for they had the three classic sources of wealth: land in abundance, sources of capital ("not enough, but some"), and labor. What must be added, he said, was a Navajo-owned private sector, good jobs, trained specialists and professionals, and credits: "We must move from a wage and welfare economy to an ownership economy." Again, he noted the limits to the advantages of bringing in non-Indian industry and emphasized the need for all kinds of training: "Every time someone says how good we Navajos are with our hands, I want to ask: 'Why not give us the chance to show what we can do with our minds?' "[7]

Many people expressed skepticism about the Navajos' ability to achieve self-determination. One seasoned BIA veteran told me: "Now, it's self-determination. They have no economy. They're utterly dependent on government. How in hell can you talk about it? Self-determination must mean being able to spend the white man's money without accounting for it."[8] Nonetheless, the Navajo national government and Navajos generally moved toward this objective in the first term of Peter MacDonald's administration through the selection of new legal counsel, continuation of legal assistance to individual Navajos, development of the Navajo judicial system, attempts to gain greater control over educational and medical services, promotion of economic self-sufficiency, greater involvement in local and state politics, exposure of conditions in border town communities, and realignment of tribal government.

LEGAL COUNSEL

As Raymond Nakai had with Norman Littell, Peter MacDonald had made Harold Mott a campaign issue in the 1970 tribal elections. MacDonald charged Mott with "no background in Indian law or matters of concern to the Navajo Nation" and claimed he had "in concert with the Chairman, too often assumed a decision making role which infringes on the powers of the Navajo Tribal Council and the Navajo people." Mac-Donald argued that a legal department ought to be established that could serve from one Navajo administration to another, since "there are major legal cases going over many years and accumulated knowledge of the cases and documents which are vital to the interests of the Navajos."[9]

The Navajo Tribal Council approved MacDonald's choice for general counsel in March 1971, the Phoenix firm of Brown, Vlassis and Bain. The choice of a firm rather than a single individual to serve as general counsel had important implications, though it represented less of a break from tradition than might be assumed. Founded by C. Randall Bain and Jack E. Brown in 1960, and joined two years later by George P. Vlassis, by 1974 the firm had twenty-four attorneys and could provide the tribe with wide-ranging talents and skills. However, as one attorney for the firm observed, the Navajos prefer particular attorneys to represent them on a consistent basis. The Navajos thus represented for Brown, Vlassis and Bain more of a personal than a corporate client, since the Navajos had not taken the corporate perspective that one attorney is really as good as another with equal training and skills. George Vlassis became the principal lawyer for the tribe, with Lawrence Ruzow, a young attorney with previous experience in Navajo matters as his principal assistant. Given the multiplicity of roles they had to play Vlassis and Ruzow seemingly inevitably became closely identified not only with the Navajo Tribal Council but with the political fortunes of the incumbent chairman.[10]

Ruzow traced the involved nature of the counsel's role in part to the character of Navajos and in part to the training of Anglo attorneys.

Navajos, generally don't like confrontation and thus there is a dearth of willingness to make decisions and take responsibility for them. Attorneys, on the other hand, are trained to thrive on confrontation. While things are changing, many Navajos have real difficulty with written English, which must be used to communicate on a daily basis with the federal government. Attorneys are used to dealing with the government and they can help with the drafting of resolutions, speeches, and so forth.

Ruzow also noted the special relationship that must exist between the general counsel and the chairman:

The Chairman is a political animal, running for reelection, and he doesn't want to share the spotlight with other Navajos. He's less threatened by Anglos, who can't run against him or really impress the electorate. Moreover, as a leader, the chairman must deal with Anglo society. The attorney can serve not as a valet or aide-de-camp, but as a natural person to ask counsel; we are thus consulted with no more than legal matters, as the Chairman can simply say, "I need to talk to my lawyer about that."

Inevitably, then, Ruzow and Vlassis drafted speeches and testimony for the chairman. Ruzow contended that he and Vlassis didn't simply put words in MacDonald's mouth: "It's not a Charlie McCarthy process. The chairman is involved with the draft, the ideas and the revisions."[11]

In addition to advising the chairman, the legal counsel fulfilled other responsibilities, including providing legal opinions on economic development and the Navajo Nation's relationship to the states, to the BIA, and to the Hopi people. The economic development questions proved particularly challenging for, as Ruzow stated, "There is flake proposal after flake proposal. There aren't many good reasons for a company to come and most outfits are not resource oriented [for example, oil or natural gas] but rip-off inclined." While attempting to avoid exploitive companies, the Navajo Nation nonetheless faced grave unemployment problems, and, in the case contracts like that between the tribe and Peabody Coal, a certain number of Navajo people received financial benefits. Any degree of willingness expressed by the counsel to sanction coal strip mining on Black Mesa, however, earned it the wrath of more militant Navajos and many DNA attorneys. Thus the general counsel became progressively more alienated from these groups, especially the Anglo DNA attorneys, "who don't have to work for a living, that is to say, produce income." Ruzow called the notion of closing down the Peabody mine or the Four Corners power plant unrealistic but felt that if enough violations of the lease could be proven perhaps the lease might be renegotiated.

In general, then, Ruzow and his colleagues took what they saw as being a pragmatic tack, working for "incremental progress" based on achievable goals. Ruzow contended the counsel must show Navajos that in fact they can succeed and that in the long run tangible, important goals can be realized. He contrasted this approach of "staying around to work things out" with that of the "reformers who want to make speeches and to write for the *New Republic,* but who aren't interested in following through."[12]

DNA LEGAL SERVICES

MacDonald's election ensured the continuation of DNA, the legal services program for individual Navajos, just as Nakai's reelection likely would have guaranteed its conclusion. In MacDonald's first term, DNA essentially continued the work begun during its first years, perhaps involving itself more deeply in the promotion of economic alternatives to existing institutions. For example, DNA won an out-of-court settlement in a class action suit against the Piñon Trading Post operators and at the same time worked with local people to help establish a cooperative store in the community. The suit charged the trading post operators with many unfair and unethical business practices, including exorbitant interest charges. The Piñon cooperative became a model venture and encouraged many other people's groups throughout the Navajo Nation to attempt similar ventures. Off the reservation, DNA sought to ensure individual Navajo rights in the consumer area through representation of individual Navajo complaints against border town merchants and in the law enforcement area through improvement of jail conditions and provisions for ensuring the rights of the accused. The Navajo newspaper *Diné Baa-Hani* carried a DNA cartoon series and articles dealing with consumer education. Additional suits against New Mexican pawnbrokers encouraged changes in pawn practices. Given the traditional use of the pawn system by large numbers of Navajos for temporary cash advances and the frequent abuses of the pawn system by brokers who charged exorbitant interest rates and did not advise their clients of their rights, reform here promised to have a positive effect on many lives.

Perhaps the most impressive DNA judicial triumph came with the U.S. Supreme Court decision of *McClanahan* v. *Arizona State Tax Commission* in March 1973. The court's decision reversed the previous rulings of lower courts against the Navajo plaintiff, Rosalind McClanahan, who had sought to prevent the State of Arizona from claiming state income tax from her wages as a bank teller in Window Rock. In addition to saving Navajos money they would be forced to surrender to the state (which most Navajos believe provides very little money or services to the Arizona portion of the reservation), the McClanahan ruling reaffirmed Navajo sovereignty. DNA attorney James Wechsler said the decision "renewed a relationship at which Arizona had been chipping away and affirmed principles I thought were there all along. . . . If the decision had gone the other way, Indian independence from state control would have been threatened."[13]

While DNA enjoyed unaccustomed support from the tribal government's administration during Peter MacDonald's first term, it still confronted two significant challenges to its continued existence during this period. Given the phase-out of most Office of Economic Opportunity programs, DNA, like other legal services programs around the country, faced complete loss of federal funding. The funding crisis reached its zenith during the summer of 1973, when Howard Philips, appointed OEO director in order to preside over its demise, ordered funds cut off for DNA, despite the OEO's commitment to DNA funding through the end of 1973. While DNA went to court to try to gain its lost funds from OEO, it had to refuse new clients in the interim.

While DNA was attempting to stay alive through regaining its financing from OEO, a new group emerged seemingly with the OEO's blessings to challenge DNA's status and indeed to attempt to replace it. This new organization, Lawyers for Navajos, Incorporated, headed by Tucson attorney Edmund Kahn, would consist of seven attorneys and six Navajos, replacing the DNA board, twenty-five of whose thirty members were Navajo. Kahn had served as an aid to general counsel Harold Mott and had consistently opposed DNA. He had resigned in September 1969 to take a job in Tucson. Kahn named six Navajos to serve on the board for Lawyers for Navajos: Howard Gorman, Harold Drake, Virgil Kirk, Roy Vanderver, Rosetta LaFonte, and Edward T. Begay. With one exception, the seven Anglo attorneys named to the new board hailed from Arizona. DNA officials protested that the six Arizona attorneys represented various off-reservation interests, including Ames Brothers Ford and Tucson Gas and Electric Company, the defendants in many cases DNA attorneys prosecuted.[14]

The general Navajo response to this alternative to DNA proved somewhat less than enthusiastic, and Gorman, Drake, Kirk, and Vanderver disassociated themselves from the new organization. Moreover, the Tribal Council's Advisory Committee passed a resolution by a 14-0 vote reaffirming its support of the composition of the DNA board of directors and executive staff and the DNA program itself, while criticizing Lawyers for Navajos: "Any attempt by the Office of Economic Opportunity to fund Lawyers for Navajos, Inc., is discouraged as an attempt to frustrate Navajo self-determination and to deny the Navajo people effective legal representation."[15]

Undeterred by the opposition, Kahn wrote to Peterson Zah, who had replaced Leo Haven as DNA director, and to Howard Gorman to re-affirm his intentions to have Lawyers for Navajos take over the direction of the legal services operation within the Navajo Nation. He said that, under the new operation, "there will be no empire building, no champion-ing of social causes; no registration or organization for political parties and no expenditures of working men's tax dollars to defend Anglos who insult Navajo leaders." Kahn called Ted Mitchell a "radical Anglo lawyer" who had "created a political empire with Federal funds and proceeded to impose his own selfish, social goals on the innocent Navajo."[16]

In the end, however, Kahn failed in his bid. DNA regained federal funding, and, with the passage of the National Legal Services Corporation bill by Congress in February 1974, stable funding for DNA in the immedi-ate future appeared assured. DNA had to change its title to DNA-People's Legal Services and expand its operation to offer legal assistance within the Hopi Nation. It also had to reduce its board of directors from thirty members to fourteen, seven Native Americans and seven attorneys.

In 1974, DNA maintained seven offices within the Navajo Nation: the central administrative office and adjoining Fort Defiance Agency Office in Window Rock, agency offices at Tuba City, Chinle, Shiprock, and Crownpoint, and an additional office at Mexican Hat, Utah. As of April 1974, the DNA staff included a Navajo director (Peterson Zah) and deputy director, twenty-eight Tribal Court advocates, twenty-two attor-neys, and additional personnel at the clerical and support level. DNA operated three service units, of which the largest was legal services. The litigation and research unit supported the legal services unit and prepared for special cases DNA chose to bring to court. The community educa-tion unit continued a basic thrust of the program: informing people about their legal rights and responsibilities.[17]

THE NAVAJO COURTS AND THE NAVAJO POLICE

Both the Navajo court system and its police department continued to evolve significantly during MacDonald's first term. The Navajo courts were blessed with a degree of stability, given the appointment system, and Navajo justices had an opportunity to learn and grow in their positions. In 1970, six Navajo judges celebrated their tenth anniversary on the bench: Virgil Kirk (the chief justice, who had replaced the recently retired Murray Lincoln), Tom Becenti, Chester Yellowhair, William·Dean Wilson, Chester Hubbard, and William Leupp. The justices faced both criticism and encouragement for better performances from the tribe's legal department and DNA. For the most part without much formal legal training upon assuming their positions, the judges then took a variety of training seminars, often under the aegis of the University of New Mexico Law School. Theirs was a demanding role, one which was to balance the dictates of Navajo tradition and custom with the demands of Anglo law. Along with the tribe's legal department and DNA, they had a responsibility to interpret the law, explain it, and make it understandable to the Navajo people.

The addition of court advocates and prosecutors improved the workings of the Navajo court system. The Navajo Nation never permitted attorneys to defend their clients in Navajo courts, but the presence of a Navajo advocate allowed the defendant the chance of capable presentation of his case. Any Navajo willing to pay a small annual fee could apply to become a Navajo advocate, but nearly all the advocates were affiliated with DNA. The presence of court advocates prompted the creation of the prosecutor's office by the Navajo government. Formerly the justice essentially played both judge and prosecutor, but with the increase in court advocates the tribe felt the need for an official prosecutor "to combat" the impact made by the advocates. The tribal prosecutor could thus determine which cases were worthy of prosecution. He was also responsible for assisting the police department in training police officers for their role in presenting a case in court. Tribal prosecutors completed training sessions to improve their knowledge of the law and their ability to perform more effectively.[18]

With the expanding Navajo population, greater population mobility, and the stress engendered within that population by poverty and socioeconomic change, Navajo law enforcement personnel faced an increasingly challenging task. The Navajo Police Academy took responsibility for the training of Navajo police officers. In 1974 the recruits, both men and women, underwent 340 hours of instruction over a thirteen-week period in state and tribal law, self-defense, first aid, riot training, and "other tools for use in the field." Guest instructors from the state highway patrols, the Federal Bureau of Investigation and Secret Service, and the Gallup police augmented academy training. The Navajo police force numbered over 200 uniformed officers. The Navajo division of law enforcement received $3.5 million for the 1975 fiscal year, an increase of over $1 million from fiscal year 1974.

Budget increases for law enforcement helped to improve police department morale, a problem in the department's short history. The increases allowed for higher salaries, more personnel, and helicopter rescue service. After considerable debate, the Tribal Council selected an Anglo, Roland Dart III, to preside over the police department expansion as superintendent. The council chose Dart over 200 applicants from across the nation, including several Navajo applicants who were rejected as too inexperienced.[19]

Given the police department's rapid expansion in size and obligations, it not surprisingly received criticism from the Navajo public. Part of the criticism may be related to the relative youth of so many policemen and policewomen in a society which customarily has granted authority to the old. Also, with the advent of a reservation-wide legal services program, Navajos had recourse to counsel against potential abuses of the police system.

In addition to the sheer size of the Navajo Nation and the inherent difficulty in adequately policing such a large region, the Navajo police faced special problems related to alcohol. The tribal ban on liquor did not begin to stem the ready supply, from both the border town liquor stores and the on-reservation bootleggers. By far the main cause for arrest within the Navajo Nation was a drunk and disorderly violation. With the increase in paved highways and motor vehicles, drunken driving problems also mounted. However, it should be noted that while the number of arrests for reckless or drunken driving increased, the arrest percentage for disorderly conduct actually declined, when the rising population rate is considered. In 1960 7,359 arrests were made for disorderly conduct; in 1972 the figure had risen to 7,741. Arrests for liquor violations declined from 1,658 in 1960 to 1,499 in 1972. For other offenses, the arrest rate remained considerably below the national average, though perhaps more comparable to that of a large rural area. As urbanism increased within the Navajo Nation, such problems as breaking and entering also grew.[20]

The fair interpretation and enforcement of the law within the Navajo

Nation was a noteworthy and essential goal of Navajo nationalism. The presence of legal assistance for individual Navajos heightened the challenge to the judicial system to provide proper treatment for Navajo citizens. Given the growing Navajo population, its mobility, and its higher urban concentration, the stress on the system would increase. However, the evolution of the judicial system was a vital indication of the Navajo Nation's ability to control its internal affairs.

NAVAJO EDUCATION

Bureau of Indian Affairs Schools

Navajo influence in Bureau of Indian Affairs schools continued to expand in the early 1970s, particularly at the few community schools, such as Rough Rock and Rock Point, which contracted with the Bureau to operate their own institutions. An increasing number of Navajos filled key administrative positions within the bureau's educational system; Rebecca Dotson, for example, became educational director in the Chinle Agency, while James Tomchee and Sam Billison assumed similar responsibilities in the Shiprock and Fort Defiance agencies. A few more Navajo teachers entered BIA ranks. Bureau school boards permitted parents to have some degree of representation, if not power, within the policy-making structures of the individual institutions.

In some instances Bureau school officials encouraged the development of bilingual programs. In 1974 staff members at schools in Cottonwood, Sanostee, Toadlena, Greasewood, and Piñon were in the process of implementing this approach. Navajo teacher aides at most schools helped Anglo teachers communicate with their Navajo pupils, a particularly pressing problem at the early elementary level.[21]

Children who attended Bureau schools were also more likely to learn something about Navajo history and culture. The College of Education, University of New Mexico, had contracted with the Bureau to provide Navajo-related texts for social studies under the provisions of the Elementary and Secondary Education Act. Thus, in the 1970s teachers had access to sequential texts that included Navajo history and to workshops designed to encourage creative use of these materials. Under the direction of Dr. Theodore Kaltsounis of the University of Washington, the staff of the

Navajo Area Curriculum Development Project also produced relevant teaching units in language arts and social studies for use in the elementary schools.[22]

Federal funding encouraged the development of other special programs. Title VII money supported the establishment of a bilingual program at Sanostee School that included the development of reading materials. Title I funds (Public Law 89-10) contributed $1 million annually to special education classes and $400,000 in the 1973-74 academic year to Consultants in Total Education, which created approaches to early language learning.[23]

Despite these changes, Bureau schools remained open to criticism for lack of Navajo control and insufficient funding of Navajo schools. Top educational officials from the bureau urged the formation of school boards for Bureau institutions, but the very isolation of the schools from the communities limited school board members' real influence on school policy. This was especially so at the larger boarding schools, where the children generally came from remote areas. In any event, board members were limited to advisory rather than policy-making roles.

The problem of the Bureau relationship to Navajo education was epitomized by the disagreements between Navajo Division of Education Director Dillon Platero and Bureau personnel. Platero clashed with bureau administrators over control of Johnson-O'Malley money and other federal funds designed to aid Navajo schools. He contended that the tribe, not the bureau, should allocate these financial resources, but BIA officials asserted that Navajos were not yet ready to do so. Platero commented, "The BIA doesn't give a hang about what we say now."[24]

Navajo Community Schools

The early 1970s witnessed the maturation of Rough Rock and Rock Point schools and the establishment of two other Navajo community schools operated through a contract with the Bureau of Indian Affairs: Ramah Navajo High School and Borrego Pass School. At Rough Rock, Bob Roessel had left for Navajo Community College, and Dillon Platero, a Navajo, was now the principal. During this period, Rough Rock became perhaps less of a demonstration effort and more of a local school. It no longer represented the sole example of Native American control of Native American education. School officials were out of the limelight and into the long-term, less glamorous effort of attempting to provide the kind of education that the parents of children in an isolated rural area want their children to receive. With the departure of Dillon Platero in March 1973 to head the Navajo Nation's Division of Education, another link with Rough Rock's first days was broken. Platero was replaced by Ethelou Yazzie, a Navajo educator who worked with Roessel and others on the publication of a volume of Navajo history issued by the Navajo Curriculum Center at Rough Rock.

Rough Rock School's directors expanded the school's facilities to provide for students' continuous education. They had added a grade a year until they had the traditional eight elementary grades; and the departure of the eighth graders from the community upon graduation inspired the school to open high school classes. The Navajo tribe loaned Rough Rock money for temporary facilities. Rough Rock officials also decided they would try to operate the high school on a day basis, making special arrangements apart from a dormitory setting for any students who would have to board. In October 1974, singer Tom Wilson led the blessing ceremony dedicating the first-phase facilities at the Rough Rock high school.[25]

After nine years the future of Rough Rock School was clouded by only one factor: money. Rough Rock had been an expensive venture. Bureau officials had not always been willing to fund it as fully as Rough Rock administrators and teachers had wished. Because of their ambitious programs, Rough Rock officials sometimes exceeded their budget. In the summer of 1973 a most severe funding crisis occurred, but since that time Rough Rock leaders appear to have worked out an accommodation with bureau personnel. The people of the community surely do not have the financial resources to support the school independently. The future of Rough Rock thus depended upon the Bureau's continued willingness to fund it or the Navajo Nation's ability to take over the support of its own schools.

Rock Point School emerged as more of a center for the promotion of traditional Navajo ways. This development was in keeping with the conservative Rock Point community, which, though somewhat less isolated than Rough Rock, is equally traditional. The employment of Barney Mitchell as a Navajo history and culture instructor was important in this evolution. Mitchell coordinated the first two annual Navajo song and dance festivals, Diné Binahagha, at Rock Point Community School on

February 14, 1974, and February 14, 1975. Diné Binahagha differed from
the typical powwow in not being a pan-Indian event; only Navajo songs
and dances could be presented.

Mitchell's explanation of the event's importance summarized the support to Navajo tradition being provided by Rock Point Community School.
He said that Navajo adults had a duty to teach their children the traditional ways and the meaning and reasons behind these ways. Presenting
Diné Binahagha helped close the Navajo generation gap: "The younger
generation copies what it sees, and when it sees the joy of acting like a
traditional, respectful, thoughtful Navajo, it will start copying that."
According to Mitchell, Rock Point community people considered Navajo
studies essential to their children's education because childhood is when
Navajo values must be introduced. Diné Binahagha, he said, provided an
opportunity for the school and community to come together to present
something for the entire Navajo Nation.[26]

The Ramah Navajo community is removed from the Navajo reservation,
south of Gallup and adjacent to Zuni. Ramah Navajo high school students
lived both in McKinley county and Valencia county and could not attend
a common school. Most attended the old Gallup-McKinley County High
School. When that school closed in 1968, Ramah Navajo students wishing
to remain in school faced the prospect of having to leave home. Some
Ramah Navajos sued the county to reopen the school. When that suit
failed, they sued the county to provide bus service for Ramah students.
The bus service proved unsatisfactory. Valencia county residents could
not use the buses at all. The community searched for another answer.

A Ramah chapter meeting on February 6, 1970 provided an alternative. The community would establish an independent high school. The
chapter elected a school board at the meeting and signed incorporation
papers; the movement to create Ramah Navajo High School had begun.
The Ramah board members hired two consultants to assist them in
soliciting funds, Michael Gross, a DNA attorney who had worked with
the community since July 1968 on the school issue, and Donald Olson
of the Robert F. Kennedy Memorial Foundation. The two men assisted
the Ramah board representatives in their meetings with private foundation officials and federal government personnel in Washington and New
York City. The board members achieved their goal in a strikingly short
period of time. By April 1970, they had won a commitment from the

Bureau of Indian Affairs to support their school on the basis of cost per student at two other BIA boarding high schools: Intermountain and Fort Wingate. This sum amounted to $2,004 per student per year. The Office of Economic Opportunity and private sources contributed additional money. The first students could thus enroll at Ramah High School in the autumn of 1970.[27]

As Ramah Navajo High School administrators and teachers sought to provide a new and creative atmosphere for their students, they soon received criticism from a variety of people for deviating from "normal" school instruction. Most Anglos from the Ramah area hailed from the old Mormon settlement of Ramah. They boycotted the school, and eleven of the seventeen Anglo students who did enroll withdrew within two months to attend Zuni High School. Some Navajo parents did not like the additional freedom given the students. Editorial writers of the Gallup *Independent* questioned the use of state tax money to support an Indian school and wondered about the qualifications of Ramah's teachers. Representatives from the education department of the State of New Mexico, Rollie Heltman, Gene Whitlock, and George McBane, visited the school and wrote an evaluation criticizing the quality of financial management at the school, the school facilities, the attitude toward Anglos expressed by school officials (for example, a poster above Abe Plummer's desk showing an Indian head nickel with the slogan "the only Indian America ever cared about"), and the amount of freedom given to students.[28]

These reactions illustrated the difficulty of providing alternative education for Navajo students. School official Abe Plummer summarized some of the school's intentions:

The Navajos believe they can train their children best because they can sense and feel the pulse of their children. Ramah Navajo High School certainly is not a maze representing ethnogenocide. The school intends to help the students to be articulate in Navajo and English. The school intends to help students attain strong egos so they can compete in anyone's society without fear of stigmas, condescension and prejudices. The school intends to help the students to be analytical and critical without fear of reprisals. The school does not intend to "lock" special students in particular grades where they finally become "turned off" as has happened at other schools.

Ramah Navajo High School directors faced several problems in common with the directors of other contract schools, but they succeeded in obtaining the promise of a new school facility. The old building was highly inadequate and nearer to the Mormon Anglo community than the Navajo community, but the new school would be more centrally located. However, while there were sufficient operating funds, more money was needed to develop new, experimental programs. School officials hoped to obtain special federal or private grants for both these purposes at a time when this assistance seemed increasingly difficult to obtain. Third, the directors also faced the problem of staff turnover, perhaps to a greater extent than other contract schools. There had not been much administrative continuity at the school, and much hiring of staff and faculty was done at the last minute.[29]

Ramah school personnel also confronted problems not faced by officials at Rock Point and Rough Rock. Ramah teachers and administrators had to deal with students who already had had a lot of schooling. These students had often been harmed as well as helped by their previous education. Because of these challenges, Ramah Navajo High School confronted a perhaps more difficult and uncertain future than did the other contract community schools.

The two Navajo communities that comprise Borrego Pass are situated twelve miles southeast of Crownpoint in eastern New Mexico. Borrego Pass gets its name from the trading post at the pass, near which the first school, established initially as a trailer operation in the early 1950s, finally came to be constructed. A decade later the two communities of Little Water and Casamero Lake obtained a three-classroom school house and teachers' quarters for a day school to serve the children.

Citizens from Little Water and Casamero Lake selected an advisory school board for their school as other Navajos in other areas had been doing during the late 1960s and early 1970s at the urging of the Bureau of Indian Affairs. According to Crownpoint Agency Education Superintendent Jack Williams, Borrego Pass community people had been the last in the agency to do so. Yet, by October of 1971, this board had requested the Bureau of Indian Affairs to be permitted to operate the day school. Administrators from Rough Rock, Rock Point, and Ramah aided the board members in formulating a proposal.

The proposal called for the school to include kindergarten through third grade at first and to have a curriculum similar to that of the other community schools. Borrego Pass school would "foster an environment that will encourage Indian children to develop positive attitudes about learning" and would "help children appreciate and retain their full heritage because it is believed that they will be stronger if they know their own way of life." School officials said they would develop a bilingual approach, building upon the language each student knew best, Navajo in most instances. The $116,800 budget allowed for a principal, three teachers, a cook and helper, two bus drivers, and community people to assist with instruction in Navajo culture.[30]

Borrego Pass School, Dibé Yazhe Habitiin Ólta, opened in September, 1972. Gary Witherspoon, a Chicago Ph.D. in anthropology with teaching experience at Rough Rock, became the first principal. Teachers at the school were supposed to be able to speak and write Navajo; Witherspoon, who like Roessel and Holm is married to a Navajo, was qualified in both respects. Control for the school was established in its board, though board members said children's parents and Casamero Lake and Little Water chapter members generally would truly control the institution.

Dibé Yazhe Habitiin Ólta had several initial advantages. It was the newest of the four community schools, and its staff could learn from the experiments and successes of their peers at the other schools. Witherspoon had experience in the community school movement and special interest and training in Navajo as both a written and an oral language. Teachers from the old Borrego Pass School could transfer elsewhere so the new school should have included only teachers who wanted to be there. As a small school, its teachers should have paid the kind of attention to individual small children desired by their parents. The small size of the school also particularly encouraged parental involvement. The main problems the school officials would face would be the lack of money for construction of additional facilities and the dependency upon outside sources to meet general financial needs.[31]

The directors and staff members of the four Navajo community schools achieved important objectives. They provided much greater local control of Navajo education and permitted a much stronger emphasis on Navajo language history and culture. They allowed the Navajo child to utilize the language he or she already spoke as a tool for learning rather than having to attempt to employ a foreign language to master other subjects and skills. While they were not widely imitated throughout the Navajo Nation, community school personnel played a central role in encouraging

Navajo parents to become more involved in education and Navajo administrators and teachers in other schools to have their institutions more
fully reflect and reinforce Navajo culture. Finally, community schools
provided leadership training for Navajo educators like the Navajo Division
of Education's director, Dillon Platero.

At the same time, there were significant problems and limitations to
the community school idea. The Navajo Nation is enormous. Rough Rock
School, for example, is important to the Rough Rock community, but it
does not change the situation facing parents thirty miles away in
Dennehotso. The success of community schools rather points to a Navajo
national approach to educational reform that will benefit all Navajos, not
just the residents of a few isolated communities.

Community schools also have had and will continue to have severe
financial problems. Without a tax base, Navajo community schools must
depend on contracting with the BIA and receiving foundation and other
forms of financial support. The contracting system had its limits. Platero,
Holm, and others pointed out that the hidden costs in a school's operation
are often not covered under such an arrangement. Holm cited as examples
the following: insurance, legal representation, postage, bookkeeping and
accounting, plant management, procurement of property and supplies,
and personnel benefits. The contracting group thus had two choices,
neither desirable: use school funds to cover the expenses and reduce expenditures on other programs or obtain more money from the Bureau and
thus reduce the amount available to noncontract Bureau schools. Private
sources were not likely to provide an escape from the dilemma since
foundation officials tend to be far more interested in granting "seed
money" for a fledgling program than in pouring in continual support
funds. For the immediate future the circle must therefore begin and end
with the Bureau. BIA administrators in Washington have shown a clear
tendency to fund contract schools not only rather minimally but on a
cautious, yearly basis. This short-term assurance does not lend stability
to any community school effort. Wayne Holm concluded:

Contract schools no sooner win a one-year contract than they must begin
to be concerned with renegotiating that contract. It is difficult to attract,
and to keep, good people under such circumstances. . . . It would be much
more desirable to set up contract schools on a multi-year basis . . . the

world does not really end each June 30th and it is not really created anew each July 1st.[32]

Navajo Public Schools

The Navajo public school system has become increasingly important in Navajo education. With the advent of federal impact funding, new public schools could be constructed and operated despite state reluctance to provide educational services within the Navajo Nation. A greatly improved, though still far from complete, road network has made possible a wide-ranging bus service for the public schools. The growth of the agency towns—Crownpoint, Shiprock, Tuba City, Chinle, and Window Rock-Fort Defiance—and other communities such as Kayenta, Tohatchi, Ganado, and Navajo promoted the development of a public school network. By 1974 a steadily growing number of Navajo children could look forward to attending public day schools for their entire elementary and secondary education.

For the major part of the period between the 1950s, when the public school system on the reservation came into being, and the 1970s, the Navajo public schools appeared quite similar to BIA institutions. The public school curriculum had a definite assimilationist bias. There were few Navajo teachers teaching Navajo children. Traders and other Anglos dominated the school boards, and Navajo parents usually remained removed or isolated altogether from the schools.

Important problems remained, but the public schools were altered in the 1960s and 1970s through the efforts of parents, teachers, students, and administrators. The degree of improvement, of course, varied considerably. But in general the school boards reflected more fully the schools' constituencies, and the schools presented more of a bicultural approach. Recruitment efforts to attract Navajo administrators and teachers became more serious, and by 1974 Navajos formed the clear majority on the school boards. Increased Navajo voter registration and participation in school board elections caused the change. The transformation of the boards in the Chinle and Window Rock school districts, for example, was remarkable.

In Chinle, new voters helped to recall several non-Navajo school board members and eventually force the departure of School District Superintendent Jody Matthews. Subsequently they recalled two school board members, one a Navajo and the other a "one-quarter" Shawnee, and replaced them with two Navajos. Two additional Navajos, Thomas Begay and Mary Ina Ray, also won seats on the board in special elections held in 1971. The Window Rock Public School Board changed similarly. In 1970, its members generally remained sympathetic to incumbent Anglo school superintendent George Burns and defended school policies against Navajo parents who complained about racist teachers and textbooks. School board member Marie Lincoln, for example, claimed, "I'd rather have racism than Communism." Mrs. Lincoln won reelection that autumn, defeating Wilbur Kellogg, Jr., an Anglo, and Lettie Nave, a Navajo. In 1972, however, the movement toward Navajo control of the school board gained momentum as Wallace Hanley defeated three non-Navajos for a position on the board, receiving 56.31 percent of the votes cast in the November election. At a special election held later in the month, Navajos Peterson Zah and Joy Hanley won seats on the board. By 1973, the Window Rock Public School Board consisted of five Navajos: Wallace Hanley, Peterson Zah, Joy Hanley, Allen Begay, and Dan Smith. Voters continued Navajo control on the board thereafter by electing Jack Jackson and Katherine Arviso to the seats vacated by Dan Smith and Joy Hanley.[33]

With the change in composition in the school boards, board members started to recruit administrators and teachers more sympathetic to a bilingual and bicultural approach to education. Chinle Superintendent Jody Matthews' departure symbolized the trend. He had believed the Navajos incapable of directing their own affairs, saying they would have buses running to each hogan. He stated he did not need to provide free lunches to a child whose parents had a new pick-up truck. The Chinle Junior High School principal, meanwhile, completely opposed the inclusion of Navajo history and culture within the school curriculum. He called the new Rough Rock School a "backward step" and labeled it "not American" to assist any "faction" to maintain its way of life. Three superintendents later, the first director of "backward" Rough Rock, Bob Roessel, headed the Chinle school district.[34] Similarly, in Window Rock a person more sympathetic to a bicultural approach replaced as superintendent an individual opposed to that perspective. Dr. Kenneth Ross, a Sioux married to a Navajo, took over from Acting Superintendent Charles Wellington, who had previously served as the right-hand man to Superintendent George Burns. One Window Rock school employee quoted Wellington as saying, "We owe no allegiance to the Tribe." Burns had balked at introducing Navajo history and culture courses, saying accreditation requirements, lack of materials, and lack of people qualified to teach the courses prevented their establishment. By contrast, within the first year of Ross' superintendency, the district school officials announced their plans to teach the Navajo language and Navajo studies. Moreover, Ross took immediate steps to encourage greater parental involvement in the schools.[35]

Navajo Community College

The first MacDonald term saw Navajo Community College under Navajo leadership and eventually in a new location. Ned Hatathli served as president of the school from 1969 to 1972, when he died in a tragic accident. Thomas Atcitty, college vice president, succeeded Hatathli. The college had begun its existence sharing facilities with the Many Farms BIA high school. In the autumn of 1973, Navajo Community College moved from these temporary quarters to a permanent, separate campus in the Tsaile-Wheatfields area, east of Canyon de Chelly on the reservation. The move was important because it symbolized the growth and permanence of the institution. It also signified the school's ability to offer a wider range of courses to its students, thus better serving their needs.

Perhaps the principal issue faced during this period revolved around the decision-making process. As it evolved at the college, the process differed significantly from that of most other colleges and universities. The regents assumed a more central role in the eyes of the Navajo people than trustees customarily do, for the board's existence served as an assurance of Navajo control. The college president had more authority than is typical as the school's spokesman to the regents and as overseer of the institution.

The college faculty possessed considerably less authority than instructors customarily exercise at most colleges and universities. The faculty also comprised the main Anglo component of the school, with Navajos making up only about one-third of the teaching staff of approximately thirty-six full-time instructors. The Anglo faculty members' positions became more tenuous in the face of the school's professed aim to recruit more Navajo faculty and replace Anglo faculty with Navajo teachers when qualified Navajo candidates became available. The college had no tenure system and no ranking system: all faculty members signed a one-year contract, had the title of instructor, and theoretically could be replaced at the end of any academic year; the fact that Navajo additions to the faculty generally did not replace Anglos who wanted to stay did little to diminish Anglo concern. Given the contemporary employment situation, if not the commitment felt by Anglo teachers to the college, some Anglo instructors did not feel comfortable about their status.

The question of faculty, especially Anglo faculty, status at Navajo Community College provided the main point of contention over the exercise of Navajo control. In her study, "Outsiders and Decolonization: Anglo Roles at Navajo Community College," Katherine Iverson summarized the problem:

Four of the first five springs of the college's existence have produced confrontations between Anglo faculty members and Navajo staff, superficially involving specific issues, but in the last analysis testing willingness to accept Navajo control over policy and Navajo control over renewal (in these cases, non-renewal) of contracts. One instructor described these annual events by saying that "the rites of spring around here seem to be orgies of insecurity." While each case involves complexities of personalities and various forms and degrees of institutional instability, all are essentially examples of outsiders insisting that they know best what is good for Navajos. What seems most remarkable is that most often the participants have failed to see the similarities in the cases. They have accepted as causal the "issues," which are really only manifestations of a pattern of social relationships.[36]

As at Rough Rock, the role played by Bob Roessel at the college provoked controversy. While Roessel maintained a close and influential relationship with the Board of Regents following his tenure as president, his impact on the everyday life of the school was frequently exaggerated by outside observers. Roessel continued to be a central figure at the college because of his responsibilities for fund raising and general promotion of the school. However, Ned Hatathli's rapid assumption of authority at the college assuredly limited Roessel's influence. Hatathli's successor, Thomas Atcitty, did not appear to be Roessel's choice for the post, and he became independent of Roessel as president of the college. Roessel became superintendent of the Chinle public school district but naturally maintained a healthy interest in the college's life. His wife, Ruth, directed the Navajo studies program, and both were directly concerned and involved in developing the Navajo studies course offerings and publications. Instructors in the Navajo studies program at Navajo Community College sought to provide students with the respect and understanding for Navajo culture, heritage, and future cited as a central goal by the regents in July 1968. Through courses in the Navajo language, Navajo history and culture, Navajo arts and crafts, Navajo creative writing, and Navajo psychology as well as courses in Native American studies the Navajo studies program offered the student extensive opportunities to reaffirm his heritage.

The curriculum in its totality represented an ambitious attempt to serve the diverse needs of the college's students. Students wishing to transfer into a baccalaureate degree-granting institution could take the appropriate courses. Students desiring more training and skills in auto mechanics, welding, secretarial studies, drafting, and commercial art could enroll in vocational-technical courses in these fields. Adults obtained instruction in basic English and mathematics in the adult basic education program.

The Navajo National Approach to Navajo Education

The movement for a Navajo national approach to Navajo education accelerated with the creation by the Tribal Council of the Navajo Division of Education on June 17, 1971. In the publication, "Strengthening Navajo Education," the division's officials contended the division's creation "signified more than a change in political climate." Rather, they said, "It implied a basic decision that the survival of a great nation and a great culture hinges upon the Navajo Tribe's ability to develop a full and rich life for all Navajos on the Reservation." They labeled the division "the primary vehicle for assuring the preservation of the Navajo cultural heritage." From the beginning Navajos headed most of the departments within the division.[37]

Dillon Platero's appointment in the spring of 1973 as director of the Division of Education showed that the division represented a major force within Navajo education. Platero had directed Rough Rock Demonstration School for five years and headed the National Indian Education Association, but his involvement in a leadership capacity with Navajo education dated back to his work on the council's education committee in 1955. Perhaps more than any other individual, Platero stood for Navajo control of Navajo education. He combined commitment to an integrated Navajo national educational effort with concern for the local community-based approach Rough Rock School exemplified.

In December 1973, MacDonald outlined the future direction of Navajo national educational planning. MacDonald noted that the Bureau, the states, the missions, and four local communities all had responsibility for providing educational services within the Navajo Nation. Each program had its own structure, levels of responsibility, lines of authority, and rules, regulations, procedures, and standards: "The net result is the present series of fragmented educational efforts with no common framework oriented toward or directly responsible to the educational needs of the Navajo people." Most of these agencies, MacDonald contended, did not really understand the basic foundations of Navajo life—the specific linguistic, social, cultural, and economic backgrounds and needs of Navajo children and their parents. Therefore, he concluded, the tribe must establish itself as an educational agency, "on an institutional level commensurate with, and supplemental to state departments of education." It would work with the state departments of education, the U.S. Office of Education, and other agencies for funding purposes. The agency would work toward ultimate control and operation of an autonomous Navajo school system but in the transition period would coordinate the educational systems in keeping with the bicultural world the Navajo child would be entering.[38]

By the autumn of 1974, the Navajo Division of Education had been reorganized into three components: planning and development, coordination, and evaluation of educational services. The division became involved in bilingual curriculum development, plans for new school facilities, implementation of research proposals in special education and fiscal resources, establishment of a demonstration program for high school dropouts, and a school board training program. But its most significant program was probably the Navajo Teacher Education Program, which was designed to alter the composition of the teaching force within the Navajo Nation.

Professors from the education departments of the University of New Mexico and the University of Arizona who joined the Navajo Division of Education officials in the Navajo Teacher Education Program started the most comprehensive effort yet attempted to train large numbers of Navajo teachers for Navajo schools. The leaders of the Navajo Teacher

Education Program decided to combine on-site educational training with summer campus residency, somewhat as the Teacher Corps staff had done at Northern Arizona University with a much smaller program. Students admitted into the NTEP could look forward to graduating in two years with proper certification. Navajo students thus could reach their desired goal promptly without sacrificing their support to their families.

The Navajo tribe's first attempt to take on the responsibility of selecting and training teachers for Navajo children began officially on September 21, 1973, with a meeting of the ninety-four program participants, university personnel, and members of the Navajo Tribal Council in Window Rock. Two Navajo educators, Dr. Robert Norris of the University of Arizona and Dr. Anita Pfeiffer of the University of New Mexico, played important roles in the new program. The Navajo Teacher Education Advisory Council, a newly formed group, served as consultants; its members included Pfeiffer, Dr. Sam Billison, Elouise Jackson, Nonabah Charley, Marjorie Thomas, and Guy Gorman.[39]

In the autumn of 1974, the Navajo Teacher Education Program entered its second year. An additional one hundred students joined the program, and their training began at sites in Tuba City, Kayenta, Ganado, Tsaile, Shiprock, and Crownpoint. The first year's class of students completed a summer program at the two participating universities and returned to the Navajo Nation to finish their undergraduate work. In several years, then, one expected significant numbers of new Navajo teachers to be trained through the program and to have an important impact on Navajo education.

That same autumn the Navajo Division of Education received a grant to train Navajos already holding bachelors' degrees as school administrators. Graduates of the program would receive a master's degree in educational administration. The growing number of Navajo teachers thus could be joined by Navajo school administrators sympathetic to Navajo control of Navajo education. Platero called the program, which would be funded initially by a quarter-million-dollar grant from the Carnegie Corporation, a "natural outgrowth" of the teacher training program. The Navajo Division of Education officials would supervise this new program, with the University of New Mexico responsible for instruction.[40]

These programs and changes described will seem limited, perhaps, to some observers. From one perspective, they are limited; they were part of a beginning that sought to alter a pattern of outside control a century old. But because that army of occupation, as Joshua Fishman would term it, was so entrenched, the changes brought about were remarkable.[41] As the Navajos participated more fully within the Navajo educational system and continued their process of obtaining more control over it, it was reasonable to anticipate escalating and often conflicting hopes and expectations among Navajos for their schools. Surely Navajos would continue to disagree about emphases and methods in the instruction of their children, but they presented a united front in their insistence upon their right to decide, in the end, these and other educational issues for themselves.

NAVAJO HEALTH CARE

Navajos sought greater control over their health care. Despite the progress that had been made in the 1950s and 1960s toward clearer communication between non-Navajo medical personnel and the Navajos and despite the greater utilization by the Navajos of medical facilities available to them, many Navajos still held stereotypes of Anglo personnel administering medical care that limited their effectiveness. Not all Navajos shared these images and the images were often unfair; still, the stereotypes persisted. Until the medical draft terminated in 1973, most Anglo doctors who came to the Navajo Area after World War II did so to fulfill a two-year military obligation. As commissioned officers within the Indian Health Service branch of the Public Health Service, these doctors had severe handicaps. Even in the 1970s they usually arrived ignorant of the land and the people and left just as they had started to become more familiar with the territory.

Their youth, relative inexperience, inability to speak Navajo, and residence in segregated housing provided by the Public Health Service all reduced their chances for success. "Interns," the Navajos called them. Richard Mike's ("N. John") cartoon series, "SuperNavajo", which appeared regularly in the Navajo newspaper *Diné Baa-Hani,* captured marvelously the negative image of the PHS doctor. Portrayed in the series as the heartless Dr. Meanie, the physician in one episode refused to aid a Navajo who sought assistance, keeping vicious dogs for the purpose of scaring off intruders. In another instance, Dr. Meanie reluctantly treated the injured Navajo rodeo cowboy Yazzie Manykids but sang "that old familiar bureaucracy tune": "We'd be a lot better off if we weren't so

understaffed. . . . We're using out-dated administrative techniques! Our
equipment is old! Too much red tape! Communication is terrible! No
community support!! Apathy!"[42]

Equally, Anglo medical personnel often had less than positive images
of Navajo singers or their patients. The Anglo doctor or nurse usually
arrived on the Navajo reservation accustomed to receiving the gratitude
of patients who accepted their services eagerly and unquestioningly.
Suddenly they found themselves less understood and their services less
appreciated. Nearly all the Navajos who sought hospital treatment produced also ritual assistance before, after, or even during their hospitaliza-
tion. Many doctors put the blame for the situation on the Indian Health
Service, their peers, socialized medicine, or "the Indians," who either did
not come to the hospital when they should or did come when they
should not.

Paraprofessional participation in medicine took on great urgency
within the Navajo area because of the limited numbers of Navajos within
the top ranks of the medical profession and the PHS hierarchy. The number of Navajo nurses had increased gradually, augmented by such training
programs as the one established recently at Navajo Community College.
But as of 1974 there remained one Navajo M.D. A Baylor medical school
graduate, Taylor McKenzie joined the Public Health Service in 1965 and
became service unit director at Shiprock in July 1970. He received a
promotion in 1972 to the equivalent of a navy captain or a full colonel
within the PHS. Several other Navajos, however, have held responsible
administrative positions within the organization. Vernon Bowman served
as a commissioned officer in the field of health education and Gordon
Denipah worked as a commissioned officer in the area of sanitation. In
1974 Marie Allen became the Navajo area assistant director for PHS and
thus the highest ranking Navajo within the Navajo area working for PHS.
However, Anglos continued to dominate PHS administration. Moreover,
talented, trained Navajos from the PHS, including McKenzie and Denipah,
moved to the Navajo Health Authority, leaving PHS even more bereft of
Navajo leadership.[43]

At the paraprofessional level, PHS personnel initiated several programs
for increasing Navajo participation. A midwife training program began
in Shiprock in 1970 as a cooperative effort between the PHS and the
University of Utah. Officials of Johns Hopkins University joined the
project to train additional midwives in Chinle and Fort Defiance. Grad-

uates of the program not only assisted at delivery but helped with pre-
natal and infant care. In addition, a most promising program to train
medical assistants, the Navajo Area Community Health Program, began
on April 5, 1971. After two years of training, its graduates, all of whom
had had previous medical experience, served as physicians assistants
capable of giving care to Navajo patients.[44] The first graduates entered
the PHS in 1973 to serve in such places as Tohatchi, where two medics,
one a former LPN and the other a former X-ray technician, ran the clinic.
The supervising physician stationed in Gallup in 1974 commented:

Since 90 per cent of PHS work is outpatient, the Tohatchi system seems
to be the route to go. The people in Tohatchi are doing a superb job. For
clinic work I am tremendously overtrained. The medics are accepted,
they speak Navajo and they can provide more personalized care.[45]

Community health representatives (CHRs) played a critical liaison
role between health professionals and the Navajo people. Over 120 Navajos
served in this capacity in 1974. After a ten-week training course, they
were prepared to perform a variety of tasks, ranging from surveys to the
provision of health care advice to people within the various communities.
Each CHR was selected by the specific chapter to which he or she was
assigned and funneled questions and complaints to the Navajo Area
Health Board chaired by the PHS area director.[46]

On May 12, 1970, the Navajo Tribal Council established the Navajo
Area Indian Health Advisory Board to provide a forum for Navajo view-
points on health care matters. The advisory nature of the area board,
however, meant that strong opinions voiced at that level might not be
translated into ameliorative action. The eight service unit boards perhaps
were more influential, but, as Sid Gilson of the PHS Gallup Indian Hospital pointed out, the issues put before the service unit boards were
usually inconsequential, "for example, should we have TV in the hospital,
or that burning issue—what about the trash in the parking lot?"[47]

Some Anglo personnel accorded more respect to traditional Navajo
religion in the early 1970s. Navajo singers performed blessing ceremonies
for the opening of new PHS facilities; medicine men obtained private
rooms at the Gallup hospital for rituals over hospital patients. PHS psychiatrists had the strongest professional interest in the relationship between the mind and general well-being. Dr. Robert Bergman has become

known as a defender of the viability of traditional Navajo healing, but Bergman was by no means alone. Dr. Jack Ellis of the PHS in Gallup headed a hospital-based mental health program which employed, in part, traditional Navajo rituals.

The most publicized reinforcement of traditional ways came with the Navajo mental health program's sponsorship of a project to train additional Navajo medicine men. Funded by the National Institute of Health and operated by the Rough Rock Demonstration School, the Rough Rock Mental Health Training Program trained a small number of people selected by the Rough Rock school board. The trainees studied after sunset every night for six to eight hours in hogans from Piñon to Chinle to Kayenta. Four students completed their training and received diplomas at a special ceremony in May 1972: Jim Hatathle and Mae Hatathle, Hozhooji (Beauty Way); Dan Yazzie, Hoocho'igi (Against Evil Way); and Billy Conn, So'tsohji (Big Star). Additional students at that time included Casey Redhouse (studying Against Evil Way), Sadie Sam (Big Star), Little Laughter and Benjamin Woody (Mountain Way), John Caboni and Bahe Tsosie (Red Ant Way), and Sam Honie and Ned Todechine (Arrow Shooting Way). The medicine men and the trainees also met every other Monday with Bergman and other Anglo doctors. These sessions informed the Navajos, none of whom spoke English, about Anglo medical practices and procedures.[48]

Why did Navajos seek to wrest authority for health care away from the PHS? Now that Navajos for the most part had become willing to utilize Western medicine for certain purposes, they wanted to determine how that medical care was provided. While the Public Health Service personnel had shown more sensitivity, their short tenure meant that for most doctors the learning process began anew every two years. The PHS also tended to be influenced by outside political pressure, which resulted in the location of the PHS hospital in 1961 in Gallup rather than on the reservation site.

Navajos also realized the internal problems that beset the PHS. The federal government did not give the PHS sufficient financial support. The PHS did not have enough doctors, or enough nurses, or enough health facilities. Also, insufficient funds halted innovative programs. Finally, PHS administrators usually did not encourage criticism from within the organization. Two nurses, Sandra Kramer and Valerie Koster wrote a letter to the *Navajo Times* in December 1974, complaining about conditions

at the Shiprock hospital—and quickly lost their jobs. While the new
Navajo area director, Dr. Marlene Haffner, denied that she fired the
nurses in reprisal for the letter, the coincidence was striking. Navajos
signed petitions in support of the nurses to indicate dissatisfaction with
hospital conditions and with the dismissal. In the meantime, Dr. Haffner
circulated a memorandum to all PHS personnel in the Navajo area for-
bidding them to criticize the PHS publicly.[49]

THE NAVAJO HEALTH AUTHORITY

Established in June 1972 by the Navajo Tribal Council, the Navajo
Health Authority is responsible for creating an exemplary health system
for the Navajo people. To meet this general objective, the Navajo Health
Authority officials began to work along several fronts to promote professional health careers, not only among Navajos but among all Native
Americans. They desired to increase dramatically the number of trained
Indian people in the field of medicine while reaffirming the value of the
traditional native healing sciences. Thus they worked to establish the
first Native American medical school while promoting traditional ways
through a department of native healing sciences headed by Carl Gorman.

The American Indian medical school would be the central element
within the Center for Health Professions Education. The Department
of Health, Education and Welfare's Bureau of Health Manpower Education granted the Navajo Health Authority, in conjunction with the University of New Mexico Medical School, a $5 million grant toward financing
the center in October 1972. The center would also attempt to
provide continuing education for health professionals now working in the
Navajo Nation, to develop new allied health training programs in cooperation with health agencies and educational institutions, such as Navajo
Community College, and to recruit and support Navajo students in the
study of medicine and other health related fields.[50]

In the meantime, the NHA's Office of Student Affairs, under the direction of Jack Jackson, offered to support students interested in careers in
health services. A sizable grant from the Kellogg Foundation already
had been put to use to give fellowships for Native American students.
The Division of Planning, Evaluation and Development's primary

accomplishment was to establish the Navajo Comprehensive Health Planning Agency, a regional agency involving Navajo consumers in planning and developing health programs for the Navajo Nation. Initially under the direction of Dr. Laurence B. Callen and then of Cecil Patrick, a Navajo who holds a masters degree in health planning, the agency pursued this objective aided by an advisory council of Navajo and non-Navajo consumers and providers of health care.[51]

Carl Gorman's efforts within the Native Healing Sciences Program promoted understanding of traditional Navajo healing and supported the practice of that healing. Gorman wrote a series of articles on Navajo health and healing and served as a liaison between traditional Navajo healers and Anglo physicians. The Navajo Health Authority's health resources directory included a list of practitioners of the Navajo native healing sciences and a list of the ceremonies each was qualified to perform, as well as a list of the instructors and trainees at the Rough Rock "medicine man school." The listing illustrated the resiliency of the traditional ways. Singers were included from each of the five regions of the Navajo Nation, with a total of forty-five medicine men listed, exclusive of the Rough Rock singers.[52]

In 1970 in a speech given to a Navajo education conference, Taylor McKenzie summarized the reasons why Navajos should control their health care services:

1. The people would identify more with their respective hospital and its problems and would be willing to help solve mutual problems out of mutual concern. . . .
2. There are certain decisions about medical and health services relating to, and affecting Navajos which only Navajos can make. . . .
3. Many helpful suggestions, instructions and requests coming from the local community would tend to improve the general quality of the medical and health services. . . .
4. There would be established a mutual working understanding between the hospital and the community.[53]

In the 1950s Navajo control of health services, let alone the American Indian medical school, seemed most unlikely. Two decades later the movement toward achieving that objective represented the synthesis of traditional Navajo and progressive Anglo ways at the heart of Navajo continuity within change.

NAVAJO ECONOMIC DEVELOPMENT

Mineral Resources

While providing an important addition to tribal revenue, Navajo uranium holdings were not considered potentially as important as oil until the 1970s. In the 1970s uranium resources provided Navajos with an opportunity to gain more control over their land's wealth. The Navajo Nation conducted its first sale of uranium in April of 1971. It brought a nearly $3 million bonus, and Navajo Tribal Council Vice Chairman Wilson Skeet called it "a first step towards self-determination."[54]

An even more promising development than the discovery of new uranium resources in the Grants, New Mexico, area tapped by the 1971 bidding came in 1973-74, as a result of negotiations between the Navajo Nation and Exxon. The joint venture between the tribe and Exxon, approved in January 1974 by the Tribal Council, had several noteworthy aspects. First, it would be a lucrative operation for the tribal government; $6 million alone would be paid for exploration rights in the 400,000 acres of northwestern New Mexico in the community areas of Shiprock, Red Rock, Two Gray Hills, Sanostee, and Beclabito. Additionally, if the amount of uranium were discovered that Exxon assumed to be present, Navajo Tribal Council Chairman Peter MacDonald estimated that the tribe would receive as much as $100 million over the next ten to fifteen years.[55]

The Exxon-Navajo Nation venture would bring other economic and certain environmental advantages to Diné. About 200 jobs per mining site were expected. Test hole drilling would help to provide many new wells for the area. The entire operation would be underground and thus would not remove livestock, displace people, or disrupt the land. These environmental and human benefits had been lacking in the Black Mesa coal strip mining operation.

Yet perhaps the most significant aspect of the entire development was that, as Chairman MacDonald observed, it would allow the "Navajo Nation to participate in a joint venture as joint owners in the production and marketing of their resources." For this reason, he labeled it "one of the most significant events in the history of Indian affairs." MacDonald also emphasized that the knowledge gained through this undertaking might help to make Diné able to utilize these resources without outside assistance.[56]

However, in February 1974, the Sanostee chapter voiced unanimous opposition to the plan, voicing concern about lack of consultation, adverse environmental impact, and failure of the chapter to receive financial benefits from the mining. Elmer Barber of Sanostee chapter argued that "a certain percentage of any revenue that comes into general funds of the Navajo Tribe needs to be put back into that community district where the revenue is coming from." He contended the chapter members would oppose exploration within its boundaries unless "our chapter is granted part of the $6 million going to general funds of the tribe."[57] While the chapter residents legally cannot block such exploration, their firm opposition would make the exploration more difficult to undertake.

Former Navajo Area director Graham Holmes characterized local opposition to mineral exploitation that would benefit the Navajo Nation as "illogical, bitter resistance" that came because of changing land use caused by overpopulation and subsequent lack of grazing land. "When the tribal government cuts across the land now," Holmes said, "it puts people's backs to the wall. It's a hell of a mean situation and it gets worse every day." Holmes also cautioned against unqualified praise for the Exxon agreement: "At the time the Peabody deal was made it looked like the best deal you could get. Now with the inflationary spiral, the royalty is cheap at today's prices. The Exxon contract will look awful cheap in ten years if the price goes up."[58]

The progressing issue of the coal gasification potential in the Burnham area showed that the Navajos were dealing with the issue of resource utilization in a much different manner than in earlier power production developments. The coal gasification question began with two leases signed by the Navajo tribe for the mining of coal for gasification. Paul Jones signed the first lease on July 26, 1957, which permitted 31,416 acres to be mined by Utah International for WESCO (Texas Eastern Transmission and Pacific Lighting Corporation). Raymond Nakai signed the second lease, which allowed more than 40,000 acres to be mined by Consolidation Coal Company for El Paso Natural Gas. Both operations would utilize Navajo water rights, but neither operation's proposed gasification plant gained approval by the tribe in the early 1970s. The gas produced would be for nonreservation, Southwestern usage. Benefits to The People would be similar to other such projects: royalties and employment, the latter mostly in the construction stage.

El Paso officials stated royalties to the Navajo Nation when the complex and mine were fully operational "will approximate $1.5 million annually." Mac Eddy, director of the Office of Program Development for the Navajo Nation believed "normal operations after three years of construction will be 700 to 800 (employees) in the plant with an annual payroll of $10 to $20 million a year." These figures would be doubled for the two plants, and as many as seven plants might be constructed. Manpower requirements for coal gasification and mining operations for two plants were estimated as follows: 130 managers and officials, 315 professional and technical, 136 foremen, 272 office workers and sales, 312 craftsmen, 686 operatives and related, 49 custodial and service: a total of 1,900.[59]

Both companies' administrators said they planned to take every reasonable step to guarantee that no part of the project would adversely affect the environment. No doubt influenced by the Four Corners emissions and the limited reclamation accomplished on Black Mesa, many Navajos were frankly skeptical. Primarily, Navajos objected to the project because of potentially adverse environmental impact and general disruption of local life.

Burnham residents' objections to coal gasification came to a head in the summer of 1973, when the chapter members voted twice to reject the proposed development. They voted unanimously to express the chapter's conviction that "any exploitation of coal resources [should] be delayed until such time that the Navajo Tribe can have more control in exploiting their own resources." In July, the chapter reaffirmed its position. Wally Davis, acting chapter secretary, traced chapter members' opposition to anxiety over potential loss of traditional means of livelihood and destruction of land as well as concern about pollution, lack of planning for future generations, and failure to provide for people displaced by the operations.[60]

In the face of this opposition, Navajo government officials would be forced to reassess the project and eventually, in MacDonald's second term, renegotiate the lease with El Paso Natural Gas and Consolidated Coal. Diné Coalition, a group of Navajos which included some Burnham residents, helped to organize the resistance. The new lease would not be approved until 1976, but by 1974 renegotiation was inevitable. Even such a proponent of coal gasification as Shiprock council delegate Carl Todacheene, upon return from a trip to Germany and Scotland, had observed that companies there took full responsibility for land reclamation. His statement in December 1973 in favor of stricter controls on the development showed a new firmness in the Navajo government's position.[61]

In the critical area of water rights and water usage, MacDonald served notice that from this point on the Navajos would assert aggressively their rights to their share of the water. MacDonald's views contrasted sharply with the 1960s, when the Navajos had traded their Winters Doctrine rights to 34,000 acre feet of upper basin Colorado River water for the life of the Page power plant in exchange for having the plant built near Page. Then the Navajos had been cajoled into believing they could not utilize much of the water from the river. In 1972 MacDonald argued along entirely different lines. He contended the tribe must claim water that it could not fully use at present in order to safeguard its future:

Our population has increased from 60,000 to 130,000 in the last 30 years. Most of this population lives in a traditional pastoral economy. We utilize for grazing a land base that was originally too small, and it has not expanded with our population. Thus if we are to retain our culture and remain as a tribal entity on our traditional lands, we must make a rapid transition to a modern agricultural and industrial economy. And to do so, we need our share of the water.[62]

MacDonald and other Navajos also reviewed the proposed use of their coal resources. MacDonald stated, "It must be clearly understood that it will no longer be accepted practice to sell the reservation off by the ton or by the barrel."[63] At hearings before a Senate committee investigating problems of electrical power production in the Southwest, many Navajos complained about the willingness of Southwestern urbanites and Southwestern energy companies to exploit Navajo resources. Peterson Zah of DNA legal services, for example, argued:

I cannot comprehend a process which allows people hundreds of miles away to use the resources of other people in a destructive manner. All religious values, as well as simple commonsense, tells us that you should not exploit and take advantage of other people. People in Albuquerque, Phoenix and Los Angeles do not dump their sewage and garbage in their neighbors' homes, nor do they cut paths through their lawns and string wires overhead.

In his testimony Zah referred to the Navajo Nation as "a foreign area," thus emphasizing the separate nature of Navajo land.[64] This new consciousness, coupled with the energy crisis of the 1970s, clearly would strengthen the Navajo bargaining position in relationship to the utilization of their land's resources.

The Tribal Enterprise

The unquestioned success of the Navajo Forest Products Industries suggested a model for developing other areas of the Navajo economy. By 1971, stumpage payments had increased for NFPI to $620,704, net profits to $691,692, and capital assets to $13,647,231; in 1972, these figures leaped to $1,281,015, $1,913,419, and $16,999,882, respectively. The year 1973 revealed continued growth. Stumpage payments stood at $1,637,956, net profit at $2,535,015, and capital assets at $18,133,649. Total Navajo earnings at the plant had increased as well. The number of Navajos employed went up to 490 in 1973, from a total of 433 the year before.[65]

NFPI, in sum, had shown a profit and demonstrated a method of controlling the operation without excluding needed non-Navajo assistance. On the basis of its success, the Navajo government moved to create other tribal enterprises as part of an overall strategy for economic development. The tribal enterprise, officials believed, lent itself well to both the development of Navajo land resources and import substitution. The primary example created in this period to develop land resources was the Navajo Agricultural Products Industries. Created by a Navajo Tribal Council Advisory Committee resolution on April 16, 1970, Navajo Agricultural Products Industries was established with the forthcoming Navajo Indian Irrigation Project in mind. It was supposed to train Navajos for agricultural work, encourage productive use of Navajo agricultural resources, expand the markets for Navajo-grown agricultural products within and outside

the Navajo Nation, and promote agribusiness. The NAPI management
board appointed by the Advisory Committee included both Navajo and
non-Navajo members. The non-Navajos, generally retired Anglo business
executives, contributed their expertise much in the same fashion as their
colleagues on the Navajo Forest Products Industries board.

The tribe provided for additional Navajo control of and participation
within the management of NAPI. The Advisory Committee approved the
general manager, who had principal responsibility for budgets, planning,
hiring and firing, and supervision. Dr. Bahe Billy, a Navajo who had earned
a doctorate in agronomy at the University of Arizona, was hired as the
general manager. In addition, "Each operating unit head, and each employee in a management position shall, if he be non-Indian, train and
otherwise prepare a member of the Navajo Tribe to replace him." "Such
a replacement," the Advisory Committee resolved, "shall occur not less
than five years following the establishment of the managerial position."
Bureau of Indian Affairs employees were forbidden to be members of
the management board, thus ensuring against potential interference from
that government agency.[66]

The tribal enterprise approach also found wide applicability in the
area of import substitution. Diné also started to utilize other methods of
replacing non-Navajo concerns and dependency on off-reservation resources with Navajo cooperatives and small business enterprises. Navajos
were spending sixty-seven cents of each dollar off the reservation. The
business community of Gallup, Farmington, Holbrook, Winslow, and
Flagstaff profited remarkably from Navajo trade, which sought these communities not because of the hospitality proffered but because needed
services were absent within the Navajo Nation. Import substitution thus
had several potential advantages: it employed Navajo people, supplied
needed goods and services more conveniently—Navajos often drive great
distances to shop off the reservation—and might supply those goods and
services more economically and with more respect for and attention to
Navajo demands.

Navajo utilization of the tribal enterprise approach in import substitution for the most part is quite recent. Chapter 5 of Title V, "Commerce
and Trade", of the Navajo Tribal Code, for example, is concerned with
tribal enterprises, and of the six enterprises listed in 1972 none falls
within the category of import substitution. The one exception to this

generalization is found elsewhere in the code, and that is a tribal enterprise of long standing: the Navajo Tribal Utility Authority. Its separate listing is indicative of its somewhat tenuous membership within the category of tribal enterprise, though it is officially considered as such by the tribe.

The Navajo Tribal Council established the Navajo Tribal Utility Authority on January 22, 1959, to bring electrical power to Shiprock. Since that time the NTUA has branched into natural gas, water, and sewer utility operations and extended its electrical services to serve eventually all of the Navajo Nation. The Advisory Committee passed a series of resolutions in 1965 and 1966 to reorganize the NTUA and alter its status to that of a tribal enterprise with a more autonomous plan of operation. The NTUA is now governed by a management board with similar powers as the boards of the Navajo Forest Products Industries and Navajo Agricultural Products Industries. As with NFPI and NAPI, the Tribal Council appoints the general manager of the NTUA.[67]

On paper the Navajo Tribal Utility Authority represents a significant example of the Navajo Nation taking over a function formerly controlled and operated by the Bureau of Indian Affairs, but in reality the NTUA is still dependent on outside concerns. Anthropologist David Aberle described the dependence quite precisely. He noted that the Navajos lease coal resources to Utah Construction and Mining Company, which receives the profits (the Navajos receive only royalties), and Utah Construction and Mining sells the Navajos back the coal in the form of electric current, courtesy of the coal-fired Four Corners power plant. The NTUA, in short, must rely on these outside companies for producing the power; it buys the power it forwards to Navajo users. Thus the NTUA does not fulfill the goal of self-sufficiency, though it has been a valuable addition to the Navajo people and certainly has been a useful source of revenue for the tribe treasury.[68]

The NTUA has continued to serve more Navajos, return a larger profit to the tribe, and place more Navajos in positions of executive leadership within the enterprise. Tribal leaders are reviewing the utility's role and place in the Navajo economy. Most recently, the NTUA has served as the agency for Economic Development Administration-Environmental Protection Agency large-scale water supply and storage and sewage facility projects at Window Rock, Fort Defiance, Chinle, Tuba City, Navajo Com-

munity College (Tsaile, Arizona), and Shiprock, with designs and contracts being prepared for the communities of Ganado and Kayenta in
Arizona, and Crownpoint and Tohatchi in New Mexico. The net return
to the tribe from the operation of the NTUA has increased steadily. For
example, in the fiscal year ending June 30, 1970, the NTUA had a net
profit of $531,614 and accumulated net revenues of $1,263,811.[69]

The first years of Peter MacDonald's administration were marked by
a strong new emphasis on the tribal enterprise approach represented by
the NTUA. Other newly created import substitution enterprises—including
the Navajo Aviation Authority—together with the others previously mentioned, formed one prong of a three-pronged attack to revitalize the
Navajo national economy. The other two were the establishment of many
small businesses on the reservation and the creation of more on-reservation jobs.

Of these new import substitution enterprises, Navajo Housing Authority
is the only other one of sufficient maturity to merit extended analysis.
The NHA is actually a tribal organization of rather long duration, but
only in 1972 did it take on the specific responsibility of full-scale administration, planning, and construction of housing facilities within the
Navajo Nation, through the Navajo Housing and Development Enterprise.
Created by a Navajo Tribal Council resolution of January 20, 1972, the
Navajo Housing and Development Enterprise was designated to find new
and more effective ways of providing housing and community facilities,
financial, technical, and other assistance for the development of housing
and community facilities, and maximum employment and training opportunities and to operate, maintain, and promote housing and community
facilities and provide a fair return to the tribe.[70]

The Navajo Housing and Development Enterprise is divided into two
main divisions. In 1974 the Housing Management Division, housed in
Window Rock, had about 300 rental units under its supervision. The
Construction Division, with offices and a housing manufacturing plant
in Church Rock Industrial Park (northeast of Gallup), built houses for
the Navajo Housing Authority and professional offices, such as the Navajo
Professional Building in Window Rock.

As of September 1, 1973, the administrator of the Navajo Housing and
Development Enterprise, the Navajo Housing Authority, had 780 low-rent
units housing 3,951 people and 365 mutual help houses housing 1,726

people. Additional residences of both types were under construction, and NHA received an $18 million appropriation from HUD in March 1973 to construct 765 new houses.[71]

Trading Posts: The Problem of Control

While it moved to regulate the extensive network of trading posts across the Navajo Nation, at the same time the Navajo government stimulated small business development at the local level as an alternative to the trading post system. It is difficult to describe to those who have never been on the reservation just how radical an alteration the transition away from the trading post monopoly would be. How did trading posts come to be so important?

The trading post's character becomes more understandable in the light of the sheep-raising economy, the quite limited geographical area in which Navajo families worked and lived, the lack of motor vehicles and paved roads, and the percentage of Navajos who did not speak English. Over the years the trader became more than a grocer; he became the main intermediary between the Navajos of his area and the outside world. He became translator, buyer, trader, and bartender. He counseled the living and buried the dead. He often encouraged new trends in weaving and jewelry making and provided a place for the people to pawn their wealth for temporary or permanent loans.[72]

The trader therefore potentially had enormous power within the Navajo economy and, despite frequent protestations to the contrary, the opportunity of gaining enormous wealth. Some of the early traders became extraordinarily influential in local affairs in the years after Diné returned from Fort Sumner: Lorenzo Hubbell of Ganado, for example, Richard Wetherill of Kayenta, and Thomas Keam, of Keams Canyon. A network of trader families spread across the Navajo area and clans of interrelated Anglos operated posts; their children grew up to take over their businesses at such isolated locales as Red Mesa and Piñon.

Over the last few decades criticism mounted against the traders and the institution of the trading post. The existence of the trading post fostered dependency and discouraged Navajo economic development. The monopolistic nature of the trading post encouraged Navajos to remain tied to the trader through exchanging sheep, rugs, and other products for credit at the post. This often meant that Diné had little choice but to accept what the trader offered, and moreover that credit rather than cash was used. The whole pawn system proved similar in practice.

The trading post remained important in the 1970s, though far less vital than in the past and substantially changed in character. A smaller percentage of Navajos depended upon sheep and sheep-related products for economic gain. Navajo families were more mobile, in part due to the vast increase in the number of paved roads and the presence of the intrepid pickup truck. Nearly universal exposure to formal schooling for young Navajos since World War II had decreased progressively the need for the trader to serve as translator-mediator. Among the rural, older, monolingual Navajo most conservative in economic pursuit, the trader's role was likely to be least changed.

This decline in dependency, the vigilance of attorneys representing Diné, and the problems of independent grocers and small businessmen in rural areas placed the average trader in a more and more untenable position. Lawyers both called attention to and did something about traders' withholding of welfare and other government checks, possible because the trader often served as the local postmaster, price fixing, and Truth in Lending Law violations. Caught in the bind of a declining profit margin the traders claimed they must raise their prices. Navajos who shopped at a trading post not only paid more than they would at an off-reservation store but also generally more than they would at the few large-volume on-reservation stores, such as FedMart in Window Rock and Imperial Mart in Chinle. A series of investigations by Navajo college students and the Federal Trade Commission documented the degree to which Navajos who patronized trading posts must be willing to pay higher prices and often obtain substandard goods for their money.[73]

Of course, some of the traders have been Navajos, and Navajos have ventured into a variety of other small business concerns. For example, in 1960 a Navajo Tribal Council trading committee inspecting trading post enterprises noted that of the 137 trading posts doing business within the Navajo reservation twenty-one were operated by Navajos, with five more Navajos having applied for trading leases. By 1970, the number of trading posts within the reservation had declined to one hundred, of which Navajos owned eighteen. In addition to this slight increase in percentage, Navajos had registered impressive gains in the ownership of other retail establishments: in 1970, Navajos owned a majority. They owned both food stores, twenty-four of forty-two gasoline service stations, nine of sixteen eating and drinking establishments, one of two furniture and home furnishing stores, the one apparel and accessory store, and one of four miscellaneous retail stores, but none of the four automotive dealerships.

Navajos also owned a majority of the wholesale and service establishments within the Navajo Nation by 1970. They owned the one wholesale operation—lumber and construction and materials—and thirteen of twenty-four service concerns: five of thirteen hotels, motels, tourist courts, and camps; three of five personal services; three of four automobile repair, services, and garage; and the one pool hall. A non-Navajo owned the one movie theater.[74]

These statistics revealed what many Navajos and non-Navajos perhaps did not fully realize: Navajos were quickly gaining control of the small business sector of the Navajo national economy. Tribal economic planners were involved in a serious effort to broaden the base of this small business sector. Many of the small business ventures one would expect to find within the Navajo Nation were either nonexistent or owned by outsiders, and a transition would require changes in attitude and in policy. Joseph R. Hardy of the Navajo Small Business Development Corporation contended there must be more delegates to the Navajo Tribal Council who "are small business-oriented rather than livestock-oriented in their thinking." He also argued there must be changes made in the "morass of red tape—all sorts of tribal and federal regulations—which discourage an individual from getting into business."[75]

Hardy and consultants to the tribe like University of New Mexico economist Gerald Boyle saw development of the small business sector as essential to the creation of a tax base within the Navajo Nation. Tribal planners viewed small business development as important in achieving the goal of "redirecting cash flow back toward reservation communities, thereby increasing the local multiplier effect of Navajo dollars spent."[76]

Many feasibility studies were conducted on the potential of Navajo-owned businesses, from an industrial laundry in Chinle—to be known, perhaps inevitably, as the Chinle Wash—to an automobile dealership in Tuba City. Many of these businesses seemed on their way to becoming a reality. The 1973 annual report for the development section of the tribe's

Office of Program Development, for example, listed thirteen small business operations at the planning stage, five more at the development stage, and three new small businesses in operation: a barber shop and a trailer court in Fort Defiance and a garage in Tuba City. For a number of years, Navajos and non-Navajos alike pointed to Fleming Begay of Chinle (operator of a gas station-trading post-cafe complex) as *the* Navajo entrepreneur, but it became apparent that in the 1980s he would have many peers, indeed.[77]

While the Fleming Begays of the Navajo nation remained few in the early 1970s, some observers of the Navajo economy questioned whether it was desirable to have them in large supply. Indeed, the traditional economy of the area, based more on extended family and community enterprise, may lend itself more fruitfully to a community-based cooperative approach. Although the cooperative is hardly a new idea, having been advocated strongly by non-Navajos for Navajos during the John Collier era, for example, only during the 1970s did it start to gain widespread acceptance among Diné.

Most Navajo cooperatives in 1974 existed as alternatives to trading posts and took the goods and services of the trading post as a model. In other words, the typical coop sold food, dry goods, gasoline, and perhaps hay or feed for livestock. It was, in short, a consumer coop rather than a marketing or producer coop, though all three varieties existed in the Navajo nation.[78]

The Piñon coop, a pioneer among Navajo cooperatives as it dates from 1971, was perhaps the most successful consumer coop and certainly served as a model for later cooperative ventures. Piñon, Arizona, is a small community forty miles west of Chinle. Dissatisfaction felt by local residents with the Piñon trading post, operated by the McGees (part of a long-time trader family), contributed to beginning the coop. Attorneys Robert Hilgendorf and John Silko of the Chinle DNA office helped the Piñon area people to file a class action suit against the trading post and then helped them to establish a coop. The class action suit eventually was settled out of court for the handsome sum of $32,500, and the cooperative has been a thriving concern ever since. Formally named the Diné-Bi-Naa-Yei Cooperative of Piñon, the coop required each of its members to pay a small yearly sum for dues. In return, the coop sold its goods at the lowest possible prices, while still making a small profit. At the end of the

year the coop returns its profits in the form of dividends to its members,
and it has paid a dividend each year since its inception.

Not all Navajo cooperatives did as well as Piñon. There were crucial
problems at several coops both in management and on the volume of
business actually engendered by the new institution. Nonetheless, as of
September, 1973, nineteen coops existed in or adjacent to the Navajo
nation. Nine provided food, dry goods, and/or hay and feed or gasoline.
Two cooperatives were basically designed to sell hay and feed. There was
one credit union and one agricultural planning cooperative. Six cooperatives were concerned primarily with arts and crafts.[79]

The arts and crafts cooperatives provided the weaver and silversmith
not only with a ready buyer, as the trader had been, but also with some
guarantees of a greater return than the trader could provide because
most (up to 90 percent) of the price paid for the craft item went directly
to the craftsperson. The arts and crafts cooperatives served the general
American public, offering high-quality goods through on- and off-reservation advertising and auctions and promised to stimulate the continuation
of crafts such as weaving long predicted to be dying out because the
monetary return to the craftsperson was insufficient.

NAVAJO INVOLVEMENT IN LOCAL AND STATE AFFAIRS

In this era Navajos also began to express greater interest in county and
state political affairs. The rapid rise in Navajo voter registration, inspired
initially by the desire to elect more Navajos to local school boards, soon
confronted several counties with strikingly increased Navajo voting power.
This movement had as its objective the assertion of Navajo rights within
the immediate area of the Navajo Nation. In Apache County, Arizona,
one of three parallel, gerrymandered Arizona counties drawn nearly 200
miles long and 50 miles wide in order to ensure off-reservation dominance
to the southern portions, Navajo voters suddenly outnumbered Anglo
voters. Southern residents wanted no part of the union and threatened
secession; they generously urged the formation of a separate Navajo
reservation county to be called Canyon de Chelly, but the Arizona legislature turned down the idea. The first Navajo elected to the Apache
County Board of Supervisors, Tom Shirley, had to go to court to be seated.

While Navajo voters had been electing a few Navajo representatives
from McKinley and San Juan counties in New Mexico since the late

1960s, they now elected three representatives to the Arizona legislature as well, Arthur Hubbard, Ben Hanley, and Daniel Peaches, an achievement also made possible by successful Navajo pressure for redistricting. Navajo voters provided the margin needed to elect Raul Castro as governor of Arizona and generally swung away from the overwhelming Republican voting pattern they had previously demonstrated. Barry Goldwater, for one, expressed dismay at this transition. He protested that Navajos were being bought off by the AFL-CIO. But MacDonald quietly commented that certain politicians had always taken the Navajo vote for granted and had voiced their appreciation for the Navajo way of life as long as Navajos had been content to play the centerfold role for *Arizona Highways*.[80]

MacDonald had indeed worked for closer ties with the AFL-CIO. Supported by a Tribal Council resolution of January 19, 1972, he forged a working alliance with the union to encourage the development of skilled Navajo workers and to increase the number of Navajos employed on various construction and industrial projects throughout the reservation. The resolution did not mention the union specifically, but it did empower the chairman "to do any and all things necessary, incidental or advisable to accomplish the purposes of this resolution," and MacDonald entered into an agreement with the AFL-CIO to set up a training program for Navajo workers. This act marked a sharp contrast with earlier Navajo relations with unionism; indeed, the tribe earlier had attempted to outlaw unions on the reservation. With the growing industrialism on the reservation and the Navajo government's desire to provide jobs for Navajo workers on various construction projects, some kind of rapprochement with unions was inevitable. The hand of tribal officials also was forced by Navajo worker dissatisfactions at Page, which culminated in 1971 in the formation of the Navajo Construction Workers Association by skilled workers in that area. The Navajo government also created the Office of Navajo Labor Relations in 1972 to oversee Navajo concerns in that field.[81]

Younger Navajos led protests beginning in 1969 over the treatment of Navajos in border town communities. Election of Frankie Garcia as mayor of Gallup heightened tensions in the early 1970s. Garcia's family held interest in the notorious Navajo Inn, a liquor store located several hundred yeards from the reservation line out of Window Rock. An inter-tribal group called Indians Against Exploitation issued formal statements against the mayor and the annual ceremonial in November and December of 1972. Following the American Indian Movement occupation of the

Gallup Public Health Service hospital in January 1973, an Indians Against Exploitation leader, Larry Casuse, labeled Gallup a "rat-hole" because of its thirty-eight bars, its pawn shops, and its police's treatment of Indians. "I don't see wrong in protecting your own basic rights," he said, "knowing the consequences of getting shot down in the streets of Gallup or getting your head bashed in."[82]

Five weeks later Larry Casuse was dead. He and Robert Nakaidineh had kidnapped Mayor Garcia March 1 and held him hostage, and Casuse had been shot as Garcia escaped their custody. The police claimed Casuse had killed himself, but other witnesses said the police had killed him. While a desperate and fatal act, Casuse's deed symbolized the utter frustration felt by many Native Americans about conditions they confronted in places like Gallup (self-proclaimed Indian capital of the world). Gallup provided as logical a target for Larry Casuse as the village of Wounded Knee did for others that same spring. A year later Peter MacDonald spoke for many who disapproved of Casuse's means but understood his ends:

The death of Larry Casuse has brought a new awareness among Indian people. Because of his untimely death, we realize that we, the Indian people, still face forces that can rob us of our culture, our resources and even our very lives. Therefore, we need one another more than ever.[83]

While Gallup received the most publicity, Farmington gained more attention in 1974 as another city with its share of difficulties in Native American-white relations. The murder of three Navajos by Anglo youths was the most tragic episode in events that brought national attention to the problems in the Farmington area. The three Navajo men had been beaten to death by three Anglo boys; all had been murdered, reportedly, while drunk. Once again, merchant attitudes, police policies, and liquor-related issues highlighted the dispute. The Coalition for Navajo Liberation led the effort to encourage better treatment of Navajos in the community, but in both Gallup and Farmington the deep-rooted problems defied immediate resolution.

TRIBAL GOVERNMENT REORGANIZATION

The Navajo tribal government succeeded in achieving substantial reorganization designed to allow it to pursue the goal of self-determination more effectively. Reorganization consisted of two parts: the revision and alteration of the council committee system and the restructuring of the tribal government framework. Through the first part of reorganization, many new council standing committees became established; in addition, the chairman received the power to appoint members to all standing committees. The council gave the chairman significant new authority immediately after MacDonald's inaugural through a resolution passed January 12, 1971.

The Health, Alcoholism and Welfare Committee established by the same resolution consolidated the work done by the Commission on Alcoholism, started in 1963, and the Health and Welfare committees, both begun in 1957. Another committee created by the January 12 resolution, the Labor and Manpower Committee, was charged with the review of "all matters relating to labor involving or affecting Navajo people . . . or involving or affecting the Navajo Nation" and the study of "employment and union practices within the Navajo Nation." The Resources Committee had its duties redefined as the study and consideration of "all matters of Tribal interest pertaining to the natural resources of the Navajo Nation," with emphasis on long-range planning for "efficient utilization of Tribal resources." Three subcommittees—Minerals, Agriculture, and Range and Livestock—were to deal with proper development of these basic resources. The Economic Development Committee, another new council standing committee, took over the previous duties of the Trading Committee and became responsible for studying and considering "all matters pertaining to economic development within or near the Navajo Nation." Finally, the council established a Transportation and Roads Committee to oversee road construction and maintenance on the Navajo Nation. With the Navajo national government responsible for this work, Navajos could become skilled in all aspects of it and derive the related economic benefits. Moreover, BIA and state jurisdiction and responsibility for Navajo roads threatened Navajo sovereignty. The committee's establishment represented an effort to begin to gain control of the Navajo national transportation network.[84]

The 1971 reorganization also significantly revised the executive branch of Navajo government. Under the altered framework, five central offices took on responsibility for supervising much of governmental business: Program Development, Administration, Controller, Business Management, and Operations. Each office was headed by a director hired by the chairman and serving at his pleasure. The purposes of each division may be

4 Organization of the Navajo Tribe, 1972

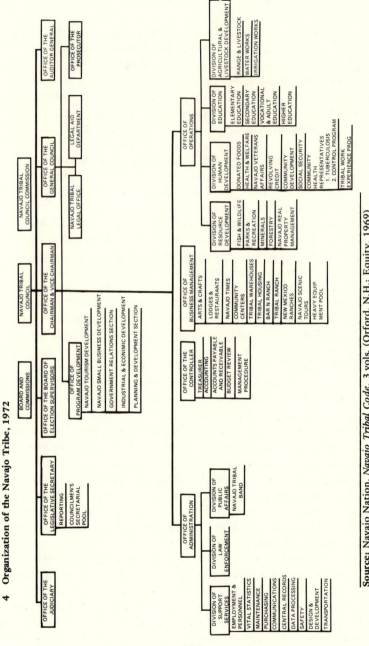

Source: Navajo Nation, *Navajo Tribal Code*, 3 vols. (Orford, N.H.: Equity, 1969) 1:24.3.

seen in Figure 4 which, when compared with the 1959 model (Figure 3), reveals the more complex nature of contemporary Navajo national government.

One may best summarize the intent of this reorganization by quoting from the preamble of the council resolution authorizing the revision:

Whereas: (1) The People of the Navajo Nation are resolved that the Navajo Tribal Council shall exercise all powers of self-government necessary to attain self-sufficiency and self-determination, and prerequisite to protecting the rights and interests of the Navajo people and their possessions, and

(2) There are vested within the Navajo Nation certain attributes and powers of sovereignty that have neither been developed nor recognized due to inadequate executive organization within the Tribal Government, and

(3) A strong and united Tribal Executive branch is essential in developing both natural and human resources; in preserving and protecting what rightfully belongs to the Navajo People; and in planning and building a future for the Navajo Nation that will realize the goals and ambitions of the Navajo people.[85]

Peter MacDonald's first term as chairman of the Navajo Tribal Council had been a significant turning point in the history of Navajo tribal government. His initial administration represented a turning away from past trends in Navajo affairs and toward Navajo self-determination. Trite though the phrase has become, it was also true. During this era Navajos did attempt to gain far greater control over their own affairs, but in many fields the attempts were only beginnings. To carry out often bold initiatives, MacDonald sought reelection in the autumn of 1974. Thus the Navajo people would have an opportunity to express their opinion of the movement MacDonald had captained. MacDonald would be opposed, to no one's surprise, by Raymond Nakai as well as Charlie Toledo and Leo Watchman.

THE SECOND ADMINISTRATION OF PETER MacDONALD

6

The theme of this second administration will be "the emerging Navajo Nation." During these next four years we will continue the program we have begun to fully develop the Navajo Nation as an important economic, social and political force in the Southwest and in the United States. We will improve the daily lives of our people; we will improve the education of our young people; we will ease the burdens of our old people; we will demand, and one way or another, we will get, the respect of the United States Government—in particular its Bureau of Indian Affairs—as well as the respect of the states which border our lands. We will neither be patronized nor insulted. We will be treated as human beings, as members of the proud Navajo Tribe, and as citizens of the United States.[1]

These words from Peter MacDonald's inaugural address in January 1975, reflected the hopeful beginnings of his second administration. Having again defeated Raymond Nakai at the polls the preceding November and having completed a generally successful first term, MacDonald could look forward to the next four years with confidence. There would be, in fact, significant accomplishments recorded during the last part of the 1970s. However, these achievements would be overshadowed sometimes and the overall potential of the period reduced by indictment, scandal, and internal criticism. For "the emerging Navajo Nation" it would be a time often troubled; for Peter MacDonald, it would test to the fullest his political skills and credibility at home, just as his reputation within the United States was ascending rapidly.

A first administration is a time for ideas and initiatives. There is a honeymoon period during which the electorate generally is willing to allow the people newly elected time to make their mark. Depending upon the era and mood of the populace, this grace period may last through much of the first term. In the case of Peter MacDonald, significant criticism of his administration would not really arise until after his reelection. The novelty was gone yet the challenges remained: unemployment, effective control over Navajo land resources and industrialization, provision of adequate health care and educational opportunities, settlement of the Navajo-Hopi land dispute, and proper administration of Navajo government. Opposition flared openly in the face of dissatisfaction with MacDonald's efforts. Apparent mismanagement of Navajo tribal funds gave ample ammunition to those seeking to discredit MacDonald. In MacDonald's view, "The success of the first term . . . really insured, or guaranteed, the forces that were set in motion which finally came at us as a backlash and as an undermining effect to the administration during the second term."[2] Despite well-publicized difficulties within the second administration, Peter MacDonald survived, neither unscathed nor vanquished.

MacDonald had emerged triumphant from the 1974 campaign. Charlie Toledo and Leo Watchman had joined Raymond Nakai in seeking to deny MacDonald reelection. While Toledo and Watchman did not mount effective candidacies, their efforts symbolized two of the important criticisms offered against MacDonald and his administration. Toledo hailed from Torreon, one of the easternmost Navajo communities, where he had served as chapter president for twelve years. Toledo drew predictable support from his region, which had always complained about its lack of representation in tribal affairs, but he emphasized the belief that the Navajo Tribal Council chairman should be an individual with less formal education and more direct ties to grass-roots people.

Charlie Toledo had run away from school in the fourth grade. "I was raised the traditional way and learned the teachings of the people," he said. "Those are the only teachings I live by." His associates claimed a man like Toledo understood the people better than the well-educated incumbent. Toledo's references were hardly subtle: "If you go to school and study engineering, all you know is engineering. Unless you live among the people, you cannot know what their needs are."[3]

Leo Watchman stressed fiscal responsibility. A third-term member of the New Mexico House of Representatives and director of administration for the Navajo Health Authority, Watchman had earned a bachelor's degree in business administration and served twice as tribal treasurer under Raymond Nakai before resigning each time over dissatisfaction with the administration's financial policies. While speaking to a number of issues, he underscored the concern shared by many Navajos about the proper management of Navajo money and the need to share the benefits of dollars flowing into Window Rock with the far-flung residents of the Navajo Nation.[4]

Raymond Nakai, in turn, promised to "return the power back to the people, not the chairman or the tribal council." Nakai disagreed with recent tribal involvement in state and county politics, with tribal efforts to reduce BIA policy-making powers, and with the ten-year economic plan and general policy of encouraging self-determination—all of which, he said, would force Navajos into the Anglo system. Once more Nakai proposed a Navajo constitution. He pledged to reduce council and chairman powers and salaries and to reduce the general counsel's salary and tribal budget as a whole. He also reminded the Navajo electorate of achievements during his terms of office, ranging from industrial development to educational change.[5]

Peter MacDonald and Wilson Skeet officially announced their intentions to seek reelection at a rally in Teec Nos Pos in June 1974. Mac-Donald labeled his first term as a time of transition "from a state of disunity and distrust to a state of renewal and hope and clarity of purpose," "from a state of dependence toward a state of self-reliance and initiative." In sum, "We have transformed our colonial status into an independent nation with greater opportunities for self-sufficiency and independence."[6]

Even given the inflated nature of campaign rhetoric, the 1974 election might well be viewed as a referendum on the growing power and ambition of Navajo national government. As the four candidates lobbied for support before the August precinct nominations, the passage by the Navajo Tribal Council of the largest tribal budget in history gave weight to this debate. The council approved a budget of $23.46 million for fiscal year 1975, which would increase expenditures in existing departments and create 518 new jobs, of which about 400 would be at the chapter level. MacDonald quickly pointed out that the tribal government had obtained more than three times as much money from outside sources than it had four years before so that "in the next fiscal year we will be spending on behalf of the Navajo people a total of $56 million."[7]

The Navajo primary election yielded the expected results: Raymond Nakai and Peter MacDonald would be on the November 12 ballot. Mac-Donald won forty-three precincts to nineteen for Nakai, eight for Toledo, and three for Watchman. MacDonald's total vote of 7,484 nearly equalled the combined totals of Nakai (4,451), Toledo (2,586), and Watchman (490). Nakai received his main support from his stronghold, the Ship-rock Agency. Toledo did well there, also, in addition to the eastern precincts in the Crownpoint Agency. In the face of Toledo's strong showing, Nakai added him to the ticket as his running mate.[8]

Incumbents tend to win reelection. The Nakai-Toledo campaign could not overtake that of MacDonald-Skeet. Interest remained high during the autumn, and 80 percent of the Navajo electorate voted on election day. MacDonald and Skeet won by a margin of over 5,000 votes: 22,500 to 17,256. While representing a sizable victory, MacDonald's percentage of the total vote had declined from the 62 percent he achieved in 1970, to 56.5 percent of the vote. He had carried fifty-two precincts in 1970; this time he carried forty-nine. Nakai's base of support remained constant. Of the twenty precincts he had won in 1970, he won all but three of them—Tonalea, Chilchinbeto, and Alamo—in 1974. Nakai showed renewed strength in District 12, winning in Sanostee, Red Rock, and Two Grey Hills; he also regained past popularity in Little Water, Blue Gap, and Nageezi. With Toledo on the ticket, Torreon, as expected, swung to Nakai. Skeet's presence helped MacDonald roll up an impressive plurality in the Crownpoint Agency. MacDonald also defeated Nakai by over 2,000 votes in the Tuba City Agency and won as well in Fort Defiance and Chinle agencies.[9]

On election night MacDonald offered the following interpretation of the results:

During the campaign my opponent argued for Navajo dependency on the Bureau of Indian Affairs and on outside development of Navajo resources. In a real sense, then, the results of this election are a referendum on Navajo dependence or Navajo self-sufficiency founded upon the treaty of 1868. By your votes, you have resoundingly chosen self-sufficiency under the treaty of 1868 and this should be the mandate of my administration for the next four years.

The chairman said his administration could not "work miracles" and noted it would have to work hard "to preserve our land, our water and our newfound influence in state governments." But, he added, "this battle is for survival and that battle no people can afford to lose."[10]

ECONOMIC DEVELOPMENT

The viability of the Navajo economy remained a central, pressing concern during MacDonald's second term. Despite MacDonald's expressed interest in promoting the Navajo private sector, little development occurred in this realm. Some small headway was achieved in small business, but this was offset by the closing of the Fairchild plant in Shiprock, one of the largest employers of Navajo workers. Navajo Forest Products Industries continued to be extremely successful, but Navajo Agricultural Products Industries encountered severe difficulties in its beginning stages of operation. Thus, as in the past, mineral exploitation had to be relied on as a critical element.

However, in contrast to earlier eras, exploitation of Navajo mineral resources could not be undertaken without severe scrutiny. Controversies erupted in the new field of coal gasification and in new areas slated for uranium exploration, as well as in established regions such as the Aneth, Utah, oil fields. Younger Navajos in such groups as the Coalition for Navajo Liberation and many Navajos of various ages from the impacted areas proved sharp critics, to say the least. Their opposition slowed significantly anticipated expansion of this segment of the economy. Peter MacDonald and a number of Navajo tribal officials sought some kind of middle ground, where this expansion took place, with increased royalties to the tribe and added environmental safeguards. MacDonald emerged as the leading figure in the Council for Energy Resource Tribes, a consortium of Native American peoples, whose lands contained an important portion of the United States' present and future energy resources.

Coal gasification was one issue that could not be resolved during this period. Opposition to the proposed plants in the Burnham, New Mexico, area had crystallized by 1973 sufficiently to alter earlier projections for their completion. Still, in April 1974, El Paso Natural Gas Company stated that its anticipated start of construction for the Burnham Coal Gasification Project would be spring 1975, and the expected project completion date would be January 1978. At peak construction they planned to employ approximately 3,500 workers. In addition, they would employ 883 at the gasification plant and 336 at the accompanying coal mine. Over the projected twenty-five-year life of the operation, an annual average 10,785,000 tons of coal would be mined. The plant could produce 288 million cubic feet per day of synthetic pipeline gas. They had requested 28,250 acre feet of water from the San Juan River, none of which would be returned, from the Bureau of Reclamation.[11]

These optimistic figures were compelling to tribal leaders eagerly seeking ways to bring in additional revenue and lower the staggering Navajo unemployment rate, but, if anything, opposition to coal gasification, had increased by 1975. In April 1975, MacDonald announced that while plans were progressing with WESCO for its coal gasification plant, it appeared unlikely that El Paso would construct its plant, "at least in the forseeable future." A week later, at a standing room only chapter meeting, Burnham residents reaffirmed their opposition to the plants by a vote of 114 to fourteen. While not binding on the council, it indicated the widespread opposition to the proposed development and probably stiffened council resolve to proceed cautiously on the issue.

Navajo opposition to coal gasification stemmed from a number of interrelated concerns. Burnham area residents worried over such matters as air pollution, removal of families, land reclamation, influx of non-Navajos, and the construction of a new town nearby. Previous Navajo experience with energy-related projects made many wary of assurances by WESCO and El Paso officials that Navajo workers would indeed be employed in large numbers and that great care would be taken in regard to environmental and social factors. By September 1977, WESCO spokesmen were expressing irritation over how slow the tribe was moving. In January and February 1978, the Tribal Council defeated a WESCO proposal and ignored a second plan. Given the mood of the current council, WESCO people decided to wait until after the 1978 council election to test the political atmosphere with revised schemes; in fact, despite all of its investment, WESCO perhaps had decided to abandon the project entirely.[12]

That Tribal Council overwhelming vote, forty-eight to eight, to defeat the WESCO proposal may be attributed in part to the social and environmental concerns voiced by Burnham residents, but dissatisfaction with the financial benefits offered must also be considered. WESCO had modified its initial resource utilization fee from 8 to 12.5 percent in view of the low royalty rates paid the Navajos by Utah International, from whom WESCO would buy its coal. The Navajo Nation would receive about $12.7 million a year for coal purchased from Utah International, $2 million for 0.5 percent of the plant's gross revenues, and $200,000 for leasing 4,000 acres. The council's willingness to turn down flatly these amounts of money indicates a greater sophistication and steadfastness than in previous times.

However, one should not interpret the council of the late 1970s as simply being anti-development. In the summer of 1976, council members debated a new agreement between the tribe and El Paso Natural Gas and Consolidated Coal Company. The revised leasing agreement clearly marked an improvement over the original pact signed in 1968. The Navajos would receive almost three times as much in royalty payments, obtaining fifty-five cents a ton, or 8 percent of the price of the coal sold at the mine. Additional changes were called for in connection with land reclamation. Opponents of the new lease either charged El Paso had failed to live up to its original agreement, argued that still better terms could be gained, or resisted any additional development of Navajo mineral resources. In August the council approved the lease forty-nine to eleven, with an amendment allowing the Burnham chapter 2 percent, or $112,000, of the $5.6 million advance the tribe would receive after Secretary of the Interior Cecil Andrus approved the arrangement. Passage of the lease prompted a lengthy sit-in in the council chambers by those protesting the agreement, and, nearly a year later, much to the chagrin of Chairman MacDonald, Andrus rejected the lease.[13]

Andrus's rejection represented yet another complicating factor for MacDonald and others favoring mineral development. Under the federal Coal Lease Amendments Act of 1975, a 12.5 percent rate of return is required for federal coal leases; the El Paso lease stipulated only an 8 percent return. Andrus contended that "12.5 percent should be the absolute minimum in any Indian lease." The secretary's action was greeted approvingly by Harris Arthur, special assistant to the Assistant Secretary of the Interior for land and water, who stated the 4.5 percent difference meant between $400 million and $500 million to the tribe. DNA Litigation Director Richard Hughes also said he was "gratified that the secretary has accepted our view as to his fiduciary duties to the tribe."[14]

While MacDonald fired off an angry telegram to Andrus protesting the secretary's action, events during the following month mollified the chairman's displeasure. Forced to renegotiate because of Andrus's veto, El Paso reluctantly complied with the essential demands he had placed

upon the revised lease. Now the Navajos would receive a 12.5 percent
rate of return on their lease, or fifty-five cents a ton, whichever was
higher. The El Paso officials at first tried to withdraw the $5.6 million
advance they had promised in return for the higher percentage. Interior
Department representatives and Navajo legal counsel refused to accept
the withdrawal, and soon the company agreed to provide the advance
as well. MacDonald praised the Interior Department:

As the members of the Navajo Nation know, for many years we have been
critical of our trustee, the United States, and in particular of the Department of the Interior for their failure to recognize and perform their
trustee responsibility. I am pleased to say that in this matter, we received
both their assistance and support.[15]

Coal gasification did not represent the only area of debate in regard
to mineral exploitation. A similar controversy raged over the Navajo-
Exxon uranium exploration, mining, and milling agreement originally
approved by the Tribal Council in January 1974. Before the secretary
of the interior would sanction the deal, six days of hearings on the draft
environmental impact statement were held in August 1976. Under the
terms of the arrangement, Exxon could drill for uranium over a 400,000-
acre area and mine up to 51,200 acres if so desired. The chapters most
directly affected would be Shiprock, Beclabito, Red Rock, Sanostee, and
Two Grey Hills, and, as might be expected, primary opposition to the
proposal surfaced from this region of the Navajo Nation in northwestern
New Mexico.

At the hearings some Navajos opposed any mining, but more expressed
disagreement with certain features of the agreement. As with coal gasification, some worried about health dangers, dislocation of families, and
general social impact; others believed the tribe was not getting enough
money, should control the operation itself, or would not use the money
appropriately. In an argument voiced ever since mineral exploitation began in Navajo country, local residents contended that more of the money
from the mining should go directly to the immediate chapters rather
than all of it going into the tribal treasury. The issue of tribal control
could be met partly by the stipulation in the contract that the Navajos
can decide with each mining of a uranium deposit whether it wants merely to accept a royalty payment or join with Exxon in a joint ownership

mining operation. This feature clearly represented an improvement over past contracts, but it did not satisfy the sharpest critics of the Exxon agreement.[16]

That winter, dissatisfied with the environmental impact statement, seventeen Navajos filed suit through DNA attorneys against the Secretary of the Interior, Thomas Kleppe, and Bureau of Indian Affairs Commissioner Ben Reifel to halt approval of the Navajo-Exxon lease. They protested specifically the adverse effects on the water table, disturbance of grazing land, and health hazards of uranium mining. Albuquerque U.S. District Court Judge H. Vearle Payne denied a preliminary injunction against Kleppe. DNA lawyers appealed to the Tenth Circuit Court of Appeals in Denver without results. With Kleppe's ratification of the lease, Exxon officials presented the tribe with a bonus payment of $6.3 million.[17]

Even with the payment, the uranium issue had not expired. The *Navajo Times* ran a series of lengthy articles in the summer and fall of 1978 questioning the region's preparedness for the impact of uranium mining and reviewing the potential dangers to human health and environment posed by this development. The Bureau of Indian Affairs came in for additional criticism for its role in mineral leasing. At the outset of 1979, DNA attorneys, together with Friends of the Earth, a leading environmentalist organization, filed a suit against the Departments of Energy, Interior, and Agriculture, the Nuclear Regulatory Commission, the Tennessee Valley Authority, and the Environmental Protection Agency to halt uranium development within the United States until a full review of its impact on the environment could be undertaken. DNA Director Peterson Zah contended the purpose of the suit was not to deny uranium mining on a permanent basis but to obtain far more information than presently was available. Thus, as of 1979, the future of the Navajo-Exxon uranium lease and other uranium development within the Navajo Nation remained at least somewhat in doubt.[18]

The third arena of conflict was Aneth, Utah, site of the great oil field boom of the 1950s, which had dramatically altered the size of the Navajo tribal treasury and significantly influenced the ambitions of the Navajo tribal government. On March 30, 1978, a group of Navajos from Aneth and nearby Montezuma Creek occupied the main pump station of Texaco, the largest oil producer in the area, and then went on to close down all oil operations in the Aneth field. The Utah chapter of the Council for

Navajo Liberation did lead the occupation, but the protestors soon
swelled to a throng of a thousand people. On April 3 those assembled
issued a total of thirteen demands, including termination and renegotiation of leases, more emphasis on the needs of local people by the tribe
and more consideration for the well-being of local people by the oil
companies, and generally more direct benefits to the area because of
oil revenues.

The Aneth occupation ended after seventeen days. After several days
of negotiation among representatives of the various parties, the four oil
companies—Texaco, Superior, Continental, and Phillips—agreed to prohibit employees from bringing alcoholic beverages on the reservation,
to dismiss any employee carrying a firearm, to begin reseeding and reclaim-
ing any area damaged, to compensate Navajo families suffering loss of
livestock or grazing area, to replace damaged wells, to protect and preserve Navajo burial sites and prevent employees from collecting artifacts,
and to give Navajos preference in hiring at the drilling site. In addition,
$20,000 would be donated for scholarships for Navajo students inter-
ested in the oil business as a career. However, the companies did not
make any alterations in existing leases. Tribal officials pledged to get
additional power lines and natural gas available to local residents. The
terms, for the most part, satisfied most of the area people, though not
members of the coalition. Yet, because the leases continued unchanged
and progress seemed slow in other concerns, tensions continued relatively
unabated in the Aneth area in the months following the occupation.[19]

These various debates and confrontations over mineral exploitation,
then, illustrated all too graphically the difficulties faced by Peter Mac-
Donald and his cohorts, who favored some form of mineral development
as a key element in their strategy for improving the Navajo economy.
MacDonald continued to be caught in an inevitable cross fire: how does
one work for progressive economic change that stands to benefit the
people as a whole but which may at the same time alter adversely the
situation of individual Navajos? MacDonald summed up his position in
this fashion in his State of the Navajo Nation address in 1977:

The developments in coal and uranium, which have been criticized by
some, are the first development that we have ever had in which we can
truly have a sense of participation. Our laws apply to these developments,
not the laws of some state, and for the first time we will receive a fair

return, both for our minerals and in terms of obtaining professional employment for the many Navajos who will be able to work on these economic developments. These proposals have been carefully reviewed with respect to their environmental and cultural impacts and decisions have been made by the Council, that neither the environmental nor the cultural impact of selective development is so great as to discourage further economic development. . . . Every time an economic development is started, it is started in somebody's backyard. The people who are located in the area of the proposed development deserve our respect—they deserve our time and our attention. Their wishes must be considered and measured against the needs of our Nation as a whole. . . . We have always said in the past that the needs of all of us are greater than the wants of a few of us. I see no reason to change our custom.[20]

MacDonald's willingness to develop Indian energy resources, but only on Indian terms, brought him to a position of national prominence in the latter 1970s. Given the energy crisis, the determination to utilize American energy resources, and the discovery that Indian reservations held substantial portions of these resources, Native Americans found themselves in a strengthened bargaining position. As we have seen, they had been advised at one time that nuclear power soon would make their coal resources obsolete; thus they had often signed leases that shortchanged their people. Now mineral exploitation promised to reduce unemployment and promote tribal self-determination. MacDonald emerged as a spokesman for this viewpoint as chairman of the Council of Energy Resources Tribes.

A consortium of more than twenty tribes, established in 1975, CERT attempted to develop Native American mineral resources in the manner most favorable to Indian welfare. The federal government balked at providing any assistance to the group until MacDonald leaked the news that CERT would approach the OPEC (Organization of Petroleum Exporting Countries) nations for money and advice. Then the BIA and the Economic Development Administration hurriedly chipped in $100,000. At the end of 1977, CERT opened its Washington office to oversee Indian energy development, with a former Energy Department official, Edward Gabriel, as its first full-time director. CERT urged the renegotiation of old leases, which offered a miserly return. MacDonald commented, "In the past, whenever the Indians were sitting on something the country wanted, the

U.S. brought out the legislative cavalry and the judicial cavalry and the bureaucratic cavalry and took it away. That will not happen again."[21]

This determination promised to make MacDonald and the Navajo Nation forces to be reckoned with in the American Southwest. In 1976 the Navajo Nation exported enough kilowatt hours to meet the energy needs of Arizona for thirty-two years. The Southwest had become increasingly dependent on these energy resources, and, as MacDonald warned a 1977 conference on "The Rise of the Southwest," "There can be no growth with more energy. And there will be no more cheap energy given away by the Indian nations who control such resources until we all can find a way of living together as neighbors with fairness and equity." Fairness and equity had not exactly been the hallmarks of American Indian policy, MacDonald reminded them:

The first conference on growth in this country occurred when the Pilgrims landed in New England and invited the Indians to a conference on growth. Such conferences have been held with great regularity as the nation expanded westward. But we were not normally the luncheon speaker; more often than not, we were cooking the lunch. . . . Every time a coal gasification company like WESCO and El Paso or a uranium company like Kerr-McGee or Exxon or United Nuclear invites me to come talk about growth, I know whose growth they are talking about. And whose resources will fuel that growth.

For growth to continue, he declared, there must be "a cessation of hostilities between the States of Arizona and New Mexico on the one hand and the Navajo Nation on the other" and the acquisition of "the technical assistance, the resources, the staff and the expertise needed to chart our future." If necessary for Navajo survival, he concluded, "we will withhold future growth at any sacrifice."[22]

That last statement one might excuse as an exaggeration, but clearly by the end of the 1970s Navajos had grown more determined to exercise what control they could over their valued mineral resources. Renegotiation of leases represented one example. The tribe also attempted to control sulphur emissions over Navajo land. In June 1977, the Tribal Council passed a resolution requiring any industry within the Navajo Nation or in "Indian Country" that discharged sulphur or sulphur compounds to purchase a tribal permit. General Counsel George Vlassis stressed that the primary function of law would be environmental protection rather than the raising of revenue but that the penalty for not complying with emission standards for the first year would be $20 million and would rise to $100 million annually after a five-year period. Both the Navajo Power Plant near Page and the Four Corners Plant near Farmington would be affected by this legislation. As of early 1979, however, the law had yet to be put into full effect and fully tested, as it had yet to win approval by the Department of the Interior and faced a legal challenge by the Arizona Public Service Company. As the Navajos' standards are the strictest the power companies would have to meet, they will not be applied without some further debate.[23]

Finally, the Navajos began serious consideration of taxing corporate interests within the Navajo Nation. After more than two years of consideration, the Tribal Council voted thirty-four to thirteen early in 1978 in favor of a possessory interest tax. Exempting possessory interest worth less than $100,000, the tax would be assessed on companies leasing Navajo land. Bearing the brunt of taxation, of course, would be energy and mineral producers. As much as $16 million might be brought in to the Navajo treasury annually through this law. Soon afterward, the council also passed a tax on large business concerns on the reservation, such as General Dynamics.

As expected, company officials howled in protest. The Navajos responded that they were trying to rebuild their revenue from energy resources, and through the possessory interest tax, for example, they could make up the difference between the lease in an open market situation and the actual royalty being paid the tribe. Russell D. Hulse, an Arizona Public Service vice president, registered a common sentiment: "Any action which unnecessarily increases the cost of electric power ultimately benefits no one, and there is no question that these proposed taxes will bring about such increases." Clearly the new taxes would be challenged in court. In the autumn of 1978, Phoenix Federal Judge William Copple ruled the Navajo Tribe had an inherent right under tribal sovereignty to tax and was thus immune from law suits questioning tribal taxation. Copple added, though, that the Secretary of the Interior still must decide about the tax waivers within company leases. At the conclusion of MacDonald's second term, then, the status of such Navajo taxation remained much in doubt, but the very creation of a Navajo Tax Commission and the direct attempt to tax such major interests as

Arizona Public Service indicated the new direction taken in this realm, one which promised to be of major importance in the 1980s.[24]

The two primary Navajo tribal enterprises related to economic development, the Navajo Forest Products Industries and the Navajo Agricultural Products Industries, did not fare equally well during MacDonald's second administration. NFPI continued its record of success while NAPI continued to have major problems. Of course, NFPI built upon an already firm foundation, and NAPI was enmeshed in the halting beginnings of the Navajo Indian Irrigation Project. Nonetheless, it is instructive to relate briefly the records of the two enterprises, if only to illustrate that the tribal enterprise may be more appropriate to certain kinds of economic development than others.

Over 600 Navajos were working for NFPI by 1977, earning $7 million in wages and salaries; hundreds more had jobs in related employment possible because of the enterprise's expansion. Employees gained many skills through their association with NFPI, and some moved into supervisory positions. Two Navajos had such posts in 1963, the first full year of operation, but by 1978 the number had grown to forty. Over $23 million in stumpage fees, more than double the Navajo total investment in NFPI, had been paid in the enterprise's history, and $14 million in earnings had been generated.

NFPI also demonstrated the value of careful management of an important Navajo land resource. All 411,000 acres of the Navajo forest had been selectively logged by 1978. Enterprise officials stated that the forest would produce 45 million board feet of new timber growth each year, now that the first cutting cycle had been completed. This sustained yield promised, then, a continuing source of income and employment for many Navajos. A new particleboard plant was added to the total operation in 1976, allowing for effective utilization of chips, sawdust, shavings, and trimmings and permitting the enterprise to operate a more fully integrated timber conversion facility.[25]

By contrast, the Navajo Agricultural Products Industries had been plagued by a variety of difficulties, financial, managerial, and directional. Established by the Navajo Nation to operate the 100,000-acre Navajo Indian Irrigation Project farm, NAPI has had a steady turnover in administrative personnel. The year 1978 marked a low point in the enterprise's existence, with its board of directors suspended by the Tribal Advisory Council after the revelation of financial problems. Art Allison, a thirty-year-old Navajo, became the latest in a series of NAPI's managers in the summer of that year. An audit by Peat, Marwick and Mitchell proved highly critical of past management, citing inexperience in agribusiness as a significant factor.

If NAPI were a private business, the auditors declared, it would be bankrupt. By mid-1978, the enterprise had lost a total of about $9.2 million, with $5.5 million disappearing within the past twelve months. The Advisory Committee bailed it out temporarily at that time with a loan of $1.5 million, and the Bureau of Indian Affairs indicated it would guarantee 90 percent of a $7.5 million loan, but only if the current management were altered. FBI and Farmington police officials were investigating financial irregularities within the operation.

The enterprise also confronted political opposition at home. Critics charged that political considerations had affected access to NAPI land and that local people were being moved out unfairly from NAPI's projected expansion. Allison admitted that grazing permits had been obtained by way of political influence. He would not cite Vice Chairman Wilson Skeet's family as a case in point, but others complained that that was a good example. Skeet indeed conceded that his son, two of his son's nieces, and two half-sisters all grazed sheep on NAPI land. In addition, approximately forty families in the Huerfano area stood to lose their lands to NAPI and were speaking out strongly against the enterprise. Before 1978, families from Burnham and Fruitland chapters had been moved off of their land. They have been complaining ever since about this forced removal.

Thus the Navajo tribal administration faced another complicated challenge in the promotion of their economic policies. Tribal officials believed that small farms, as originally envisioned for the project, simply could not work. They were not economically feasible. The corporate approach, as embodied in NAPI, looked more promising. And yet, a study authored by economist Phil Reno and Navajo agronomist Bahe Billy argued to the contrary: "The vital requirements for farm productivity are incentive and opportunity. Family farms provide a broadly based incentive and, as a rule, state farms and corporate farms do not." Allison and others, however, contended that across the nation the small family farm was in trouble. With proper management, the future of the Navajo Agricultural Products Industries might become brighter. The future of those who have been and would be relocated remained problematical. As with those who faced relocation from the Navajo-Hopi joint use area, they really had no-where to go.[26]

MacDonald and his associates also had looked hopefully at the beginning of his second term to the private sector as an integral part of the Navajo economy. However, a significant breakthrough could not be achieved in this area. There were some notable beginnings, such as Donald Davis' Chevrolet dealership in Tuba City. With the help of the tribe's economic development division, which had worked with General Motors for several years in the hopes of establishing a dealership within the Navajo Nation, Davis opened Davis Chevrolet in December 1978. Mike Nelson, also a Navajo, formed Mike Nelson and Associates with his brother and brother-in-law to operate Navajo Westerner shops in Window Rock and Tuba City and a gas station in Tuba City. Additional enterprises were being considered in 1978 by the thirty-six-year-old from White Cone, who had earned a bachelor's degree in business administration from Fort Lewis College.

These examples were exceptions to the general rule. Part of the difficulty stemmed from the bureaucratic hurdles looming in front of the potential entrepreneur. Twenty-four different clearances must be received, from the chapter grazing committee up to the tribal chairman, and gaining approval at the chapter level often represented the most challenging task. A new business might offer needed services and employment to the local community, but it also would consume land desperately coveted by chapter residents. Given the large numbers of Navajos who still rely at least partially upon livestock grazing and given the population growth in Navajo country, which has not been matched by the acquisition of additional land, the land issue becomes a touchy matter at best for chapter officials. Some tribal officials advocated zoning chapter land for business development. But as of 1978 that step had yet to be taken. Surely other problems were important as well, including capital, training, and continuing technical assistance.[27]

Substantial investment by outside companies also apparently had peaked in the Navajo Nation by the late 1970s. With more critical legal advice available, the Navajos were unlikely to repeat earlier gambles on marginal concerns. On the other hand, given the isolation of the Navajo country and the knowledge that the tribe would be less extravagant in its inducements to companies, company officials tended to shy away from locating on the reservation. In some ways, the closing of the Fairchild plant in Shiprock may have set the tone for this period. In February

1975, over forty men and women, most of them Navajos, occupied the Fairchild site in protest of the layoff of 140 workers the previous week and of the general reduction in the work force over the past year. The Fairchild Semi-conductor Corporation seized upon the American Indian Movement-led takeover as a pretext to abandon entirely their operation of the tribally owned plant. While the occupation ended peacefully, Fairchild did not return. Though outside companies may continue in a small way to establish operations on the reservation, it would appear that the tribe cannot rely to a major extent on such investment as a central component in the Navajo economy. One of the few exceptions may come in the area of tourism, where restaurants, motels, and other tourist facilities may emerge in the Lake Powell region as well as more populated Navajo centers such as Window Rock, Tuba City, Chinle, and Shiprock.[28]

THE NAVAJO-HOPI LAND DISPUTE

While the controversy over land claimed by both the Hopis and the Navajos had been brewing for many years, the longstanding disagreement reached a critical stage during MacDonald's second administration. In a sense the dispute dated back nearly a century, to 1882, when President Chester Arthur in an executive order provided reservation land "for the use and occupancy of the Moqui (Hopi) and other Indians as the Secretary of the Interior may see fit to settle thereon." This portion of land, 2.4 million acres, formed the main basis for the land dispute. After Navajos and Hopis quarreled over its disposition, the Secretary of the Interior in 1891 set aside 300,000 acres for exclusive Hopi use.

Developments in the twentieth century complicated the land issue. In 1934, congressional legislation added a small amount of land, 243,000 acres, to the Navajo reservation. This additional land immediately east of Tuba City included the Hopi village of Moencopi. According to the law, the land is for the benefit of Navajos and "such other Indians as are already settled thereon." The Hopis later claimed the entire addition as compensation for Navajo occupancy within the joint use area. Navajos argued that the Hopis should be limited to the acreage they occupied in 1934, which the Navajos estimated at 35,000 acres. In 1943, the Hopi reservation more than doubled in size through the creation of land management district 6 and its simultaneous limitation to Hopi use. The remaining 1.6 million acres remaining in the joint use area remained disputed. Hopis claimed the entire area for themselves, while Navajos claimed their rights on the basis of traditional occupancy and their inclusion, as they believed, as the "other Indians" of the 1882 order.[29]

In 1958 Congress created a special three-judge court to resolve the dispute. In 1962 in *Healing* v. *Jones,* the court ruled the Navajos and Hopis had "joint, undivided and equal rights and interests" in the remaining portion of the 1882 executive order area and ruled it could not properly partition the land. The U.S. Supreme Court affirmed the ruling in 1963. However, partition acceptable to both parties had not been provided. Equal partition of the land would force many Navajo families to move, just as one hundred Navajo families had been evicted by the creation of district 6.

Navajos strongly opposed three congressional attempts to settle the land dispute in MacDonald's first term. The three bills all failed to gain passage, in part due to the lobbying efforts of the MacDonald administration, the Navajo Tribal Council, Brown, Vlassis and Bain, and a Washington law firm. In the waning moments of 1974 a bill emerged from Congress providing for a six-month period of negotiations between the Navajos and the Hopis, with the aid of a federal negotiator. The district court would receive the matter if no agreement could be reached. Relocated Navajo families would get financial assistance and time to find new homes. The legislation was the most favorable the Navajos could have hoped for and represented a victory for the tribe. Navajo officials such as Sam Pete predicted hopefully that "left alone without outside intervention by Congress or attorneys, the two tribes could work it out."[30]

Talks between the Navajos and the Hopis concluded in September 1975, without agreement, however. In December the federal mediator suggested to U.S. District Court Judge James Walsh that the tribes each receive half of the disputed territory. Under such a settlement, 3,495 Navajos would have to relocate. The Navajos would also obtain $6 million for purchase of 520,000 acres of land for relocation. MacDonald quickly expressed his dissatisfaction with the proposal, calling it "a failure to understand Indian people," with property rights "considered at the expense of human rights." Hopi Tribal Chairman Abbott Sekaquaptewa labeled it "a big giveaway program primarily for the Navajos." Both chairmen protested more the drawing of the boundary line than the equal partition per se, with Sam Pete conceding that the mediator's report represented

"the best comprehension of the problems of the Navajo and Hopi people"
yet exhibited by any government official.

In September 1976, Judge Walsh concurred with the recommendations
of the federal mediator. He issued his order in February 1977, stating
that the partition line should be drawn as suggested and the relocation
of 3,495 Navajos and about forty Hopis should take place. The Navajo
Nation appealed this judgment in April, with the Tribal Council unanimously authorizing the general counsel, despite the counsel's admission
that the chances for a successful appeal were not good. In May 1978,
the Ninth Circuit Court of Appeals in San Francisco ruled that the southern
and western boundaries of the joint use area had not been finally determined, thus in part overruling the partition ordered by Walsh. An error
in a 1914 survey accounted for 50,000 acres being included within the
1.8 million joint use area; this parcel, the court decided, should not be
a part of the overall partition. Yet the court agreed with the balance of
Walsh's decision, including the choice to divide the area equally.[31]

Congressional debate seemingly entered its final stages on this issue
in the autumn of 1978. Navajos continued to be extremely critical of
Barry Goldwater, both for his perceived support of the Hopis and what
they saw as his unfamiliarity with the details of the controversy; a
Goldwater visit to Big Mountain particularly provoked such sentiments.
Members of Congress seriously considered a proposal that would have
permitted life estates for residents of the area threatened by relocation,
but eventually this provision was deleted from the final bill. The bill,
originating in the House and accepted by the Senate, essentially ratified
the arrangements posited by the courts. However, the legislation included
a provision allowing for either house to veto the arrangement that would
be put into effect by the relocation commission, and to President Carter
that stipulation proved unacceptable. Carter vetoed the bill in November
1978. Navajo officials thought the veto also would forbid an increase in
money to carry on the relocation effort and so in that sense they were
not disappointed.[32]

Thus at the end of 1978 the Navajo-Hopi land dispute had yet to be
resolved. While one anticipated that a final arrangement would be affirmed
in Washington in 1979, the controversy obviously had dragged on far beyond the point one could have reasonably expected. Surely this issue defied reasonable expectation and reasonable solution. Because no arrangement could be engineered satisfactory to both parties, an imposed partition,

sadly, was perhaps inevitable. Navajo efforts had secured the best deal the Diné could have obtained, but in the 1980s it appeared that thousands of Navajos would have to move from their homes. Where they could go had not been determined and could hardly be predicted.

EDUCATION

Important developments in Navajo education in the late 1970s included the start of the Native American Materials Development Center, the continuation of special programs to increase the number of Navajo teachers and school administrators, and troublesome questions of leadership and growth at Navajo Community College. Education marked a good case in point in the difficulty of translating the idea of Navajo control into a reality. While the materials center and the teacher-administrator programs represented hopeful signs, financial difficulties and overlapping educational jurisdictions remained basic dilemmas.

Under the supervision of Gloria Emerson, the Native American Materials Development Center began to produce books, magazines, posters, and other classroom materials for Navajo children. Located in Albuquerque and sponsored by Ramah Navajo School Board through a grant from the U.S. Office of Education, NAMDC opened in 1976. With the assistance of such prominent Navajo linguists as William Morgan and Paul Platero, the center staff moved to develop the kind of curriculum that would effectively utilize the language spoken by most Navajo children, Navajo, throughout the Navajo schoolchild's educational experience.

One staff member voiced a viewpoint that William Morgan indeed had been espousing for forty years:

Educational psychology shows how much kids learn early in life. The vehicle they use is language. Concept development is interrupted by having to go to school in a language they don't understand and the damage is permanent. What makes sense is to teach content and the skills of reading and writing in the mother tongue and then transfer these skills to English.

Moreover, as Morgan added, reading, writing, and learning in Navajo is critical to the reaffirmation of Navajo identity.

While such schools as Rough Rock and Rock Point have produced some material in Navajo and the tribe's Navajo Community College as well as the successor of the old Ganado Mission High School, the College of Ganado, have promoted written Navajo through instruction, NAMDC promised to evolve as a central clearinghouse for the integration of the Navajo language in Navajo schools. Certainly there had been a need for the development of a workable, coordinated curriculum from kindergarten through high school. Now, through a wide-ranging utilization of contemporary media, center personnel proposed to fill that need. Many of the key people involved were veterans of the past decade of change in Navajo education. Drawing upon lessons learned through the pioneering years of Navajo community schools, they hoped to move as quickly as possible toward implementation of thorough bilingual instruction across the Navajo Nation.[33]

With only one of every fourteen teachers within the Navajo Nation a Navajo, this process would take years to implement. However, the continuation of cooperative teacher and school administrator programs at the University of New Mexico and the University of Arizona signaled that the proportion might be reduced in the near future. The school administrator program at the University of New Mexico began in the spring semester of 1975, courtesy of a grant from the Carnegie Foundation to the Navajo Nation, which contracted with the university to provide the training for a master's in educational administration. Program personnel estimated in the fall of 1978 that by the spring of 1979 forty Navajos would have graduated. In April 1978, program graduates and enrollees met in Gallup and formed the Navajo School Administrator Association. The University of Arizona teacher education program also revealed impressive results. As of June 1977, 105 Navajos had been graduated in the first four years of the joint effort of Arizona and the Navajo Division of Education, with ten additional people expected to graduate at the end of the summer.[34]

Another important potential source for Navajo teachers, Navajo Community College, was beset by internal troubles. The college had moved two years before from its temporary location at Many Farms to its permanent campus at Tsaile, and many had hoped the Tsaile site would cure some of the school's nagging problems, yet basic difficulties remained. Enrollment continued to lag, and both faculty and student morale suffered. After the college's first Navajo president, Ned Hatathli died, another

Navajo, Thomas Atcitty, took over at the helm. By 1975 Atcitty had
come under increasing attack by many at the school. Eleven Navajo students penned an angry letter to the *Navajo Times* in October, charging
that the administration was "not qualified to run a community college"
and calling for "someone who knows college problems" and who had
"the Navajo people at heart." They particularly castigated the administration for "taking over" the new cultural center named after Hatathli.

NCC Vice Presidents John Tippeconnic and John Martin gamely responded to the student charges the following week. While dispelling some
of the complaints, they admitted that the administration was utilizing
part of the center's top floor for offices. While the college's Board of
Regents had approved such use, the appropriation of any of the cultural
center for the administration seemed to many observers to run contrary
to the spirit in which the building had been created, as a place for spiritual
and cultural observance and study. Lucy Draper, the wife of Navajo
language instructor Teddy Draper, followed in December with a lengthy
critique of top personnel at the college. She argued that Tippeconnic,
Martin, and Atcitty knew nothing about Navajo history and culture and
did not value it. Draper said a change in administration was needed but
that Peter MacDonald would not take action because of political ties between him and the Atcitty family.[35]

Navajo Community College received full accreditation from the North
Central Association in July 1976. This landmark, which the school had
worked toward since its inception seven years before, was partially overshadowed by the continuing controversy on campus. The situation reached
a crisis stage in January 1977. Angered at the administration's decision
to end the Navajo studies department while maintaining courses in this
area, Teddy Draper bitterly complained that "the heart and core of the
college is dead" and now "our college will be just another Whiteman's
Junior College, not a Navajo college." Several days later, on January 12,
the Board of Regents dismissed Lawrence Isaac, vice president for academic
and student affairs. Dismissal of the popular Isaac, who had been the first
student body president at the college and had returned recently to work
at the school, sparked a mass meeting on January 17. There many faculty,
staff, and students called for Atcitty to resign the NCC presidency. They
drafted a statement, which in part claimed:

For the past four years conditions at Navajo Community College have
been deteriorating to the point where the future of the college in realiz-

ing its mission to the Navajo people, their youth and communities, as mandated by the Navajo Tribal Council, is in serious jeopardy due to certain conditions which we believe are the responsibility of the office of the President.

Peter MacDonald issued a statement decrying confrontation tactics and the taking of issues outside the confines of the college community to the media and to the politicians. MacDonald said the college had strayed from its original objectives so that true education had been "replaced by selfish indulgences and misguided endeavors." Therefore, he concluded, the "entire faculty personnel must be reevaluated" and "the college administration must undergo drastic change." With that handwriting on the wall, Atcitty's days as president obviously were numbered, and he soon resigned, to be replaced by Donald McCabe.

Appointed initially as an interim president, McCabe was inaugurated officially as president in July 1977. A Navajo who had completed all requirements but the dissertation for a doctorate in education from Stanford, McCabe brought wide experience in Indian educational programs to his new post. As a relative outsider who had not been entangled in earlier NCC issues, McCabe was free to move on his own. Morale at the school lifted perceptively. McCabe spoke confidently about the progress being achieved. By May 1978, the *Navajo Times'* feature story headlined the school as "a whole new place." Faculty members praised McCabe and new Vice President Joy Hanley for their leadership in helping to create a new, more open atmosphere on campus.

Yet even in May, McCabe indicated some problems with the Board of Regents. Faculty turnover continued to be high, if not necessarily for the same exact reasons as before. Two months later, in July 1978, McCabe resigned the presidency, contending, "The Board of Regents continued to meddle and interfere with my administration of the college." McCabe argued that the board did not understand the difference between making policies and executing policies, and, until it did, any president would have problems. Joy Hanley assumed the duties of interim president, with McCabe that fall becoming the president of the BIA's Southwestern Indian Polytechnic Institute in Albuquerque.[36] In 1979 Dean Jackson was selected as the college's new president.

If Navajo Community College had not solved the boundary lines of authority, neither had the Navajo Division of Education overcome the problem of overlapping school jurisdiction and overall direction of Navajo educational programs. In MacDonald's first administration, the division had issued publications detailing programs for strengthening Navajo education. But in his second term little headway seemed to be made to implement these ideas. The division did take over the administration of Johnson-O'Malley funds in 1976. Yet with the continuing programs offered for Navajo children by the Bureau, the public schools in Arizona, New Mexico, and Utah, mission schools, and community schools, the Navajo Nation still had a great range of educational goals, and the Navajo Division of Education exercised no more control over that process in 1979 than it did in 1975.

The Navajo educational picture also was clouded over by financial limitations. The public schools did not have an adequate base. With burgeoning enrollments, they struggled to stay afloat. In 1978 the Ganado and Window Rock school boards voted to abolish their high school programs in order to force the Apache County High School District to include Ganado and Window Rock high schools as part of its financial responsibility; formerly the reservation schools had been funded out of elementary school districts. At the college level, Navajo students contended for an inadequate number of tribal scholarships. An increasing number of Navajo college students could not receive aid from the Navajo Nation, and those who did obtain assistance complained that they needed additional help.[37]

In 1977 Peter MacDonald summarized the dilemma still faced by the Navajos. We must, he said, gain control over our own educational system, set our own priorities and goals, and create a total education system, capable of meeting those goals and producing results. The implementation of "those fundamental principles," he added, would be essential "to produce the kind of leadership, the kind of professionals, the kind of human capital that our people will need to guide them to self-sufficiency and to assure them of survival once our coal and uranium and gas and oil are depleted." Education was central to a Navajo strategy of survival, he concluded, but time was running out.[38]

HEALTH CARE

As in education, Navajo initiatives in the area of health care during the second administration of Peter MacDonald were not followed by striking success. The much ballyhooed American Indian Medical School, if not stillborn, had been delayed to a virtual standstill. The Indian Health

Service branch of the Public Health Service still controlled the health care facilities and basic programs for Navajos, though the Navajo Nation perhaps was beginning to move in the direction of controlling funds to be dispersed within the reservation. Marlene Haffner, area director, received some criticism for her performance, though she still seemed firmly ensconced in her post in 1979. Some Navajos did receive additional training or responsibilities in health care, including three who completed medical school. Finally, medicine men within the reservation formed an organization to support their traditions and ensure the continuity of their ways of healing.

Perhaps the most significant development came with the establishment in 1977 of the Division of Health Improvement Services, the Navajo Nation's health department. This agency began to serve as the coordinator for planning and organizing health care delivery. In 1978 the Navajo Tribal Council approved three resolutions which outlined the immediate tasks of the DHIS: to help develop a comprehensive health plan for the Navajo Nation, ensure that all agencies providing health care do so in harmony with Navajo beliefs, and manage and evaluate all health programs in the Navajo Nation. Congressional passage of the Health Planning and Resource Development Act of 1974 and the Indian Health Care Improvement Act of 1975 helped prompt such action by the council. In the spring of 1979 the council would be presented with the first comprehensive health plan ever designed for the entire Navajo Nation. Thus there was some indication that the 1980s might be a time of important progress toward better health care for all Navajos and greater control by the Navajo Nation over this care.

The American Indian Medical School gained approval by a Navajo Tribal Council resolution of February 24, 1977. Approval did not connote full financial support, however, and funding sources must be guaranteed before medical schools can be established and accredited. Dr. Taylor McKenzie, president of the proposed institution, did not favor seeking Navajo funding "since the federal government funds the operation of most medical schools in the United States." Secretary of Health, Education and Welfare Joseph Califano deliberated over a year before turning down the feasibility study presented under the terms of Title VI of the Indian Health Improvement Act. Thus the school sought foundation support while continuing to urge Congress to fund the institution.

Even without full support, the American Indian Medical School planned to begin early in the 1980s with thirty-two students. The students would start their preparation at Northern Arizona University in Flagstaff, then focus on a specialized field through additional training in Phoenix, and complete their work with practice on the Navajo Nation and perhaps other reservation communities in such areas as Alaska, Oklahoma, and the Dakotas. McKenzie argued that statistics proved adequate Native American interest in medical training; in 1978, forty-three Indians gained admission to medical schools of 125 who passed entrance exams. As of that year, there were only 125 Indian physicians, hardly a sufficient number to serve adequately a growing Native American population.[39]

At the close of MacDonald's first term, Marlene Haffner, area director for the Public Health Service, had become embroiled in a controversy over the firing of two nurses. While their reinstatement was later recommended, Haffner declined to return the two to their positions, though she did agree to transfer them elsewhere. Dr. Haffner received other substantial criticism in the late 1970s. Many members of the Navajo Area Health Board complained publicly about her performance and urged that she be replaced. However, Chairman MacDonald's support and the gradual movement toward greater communication between tribal health departments and the Public Health Service seemed to reduce the amount of pressure being applied to remove Dr. Haffner from the directorship.[40]

Three Navajos completed their medical degrees in this era: Roger Greyeyes, Ervin Lewis, and Orville McKinley. They joined Taylor McKenzie in the ranks of Navajo physicians. A dozen other Navajos were studying in medical schools across the country. McKinley symbolized the new generation of doctors from the Navajo Nation who had entered the Anglo medical world without denying a more traditional heritage. "Navajo have always had doctors," he noted, "they just weren't recognized by the AMA." After his graduation from the University of Arizona, his eighty-nine-year-old grandfather gave a Navajo mountain chant; McKinley soon returned home for an observation of the Blessingway ceremony. He hoped to work for the Public Health Service in the Navajo Nation: "Health care on the reservation is poor and the Indians are the ones, in the spirit of self-determination, to improve it."[41]

McKinley's continued attachment to the old ways of healing reminded one that those ways did perservere through the 1970s. In December 1977, the medicine men of the Rough Rock area moved into their new offices at the Rough Rock Community Health Center. A year earlier, the community had started as the first Indian community to contract with the Public Health Service; now the doctors from both cultures could work to-

gether in the same facility. At the dedication, one of the singers, Fred
Stevens, remarked that he very much looked forward to working with the
Anglo physicians and noted as proof of his bicultural flexibility that when
he got a headache he took Anacin.[42]

Following two years of planning, medicine men approached the Navajo
Tribal Council in the spring of 1978 with a charter for the Unity of Navajo
Medicinemen (Diné Be'Azeeiileehini Yee'A Hot'A). The new organization
would attempt to improve the quality of the ceremonialists, preserve
their tradition, and "develop new health care systems which combine the
healing arts and skills of trained Navajo healers and medicinemen in conjunction with practitioners of Western medical science, and thereby improve the health and well-being of the Navajo people." In part the organization represented an attempt to stop the erosion of old ceremonies through
disrespect and direct attack by Pentecostal missionaries. Following approval
by the council, the organization adopted articles of incorporation and
elected its first officers: Miller Nez (White Cone), Hoskie T. Becenti
(Thoreau), Fred Stevens, Jr. (Chinle), and Mike Mitchell (Tsaile). The
formation of Diné Be'Azeeiileehini Yee'A Hot'A augured well for the
continuation of a vital element in Navajo culture.[43]

GOVERNMENT

Navajo political affairs were troubled indeed in MacDonald's second
term. The Navajo Nation did attempt to strengthen its jurisdiction over
non-Indians, continued to be active in local and state affairs, and began
to exert more influence over large corporate interests, but scandal within
the tribal government and the indictment of MacDonald halfway through
his second term helped to create internal turmoil. Though the jury did not
find MacDonald guilty, the disruption caused by indictment came fresh
upon the mismanagement of tribal funds, and together they limited to
some extent MacDonald's influence through the remaining months of his
administration. Such vital issues as reapportionment and the judicial
system were mired in controversy. Many Navajos campaigned publicly
for governmental reform. The damage done to MacDonald, however,
ultimately proved more apparent than real.

Until the Oliphant decision of the United States Supreme Court finally
limited Navajo assertion of sovereignty over non-Indians within the
Navajo Nation, the tribe moved strongly to gain more control over out-

siders. In the autumn of 1975, for example, the Department of the
Interior ruled non-Indians within the Navajo reservation were bound not
by state laws but by Navajo regulations, affirming a Tribal Council resolution of June 18, 1976. The Navajos then moved to allow non-Indians
guilty of misdemeanors to be tried within the Navajo court system. By
the summer of 1977 the Navajo police began to issue tickets on a limited
basis for traffic violations to non-Indians, who then were summoned to
tribal court. That fall Tuba City Tribal Judge Robert Walters sentenced
a non-Indian, Kenneth Sykes, to thirty days in the tribal jail for trespass
on Navajo lands; Sykes, who had exercised squatters' rights for a time
near Kayenta, served three days in jail and then was released, contingent
upon his promise to leave the reservation. However, the U.S. Supreme
Court ruled in March 1978, that Indian tribal courts did not have criminal
jurisdiction over non-Indians unless Congress could find a manner that
would be acceptable. The decision, authored by Justice William Rehnquist,
thus voided the revised criminal code approved in December by the Tribal
Council. In October 1978, the council rescinded its earlier decision and
voted to end the attempt to have jurisdiction over non-Indians.[44]

As noted earlier in this chapter, the tribe also began at this time to
try to control sulphur emissions over Navajo land and to consider a more
comprehensive taxation of corporations doing business within the Navajo
Nation. These initiatives had, of course, great potential repercussions
within the Southwest. Earlier in the decade Navajo political activity also
had sent reverberations through the region; the Navajos helped elect Raul
Castro, a Democrat, governor of Arizona and had become far more active
in county politics. Peter MacDonald reaffirmed his belief that his people
must become fully involved in the political arena. His working alliance
with the AFL-CIO to encourage Navajos to register and vote dismayed
several leading council delegates. MacDonald supported the leading Democratic candidates in Arizona and New Mexico in the 1976 elections, and
the tribe turned out to vote in record numbers, with the Democrats
generally reaping the benefit of the turnout. Concomitantly, DNA head
Peterson Zah had led a movement to endorse candidates for office
within Apache County, Arizona. Given the increasing Navajo population
and the impressive participation by the people—75 percent of those
registered voted on election day—the 1976 election reinforced the impression that the Navajo vote mattered in Southwest politics. Between 1974
and 1976, the number of Navajo voters had increased from 11,500 to
over 38,000.[45]

While observers noted the Navajo vote, they could record in November that three Navajo officials had been indicted for their role in investments made by the Navajo Housing Authority, a story which had started unraveling early in the year. On February 27, 1976, Barry Goldwater demanded that an immediate audit of the fiscal affairs of the Navajo tribe be made by the General Accounting Office. A week later, the public learned of an investigation of the investments by the Navajo Housing Authority. NHA, it seemed, had invested nearly $10 million in American Funding Corporation, a Beverly Hills investment company. Unable to pay approximately $5 million demanded by the Navajo Nation, the company was placed in receivership by a federal district court judge. Department of Justice officials revealed three Navajos, Pat Chee Miller, Carl Todacheene, and Marshall Tome, had been given checks totaling $115,000 by the company. The checks, allegedly personal loans, bounced because of insufficient funds. Miller, the NHA director, quickly resigned. Todacheene, NHA board chairman, and Tome, director of the tribe's Office of Operations, were later vindicated, but Miller plead guilty in March 1977 of conspiring to defraud the government in a kickback scheme supposedly involving the misuse of $13.3 million of NHA funds.[46]

The NHA scandal in part influenced the Navajo Tribal Council to take action to investigate Navajo finances. But, as Chairman MacDonald had protested so strongly against Goldwater's request for an audit, the issue became clouded. In a rare, close vote, thirty-two to twenty-eight, the council decided in April 1976 to hire an auditor. Two months later, council members unanimously approved a resolution authorizing a GAO audit of the tribe. All of the subsequent audits did not unearth additional examples of financial irregularities. During the examinations and afterward, MacDonald remained angry about the role played, in his opinion, by Goldwater in instigating all the scrutiny:

Goldwater began to put in early 1974 on the U.S. attorney to get something on MacDonald and this began to continue to mount as the Navajo-Hopi legislation was being discussed, as the mineral resources of the tribe was being held back, all of these self-interest groups began to drum up opposition to this administration and finally they began to find bits and pieces here that they want to embarrass the Tribe with . . . during the three year period during my second administration there were approximately 176 audits by the government of various types and of all those 176 audits they did not find any kind of wrongdoing.[47]

MacDonald's thesis that Goldwater was simply out to get him in reprisal for the Navajo vote against the Arizona senator in 1974 clearly was shaped in part by the chairman's own indictment in February 1977. MacDonald had been subpoenaed by a federal grand jury in Phoenix looking into the possible misuse of federal funds in the Navajo Nation. The eventual eight-county indictment alleged essentially that MacDonald and former assistant William Moore had schemed to defraud Tucson Gas and Electric Company by submitting false traveling invoices while MacDonald and other Navajo officials talked to groups protesting the completion of a company power line through the Navajo Nation. In MacDonald's perspective, given a year after the indictment: "So finally, I guess, the word from Goldwater was that by golly you've got to get something on MacDonald. So they kept on going, they kept on going, and finally they came to the situation which to this day I think was very much framed."[48]

For the most part, Navajos rallied to MacDonald's defense. The Tribal Council appropriated $70,000 for his legal defense and passed a resolution in his support. By mid-April 1977, eighty-five of the 102 chapters in the Navajo Nation had also approved resolutions backing the chairman and his legal battle against the indictment. One chapter, Shiprock, called for his resignation. MacDonald hired F. Lee Bailey to defend him. The trial began on May 10, 1977. After a week's proceedings, visiting Pennsylvania Judge Herbert Serg ordered acquittal. The jury had not been able to reach a unanimous decision, and Serg ruled that no jury could have deemed MacDonald guilty based on the evidence presented. One jury member revealed that the jury had voted eight to four for acquittal before announcing itself as deadlocked.[49]

The chairman put the best possible face on the trial, calling it a test of the unity and strength of the Navajo people: "I am happy that when difficulty afflicts us, we still have the strength and determination to prevail over such difficulties." Indeed, in the long run, the indictment and trial may well have worked to MacDonald's political advantage. By casting himself as a Navajo being persecuted by powerful outsiders, MacDonald ultimately probably gained. But in the immediate months surrounding the trial there can be little question that the indictment delayed and hampered his efforts in some critical areas. Economic development and the Navajo-Hopi land dispute, already considered, were two cases in point; tribal government reorganization ranked as another.

Reapportionment stood out as perhaps the most controversial element in Navajo government reorganization. Given the one man, one vote dictum provided by the United States Supreme Court, the Navajo chapter system had to be revised in some fashion. Some chapters, such as Shiprock, had grown enormously in population, while others, such as Le Chee, in the most remote reaches of the Navajo Nation remained lightly populated. The tribe had moved very slowly on this delicate matter, and finally by the summer of 1976 federal officials were threatening to sue the Navajos to reapportion. In 1976, seventy-four council members represented 102 chapters. Most of them, fifty-seven, represented one chapter. Twelve were elected from two chapters, two from three chapters, and one from seven chapters. The aforementioned fifty-seven delegates, however, could be in Window Rock in behalf of as few people as 463—in the case of Le Chee— or as many as 7,997—in the instance of Shiprock. If, as Board of Elections Supervisor Benjamin Hanley estimated, the Navajo Nation included 151,627 people, each councilman should represent about 2,049 people. Obviously, this was not the case.[50]

Even if the tribe had not moved decisively on the issue, it had at least moved a little by this time. On March 20, 1974, the council had passed a resolution to initiate reapportionment on the principle of one man, one vote. This resolution was but the first of several expressions of interest in the matter, but little results could be perceived. By August 1977, the *Navajo Times* would run a full front-page cartoon of MacDonald juggling the different Navajo agencies, under the headline, "Reapportionment: The Great Juggling Act." MacDonald, to be sure, had been preoccupied until quite recently with other concerns during 1977, and other factors complicated the situation, including precise population statistics and place of voting. Census figures for the Navajo population have always been considered unreliable, at best. But reasonably accurate totals seemed a necessary prerequisite for proper reapportionment. In contrast to the residency requirements imposed in non-Navajo elections, the tribe had always permitted one to vote in one's home chapter, even if an individual had not actually lived there for many years. Many Navajos thus voted where they were born rather than where they presently lived. Should this tradition be changed?[51]

Not surprisingly, each chapter would fight to maintain what it regarded as its correct boundaries and corresponding influence within the Navajo Nation. An inevitable struggle erupted over these boundaries in connection with reapportionment. In the fall of 1977, MacDonald relieved Ron Faich, director of the tribe's Research and Statistics Department, from further duties in mapping the reapportionment of the council districts and for the 1980 federal census on the Navajo Nation. Faich had had various confrontations with other tribal employees over the carrying out of his duties, but ultimately he was simply a casualty of this complicated and emotional issue. At the end of the year, as many as thirty-six different boundary disputes loomed to be settled. As in the 1930s, when Commissioner of Indian Affairs John Collier helped institute grazing districts within the Navajo reservation, there appeared to be massive confusion about the reapportionment and its precise purposes. This time, many Navajos worried that reapportionment would somehow affect future grazing areas.[52]

In March 1978, the Navajo tribal court released its decision upon the boundary disputes. Judges Charley John of Shiprock and Marie Neswood of Crownpoint took great pains to deny that the court ruling would change "customary grazing or other land usage rights." The Navajo Court of Appeals in April upheld the reapportionment plan, which conflicted with an earlier plan approved by the Tribal Council. The council had called for eighty members of the council representing ten districts, with some chapters to be combined with others. The court plan, which had been shaped by the suggestions of DNA attorneys and a variety of tribal officials, maintained the seventy-four-member council and traditional boundaries. It would have twenty-five single-member districts, fourteen two-member districts, three three-member districts, and three four-member districts. After considerable debate, the council in June devised yet another plan for an eighty-seven-member council, providing for additional representation for such larger communities as Shiprock, Tuba City, Fort Defiance, Chinle, and Saint Michaels. This compromise provided something for everyone: it permitted continued representation from the very small chapters yet allowed the large chapters to have extra representatives. Perhaps this latest arrangement would be satisfactory to all sides, and reapportionment, for the time being at least, would have been settled.

The reapportionment debate, in the eyes of some onlookers, influenced the formation of a third tier in the Navajo judicial system: the Supreme Judicial Council. Some contended that because of administrative dissatisfaction with the way the existing court system had handled the reapportionment question and other matters Chairman MacDonald decided to create a higher court more responsive to his beliefs. For example, in January 1978 the Navajo Court of Appeals had upheld a Shiprock court ruling overturning the decision by the Tribal Council to pay F. Lee Bailey $70,000 for his defense of MacDonald. By the time the ruling had been made, $51,000 had already been paid Bailey, but the remaining $19,000 was withheld. In addition, the council voted at this time that the courts could not review council decisions. This conclusion, prompted by the reapportionment issue, in turn encouraged the courts to file suit against the council. Members of the general counsel for the tribe, George Vlassis and Larry Ruzow, clashed as well with judicial counsel Steve Gudac on how the courts were handling reapportionment.[53]

The Supreme Judicial Council came into being in May 1978. The Navajo Tribal Council empowered it to hear cases on appeal from lower courts. The 35-22 vote by the council to create this body indicated the strong division of opinion existing within the Navajo Nation. The council eventually approved the idea, originally presented by Edgar and Jean Cahn of the Antioch Law School, as one final place of review before hearing by a federal court. Two retired justices, one Tribal Council member from each agency, and the chief justice would sit on the Supreme Judicial Council, with the chief justice voting only to break a tie. The Tribal Council ultimately could overrule the Judicial Council, but only within sixty days of a decision; otherwise, the Judicial Council's decision would stand.

Several features of the Judicial Council immediately came under severe criticism. The ability of the chairman to appoint the five Tribal Council representatives as well as the two retired justices proved to be one of the more controversial points. Surely, critics argued, this would strongly influence the composition of the council in the direction of favoring the current chairman's views. In addition, many Navajos complained that the Judicial Council had to be supportive of the Tribal Council, given its majority council delegate vote. Third, the existence of an additional court of review by definition undercut the power and authority of the existing court system.

Support and criticism of the new judicial group primarily fell along partisan lines. MacDonald, the general counsel, and MacDonald supporters within the Tribal Council favored the Judicial Council; MacDonald opponents in the Tribal Council, the judicial counsel, and DNA attorneys generally opposed it. Fuel for the controversy was provided during the remainder of 1978 by the Judicial Council's first three decisions, all of which went against the lower courts. Vlassis's new role as advisor to the Judicial Council also sparked heated discussion. At the end of 1978, the Supreme Judicial Council seemed destined to lead a lively existence; it would be difficult to reach a consensus about its merits.[54]

The Supreme Judicial Council, reapportionment, mineral exploration

and exploitation, and other disputed questions combined to inspire
significant protest within the Navajo Nation in the late 1970s. While
demonstrations had occurred before on the reservation, this era particularly was characterized by sit-ins, takeovers, marches, and other modes
of publicizing discontent. The American Indian Movement, the Coalition
for Navajo Liberation, and other groups actively protested expanded
mineral development by, for example, taking over the Aneth oil fields
or sitting-in within the chambers of the Navajo Tribal Council. Young
people composed a significant percentage of the protestors, but by no
means all of those disenchanted were young. Shiprock definitely marked
the center of opposition, but it was not the sole location.

The "Walk for Better Government" held in Window Rock in May
1976, symbolized widespread concern felt midway through MacDonald's
second term for financial irregularities, mineral development, and the
organization of tribal government. March organizer Peterson Zah and
others asked searching questions about the contemporary state of affairs
within the Navajo Nation. Chairman MacDonald bore the brunt of much
of their criticism, and it appeared in the summer of 1976 that his political
stock was at an all-time low. The evolving scandal surrounding the Navajo
Housing Authority coupled with MacDonald's indictment for a time
seemed to have crippled his chances for an unprecedented third term.
Challengers to his reelection began to gather rather early in the wings.

Eventually no less than twelve people would emerge to battle for the
chairman's position. They would include former political allies, such as
Vice Chairman Wilson Skeet, and former top administrative official James
Atcitty. The well-known Navajo physician, Taylor McKenzie, announced
his candidacy in September 1977. The ubiquitous Raymond Nakai also
entered the fray. After much soul searching and considerable pressure
from friends to seek the office, Peterson Zah finally decided not to run.
And in the end, as expected, Peter MacDonald did decide to seek four
more years in office. Given the difficulties he had encountered in his
second term, few expected him to win reelection easily. Yet his past
election showings combined with the support he had attracted during his
indictment and trial promised that MacDonald's challengers definitely
would have their work cut out for them.

THE PAST, PRESENT, AND FUTURE OF THE NAVAJO NATION

7

As in the United States, elections in the Navajo Nation have become progressively more costly and prolonged. More candidates seem to seek the top elective office with each passing campaign. The race for the tribal chairmanship in 1978 began earlier than any previous contest and ultimately involved a record number of aspirants. It may be concluded that the early beginning of the political race was influenced partially by the prospect of Peter MacDonald seeking a third term. Given the difficulty of defeating an incumbent and given MacDonald's strong showings in 1970 and 1974, a potential challenger would be well advised to start well before November 1978. Surely this would be particularly true for a newcomer to Navajo politics. More seasoned veterans such as Raymond Nakai need not enter the fray as quickly.

The Navajo physician, Taylor McKenzie, became the first announced candidate for Navajo chairman. McKenzie started his campaign in the autumn of 1977. He struck some familiar chords, promising he would not force a program of stock reduction and calling for more local influence in the decision making of the tribal government. He spoke cautiously on the issues of coal gasification and tribal taxation, saying that the people needed to be fully informed before a final decision on coal gasification could be reached and advocating taxation of industries but not individual businessmen. When asked if he would remain in medicine, given the shortage of Navajo physicians, McKenzie stated he was presently serving as an administrator with the Navajo Area Indian Health Service and thus was already divorced from clinical medicine. The most important administrative post in the Navajo Nation, he noted, was chairman.[1]

While a political novice, McKenzie held the advantage of being well known throughout the Navajo Nation. When coupled with his early announcement, he seized the position of being the first prominent person to oppose MacDonald. A year before the election he thus had emerged as one of two viable alternatives to the incumbent. No one doubted that the old war horse, Raymond Nakai, ultimately would be a candidate. And, despite his often troubled second administration, few believed that Peter MacDonald would not try for a third term. The real question in the minds of observers was whether DNA legal services director Peterson Zah also would run. The thirty-nine-year-old from Low Mountain, so his friends believed, would be the only individual who might defeat MacDonald.

Zah maintained firmly in October of 1977 that he would not attempt to gain the chairmanship. He contended that in five years as DNA director he had accomplished some of his goals but not all, and thus he wanted to continue in his present post. A fire the previous summer of undetermined origins had destroyed his home, and Zah said that the loss had made him feel a greater responsibility to his family. Moreover, Zah had become increasingly critical of the contemporary structure of Navajo government. He argued that one could be influential without being chairman and that "the idea that you can change a situation through politics overnight is a myth."[2]

Despite much public pressure—including the formation of a Peterson Zah for Chairman committee—Zah held fast to his decision not to run. While depriving the anti-MacDonald forces of their perhaps most attractive candidate, Zah's abstention hardly left the campaign bereft of people avidly pursuing Navajo politics' top prize. In the end, twelve Navajos sought the chairmanship: MacDonald, McKenzie, Nakai, Wilson Skeet, Raymond Smith, John Pinto, Raymond Tso, Perry Allen, Rex Kontz, James Atcitty, Tonney Bowman, and Cecil Largo. The remaining nine candidates, for the most part, did not announce their candidacies until the summer of 1978, and by that time it was too late to mount an effective campaign prior to the August primary. Wilson Skeet, of course, had served for two terms as MacDonald's vice chairman and could count on some backing even when limited to a brief period to generate support. Raymond Smith, a sixteen-year council member from Houck, earned some endorsements but few votes in the primary itself.

The multiple candidacies worked to MacDonald's advantage. The other eleven office seekers cut into each others' bases of support, making it difficult for any one of them to garner a substantial vote in the primary. Nakai had held on to a reliable constituency over the years, but he had already been defeated twice by MacDonald. McKenzie had firm backing from his home chapter of Shiprock—a mixed blessing, given Shiprock's image elsewhere—and some additional allegiance in northern New Mexico but had not generated reservation-wide enthusiasm. MacDonald ran a highly organized, well-financed campaign which included sophisticated media advertisements emphasizing Navajo advances in the 1970s. Such advertisements appeared often in the *Navajo Times* during this period:

He knows how. Nobody else has done that before.
No one else sustains the growth he has created.
No one else is as feared by our enemies.
No one else is as respected by our friends.
No one else has made the federal government honor its promises.
When he speaks, others listen.
IT DIDN'T JUST HAPPEN, MACDONALD MADE IT HAPPEN.

By mid-July, thirty-eight chapters had officially endorsed MacDonald. They represented all regions of the Navajo Nation and gave a firm indication that the chairman would be the clear front-runner in the primary. Despite his well-publicized problems and the alienation of some former associates or supporters, who scored his record, MacDonald remained able to attract general popular endorsement.[3]

Peter MacDonald won the August primary in what can only be described as a landslide, gaining 20,695 votes. Raymond Nakai came in second, trailing badly with 6,203. The only two other candidates to collect more than 1,000 votes were Taylor McKenzie with 5,017 and Wilson Skeet with 2,736. Under the terms of this first primary election (in the past, there had been a convention where the two candidates holding the most chapters would be nominated for the fall election), MacDonald and Nakai thus once again would confront each other. While MacDonald could not hope to win the general election by such a margin, it seemed impossible that Nakai could close the gap between the two men. MacDonald had received the most votes in eighty-six of the 104 chapters, including every chapter in the Tuba City Agency. Nakai had won eight chapters, mostly adjacent or near to his home of Lukachukai; McKenzie had won six, generally near his Shiprock base. But even in the Shiprock Agency, Mac-

Donald led Nakai and McKenzie by counts of 2,541 to 1,854 and 1,973, respectively. In the remaining agencies, he defeated Nakai by nearly four to one in Fort Defiance, over ten to one in Crownpoint, four to one in Tuba City, and three to one in Chinle.[4]

The three months of campaigning between August and November contained few surprises. MacDonald selected Tuba City Agency Superintendent Frankie Paul, forty-four, as his running mate, while Nakai chose Reginald A. Begaye, forty-four. Paul, from Ramah, had known MacDonald from the time the two had worked in southern California. He had gained administrative experience through tribal and BIA positions and helped balance the ticket, with MacDonald following tradition in choosing someone from the eastern region. Begaye, of Coyote Canyon, was director of School for Me, a center for special education in Tohatchi. Probably neither Paul nor Begaye significantly affected the course or the outcome of the campaign and election. Navajo voters would decide between two men they believed they knew well, both two-term chairman whose basic views had been well publicized.

Nakai and his supporters stressed government reform as their key issue. Arguing that "the present system of government has been formed after a non-Indian government fifty years ago," Nakai sharply criticized as well the recently created Supreme Judicial Council and returned to his advocacy of a tribal constitution. Only a constitution, he contended, would ensure individual rights, due process, and a check-and-balance system within Navajo government. In addition, Nakai and Begaye attacked MacDonald and his record with increasing severity in the final weeks before the election. They charged MacDonald with conflict of interest for his involvement with Denay Insurance, with which the tribe had contracted for a good deal of business. They asserted he had done little to protect Navajo water rights and little to create permanent, non-federally funded jobs within the Navajo Nation. Their ads represented them as an alternative to "an aircraft engineer and a BIA bureaucrat."

MacDonald, in turn, attempted to refute these charges and to critique the record of Nakai as chairman during the 1960s. The "great Nakai giveaway" of the Armex tennis shoe factory, the Page power plant, the Westward Coach company, and the transfer of water rights at Page all came under fire. MacDonald and Paul argued that the tribe had greatly increased federal funding during their administration, "stopped the give away of precious resources," protected the land base, reduced unemployment by 20 percent, and moved to exercise Navajo sovereignty through the sulphur emissions fee, business activity tax, and possessory interest tax. Full-page advertisements also trumpeted endorsements or praise from Arizona Senator Dennis De Concini, Arizona Governor Bruce Babbitt, and other political leaders; MacDonald, for example, was pictured shaking hands with Jimmy Carter, with the caption reading "Peter MacDonald is the most powerful and influential Indian in the United States."[5]

Just before the election, Larry Anderson and other members of the Diné Bii Coalition took over tribal headquarters in protest of the MacDonald and Nakai campaigns. MacDonald aides charged Nakai with encouraging the takeover, while Nakai supporters called the allegation ridiculous. The impact of the takeover cannot be ascertained, though Nakai assistant Perry Allen would label it a significant factor in the MacDonald triumph at the polls. This assessment seemed questionable. The reelection of the incumbent indeed had appeared assured, but the action of the young men may have reflected a bit of the frustration shared by some of the people over the choices available to them.

Peter MacDonald did not receive many more votes in the general election than he had in the primary, but they proved more than enough to swamp Raymond Nakai in November. Nakai picked up quite a bit of support from his initial showing, but MacDonald still won by about three to two; nearly complete totals showed a margin of 21,861 to 14,060. Nakai and Begaye cut into MacDonald's majority in many chapters and made major gains in about twenty chapters: Inscription House, Dennehotso, Blue Gap, Many Farms-Rough Rock, Mexican Springs, Greasewood, Steamboat, Ganado, Cornfields, Crystal, Sawmill-Red Lake, Oaksprings, Houck-Lupton, Rock Point, Mexican Water-Red Mesa, Hogback, Sanostee, Two Grey Hills, and Nenahnezah. MacDonald, however, rolled up remarkable landslide wins in the far western and eastern reaches of the Navajo Nation and in many other sites engineered impressive victories. It may have marked the end of Nakai's long political career, a career which had included seven different candidacies for the chairmanship. Yet, if MacDonald were not to seek a fourth term in 1982, one suspected the old campaigner from Lukachukai might be tempted to give it another try.

But for Peter MacDonald, it was, of course, a triumph worth savoring. He was, after all, the first person ever to gain a third term as Navajo tribal chairman, despite difficulties that had plagued much of his second administration. On a cold and cloudy January day, in his inaugural address he outlined three main objectives that he would seek beginning in 1979:

First, we must claim what is ours—actively and aggressively. We must assert our rights and continue to press for what is due us.
Second, we must seek unity within. The time for division and dissension is over. We must reach out to each other, come together and unite.
Third, we must dare to dream great dreams—and then we must dare to put them into action.

MacDonald claimed that the Navajos "made great strides during the past four years" but acknowledged "we have lived under a shadow . . . created by those who oopose our well-being." This shadow of suspicion; of federal audits and investigations, of unproved accusations, of indictments and prosecutions . . . of backlash against Native Americans . . . of retaliation for the progress we dared to make as a people . . . of intimidation—for the voter registration drive we conducted—for the energy resources we have—for the leadership we have exercised on behalf of all Native Americans must be dispelled.

The chairman promised the tribe would move forward in guarding its resources and asserting its power. All leases for minerals would be reviewed and negotiated. All promises to preserve the land, water, and air would be enforced. Taxation and regulation would be pursued. A fair share of funds and services from the state and federal government would be insisted upon. "As joint owners of the Joint Use Area," the Navajos would "be accorded at least the same treatment as the people of Maine who are not joint owners of the land."

"Never before has Navajo attacked Navajo in the way we see going on today and never before have Navajos invited outsiders to take up their cause against other Navajos," MacDonald concluded. He argued that "we attack each other with such bitterness because we are afraid to attack our true enemies, those who oppress and exploit us." Urging that Navajos not "fall into the trap that has always been used: 'Divide and Conquer,' " MacDonald proposed a number of measures aimed particularly at the young: a youth assembly modeled after the Tribal Council, a government internship program for youth, and an office of youth affairs. He also said the Navajo government must have "greater accountability and fewer excuses"; government structure needed review and governmental personnel required more training and technical assistance.

The first part of MacDonald's great dream would be to "move immediately to designate six locations as economic growth centers, magnets to draw the dollars that now drain off the reservation." These centers would include shopping centers, recreation complexes, social service centers, health care centers, and modern homes. He targeted groundbreaking the first of the centers for August 1979, with it being open for the public by June 1980. But, in addition to material growth, the chairman called for a new capital with a cultural center at the core to aid in the transmission of Navajo life and culture to future generations. This city, ideally, would be a true community, with disputes solved by consensus and mediation and with people helping and trusting each other, a place where people would not live as strangers but rather where all Navajos and indeed all Americans could learn how to walk the Beauty Way.[6]

What, then, of the past, present, and future of the Navajo Nation? The degree of Navajo continuity shown over the past century would have surprised, indeed dismayed, most Anglo-American observers of a century ago. With the rapid expansion of the United States into what had become the American Southwest following the Mexican War, the Navajo position had been drastically changed. General James Carleton and others moved to squelch Navajo independence. The military campaigns and the long winters combined to force the surrender of a great many Navajos and bring about the tragic Long Walk to Fort Sumner in eastern New Mexico. Carleton envisioned the Navajo incarceration as necessary to remake the people into the Anglo American mold. But unlike many Native American peoples, whose military defeat in the nineteenth century resulted in permanent banishment from their homelands, the Navajos were not forever exiled.

Through the Treaty of 1868, the Navajos could return to a reservation that encompassed a portion of their country, and through additions to this initial land base of 3.5 million acres the Navajos claimed by far the largest Indian reservation in the United States. The consolidation of their land holdings clearly proved vital to the Navajo future. It allowed them, of course, an ongoing cultural tradition, with key events in their history focused in familiar surroundings. It permitted them the relative isolation to flourish in the sparsely settled Southwest at a time when most Native Americans were far from prospering. This isolation gave them precious time to adapt and adjust in the years following Fort Sumner. Their population expanded and migrated. Their economy diversified. Their language and religious traditions were maintained. Politically, they may not have envisioned themselves as one unit, but given their relative degree of cultural unity and the tendency of the United States government to treat them as one political entity, the movement in this direction could not be doubted.

The twentieth century marked a period of steadily increasing pressure on the Navajos and their land from forces beyond the boundaries of the reservation. As the United States in general and the Southwest in particular developed, Navajo resources became progressively more valued. Navajo oil, uranium, and coal altered how the outside world perceived land once seen at best as picturesque, barren desert. Mineral wealth would inspire creation of the Navajo Tribal Council as a body authorized to approve oil leases. Mineral wealth several decades later would bring in a deluge of dollars into the Navajo treasury and thereby change what the Navajo government could attempt to achieve. It was a two-edged sword, this growing interdependence and more complicated relationship with the non-Navajo world. Nowhere was it better illustrated than during the traumatic years of the livestock reduction era. Here the Navajos confronted John Collier, a commissioner of Indian affairs who may have been genuinely interested in the Navajo well-being but whose cure seemed worse than the illness itself.

World War II ushered in the contemporary Navajo world. Thousands of Navajos gained their first long-term exposure to societies beyond their homeland. The termination era also encouraged many Navajos to relocate on a temporary or permanent basis in American towns and cities. These experiences convinced many prominent Navajos of the need for formal education for their children. Passage of federal legislation made possible the building of a network of public schools across the Navajo Nation. In addition, the Navajo-Hopi Long Range Rehabilitation Program provided millions of dollars for highways, schools, and other programs boosting Navajo economic development. The great oil strikes in the Aneth, Utah, area highlighted growing utilization of Navajo mineral resources. The royalties and other returns from mineral exploitation came flowing into the Navajo tribal treasury and altered the potential of the Navajo government.

The heightened ambition of the Navajo government came as a response, too, to economic, social, and political challenges within and from outside of the Navajo Nation. Navajos were beset by overwhelming unemployment, and the tribal government reached out to help. In its almost desperate search for jobs for its people, the government made some questionable decisions with regard to coal mining and electrical power production. These choices would come under increasing scrutiny and eventual attack at the end of the 1960s and into the 1970s, but at the time they were made few Navajos objected. The Office of Navajo Economic Opportunity generated hundreds of jobs and worked to provide funds and training for grass-roots people. At the reservation level, it allowed young Navajos such as Peter MacDonald a chance to exercise leadership and gain administrative experience. DNA legal services attorneys had an important impact not only upon improving legal representation for individual Navajos but also upon the workings of tribal government. DNA legal services became a forum for the exploration of ideas about the functioning and purposes of that government.

The Navajo government moved into various areas in part because the state and federal governmental agencies both seemed to be doing too little and threatening to do too much. The Long Range Rehabilitation Act had been devised in the spirit of the termination era: to provide short-term assistance for the Navajos so that the federal government could spend less on the tribe in the long run. If the federal government appeared to be moving away from involvement, then what would move in in its place? It would be the state governments, of course, that would suddenly begin to exercise greater jurisdiction, the very governments that had been notably unwilling to assist in Navajo education, health care, or economic development. If the Navajos failed to produce a judicial system of their own, a tribal attorney warned, then increasingly the state judicial system would be involved. So, for example, we see the evolution of the Navajo court system as a response to that incipient challenge.

But the Navajo government became more active in various areas primarily because the Diné deemed work by outsiders inadequate and because they wanted, quite simply, to take greater charge over their own lives. The Navajo tribal enterprise represented one approach to economic development through which they not only could provide employment and leadership training but also exercise control over vital resources. The Navajo Forest Products Industries proved to be the most successful example of this kind of endeavor. In education, the Navajo government's division of education encouraged the evolution of a bilingual, bicultural approach to the teaching of the young. The tribe founded its own community college and supported efforts at such innovative institutions as

Rough Rock Demonstration School, Rock Point School, and Ramah
Navajo High School. In health care, the Navajo Health Authority promoted
cooperation between traditional Navajo healers and Anglo medical doctors.
The NHA also helped to sponsor young Navajo students interested in
health careers.

Peter MacDonald, the elected leader of the Navajos throughout the
1970s, escalated the rhetoric and to some extent the reality of Navajo
self-determination. The chairman spoke out strongly about the need for
Navajos to claim what was theirs, develop what they had, and seek what
they did not have but desired. Under MacDonald's aegis, the Navajos did
move to assert more strongly their rights to their land resources. Given
the extent to which previous administrations had made long-term leases
of coal and other mineral resources and commitments to electrical power
production, MacDonald and his legal counsel felt limited in what the
Navajos could do to alter this general situation. They attempted to press
for the best possible deal in new leases. By the end of MacDonald's second
administration, however, public insistence had grown markedly for renegotiation of existing leases; MacDonald's inaugural address in January
1979 indicated that he would move more strongly in that direction.

While he became increasingly recognized as a national Native American
leader, MacDonald came under growing fire at home. Part of his dilemma
stemmed from the predictable erosion of support that accompanies most
incumbents during their second term of office. MacDonald stubbornly
clung to what he perceived as a middle ground, between those who wanted
to prohibit any development in areas such as mineral exploitation and
those who argued he was not exerting sufficient pressure on outside
companies and Anglos in general, who were profiting from the utilization
of Navajo resources. The chairman also bore the brunt of the criticism
that had echoed for half a century over sectional versus national Navajo
interests. Should not the local impacted area receive greater benefits than
it had? Was too much of the money flowing solely into Window Rock?

These two issues would continue to be debated within the Navajo Nation. They were at the very heart of the Navajo future. On whose terms
would future development be gained? To what extent could or should
the trend toward greater concentration of power in Window Rock be
reversed? Here we have seen and will see questions raised about the essence
of Navajo well-being. As Peter MacDonald once noted, when Navajos
talk with Kerr-McGee or United Nuclear about growth, he knows whose

growth they are talking about. And what about the bitter resentment from the areas of mineral wealth? What about the strong feelings emanating from Shiprock? Can Navajos agree on who will receive the money and how and where it will be spent? Or will the internal divisions intensify with time if the population continues to grow while the land base does not?

Clearly the answers to these questions have yet to be made and cannot be predicted with any degree of certainty. However, when we look to the future of the Navajo Nation, certain factors appear likely to be present that would centrally affect that prospect. First, the Navajos cannot expect to gain any significant amounts of land. Second, the population for the immediate future is likely to continue to grow more rapidly than that of the United States. Third, a great many Navajos will continue to want to spend some or all of the year within the boundaries of the Navajo Nation. In addition, the main source of revenue for the workings of Navajo government, mineral wealth, stands to be depleted after a certain period of time. Yet given the heightening dependence upon domestic energy sources, the Navajos will face unprecedented pressure from the American public for those sources to be utilized very fully as long as they last.

These considerations have been evident for some time. The first three factors, as we have seen, directly affected Navajo economic development policy. The Navajos have wanted jobs and wanted their young people to be able to make a living at home. Rapid expansion of mineral depletion promised some relief. In the short run, again from a purely economic standpoint, it has achieved that, if not to the extent perhaps envisioned by some Navajos. But in both an intermediate and long-term sense there already have been negative repercussions. Mineral exploitation implied wider and more enduring prosperity. When many young Navajos could not enjoy that condition, they understandably were embittered. Who, they asked, was benefiting from that exploitation?

It became more and more apparent during the 1970s that not only could the Navajos not count on depending as exclusively as they had upon their mineral resources but they also might not be gaining as much as they could even presently from those resources. Perhaps the most perceptive analysis of this state of affairs came in a study by Michael Benson sponsored by DNA Legal Services entitled "Sovereignty: The Navajo Nation and Taxation." Benson's critique of contemporary Navajo policy touched upon many critical points germane to this discussion and will be utilized during the ensuing paragraphs.

While coal and uranium have gained widespread attention, oil and gas revenues actually have been by far the most important for the Navajo economy. In fiscal years 1972 through 1975, these revenues comprised from 76.8 to 84.4 percent of mineral returns. However, oil and gas reserves have been greatly reduced and cannot be relied upon as they have in the past. Coal and uranium obviously will take up an increasing percentage of Navajo mineral return.[7] Given inflation, changing attitudes, and the heightened value of Navajo coal, old leases appear extremely inadequate. The extent to which they may be renegotiated is a moot point. Some improvement, at least, may be expected in the various arrangements. New leases, of course, will be more favorable, though the most promising coal mining areas may already be committed. Future uranium exploitation had been keyed to nuclear power. With the accident at the nuclear power station near Harrisburg, Pennsylvania, in the spring of 1979, nuclear power became a more questionable source of energy. Increasingly, Navajos are protesting about the hazards of uranium mining. Still, increased mining of uranium may be expected, with greater dividends to the Navajos.

Eventually, perhaps as early as the year 2000, the Navajo coal and uranium reserves will be markedly reduced, and the tribe will be forced to turn elsewhere in the twenty-first century for a steadily higher portion of its operating expenses. With that eventuality looming ever nearer, what will the Navajos do? In the 1980s and 1990s, Navajo leaders assuredly will work doggedly to diversify the economy. Large-scale industry may remain difficult to attract. Smaller investments may prove more common and, indeed, in the end more desirable. The Navajo Agricultural Products Industries, to this point plagued by difficulties, may prove to be a vital element within the economy. But even given small business development and more effective employment of the tribal enterprise approach, the present imbalance in the Navajo economy is genuine cause for alarm. It poses the most fundamental challenge to the future of the Navajo Nation.

In the meantime, given the fact that diversification of the economy will take considerable time, how can the Navajos take best advantage of the resources they do have? For a growing number of Navajos, taxation holds much promise as a tool to ensure maximum return to the tribe on outside investment within the Navajo Nation. The Navajo Nation is familiar with other governments collecting taxes. The United States government, the States of Arizona, New Mexico, and Utah, and six counties—McKinley and San Juan in New Mexico, Apache, Navajo, and Coconino in Arizona.

and San Juan in Utah—all collect taxes of various kinds. Navajos are immune from some forms of taxation, including county taxes and state
taxes on income earned within the Navajo Nation. Nonetheless, the governments reap remarkable windfalls. From 1972 to 1974, for example, New
Mexico collected $2,466,309.84 in taxes on oil and gas produced in the
Navajo Nation. As Benson notes bluntly: "It is no big secret that the
non-Navajo governments receive more money in taxes from the development of Navajo Nation resources than the income realized by the Tribe
from these developments." The Four Corners and Navajo power plants
are two of the more blatant cases in point.[8]

Taxation may provide the medium for financing the progessively more
expensive government of the Navajo Nation. On January 10, 1974, the
Navajo Tribal Council authorized a Navajo Tax Commission. While it took
considerable time for Chairman MacDonald to nominate commission
members and more time for the members to be approved, nonetheless,
by the end of the 1970s, the Tax Commission represented an entity which
may well be extremely important in its effect upon the daily lives of all
Navajos. The sulphur emission tax, which the tribe attempted to levy
during MacDonald's second administration, showed the potential of the
Navajo Nation to move in this area. It also revealed the degree to which
non-Navajo corporate interests will resist such movement. Considerable
legal battles remain to be fought here, with the outcomes of utmost
importance. If the Navajo Nation can tax such interests, then it will make
a great difference in how the Navajo government may be supported. It
should be added that pressure undoubtedly will grow for wealthy Navajo
individuals to be taxed as well. The income derived from new taxation
should in turn free royalties and other forms of Navajo tribal income to
be invested in bolstering the entire Navajo economy rather than being
swallowed by general operating expenses of the Navajo government.

This sort of alternative approach to their government and economy
symbolizes the positive effect that the creative thinking of present and
future generations may have on the well-being of the Navajo Nation.
If there can be substantial numbers of professionals who can apply their
education, imagination, and sensitivity to Navajo needs, then the future
of the Navajo Nation should be bright indeed. It will be a future lived,
like their past, not in isolation. Their mineral resources alone guarantee
that such will be the case. Outside companies and concerns have exerted
and will exert influence over Navajo life, but they have not and will not

control existence in the Navajo Nation. We have witnessed during the past few decades the continuity of cultural institutions and seen Diné efforts to effect change in their economy, education, government, and health care. Thus we may conclude that the Navajos can hold the answer to their own destiny. Time and again, they have been pictured as a vanishing race or a people who could not continue to live on their own land, and time and again they have defied the informed judgments of others who predicted their decline or demise. If their past and present teach us anything, it should be not to underestimate their strength, resilience, and persistence.

NOTES

INTRODUCTION

1. Brian W. Dippie uses the Curtis photograph in his article, "This Bold But Wasting Race: Stereotypes and American Indian Policy," *Montana* 23 (January 1973): 2-13.

2. Clyde Kluckhohn and Dorothea Leighton, *The Navaho*, rev. ed. (New York: Anchor, 1962), pp. 122-23. "Navaho" has been the spelling preferred by many anthropologists, but I use "Navajo," the official spelling adopted by the Navajo tribe.

3. Edward H. Spicer, "Plural Society in the Southwest," in *Plural Society in the Southwest*, eds. Edward H. Spicer and Raymond H. Thompson (New York: Weatherhead Foundation, 1972), pp. 54-55.

4. Navajo Nation, *Navajo Tribal Code*, 3 vols. (Orford, N.H.: Equity, 1969): 1:7-8.

5. Ibid., p. ix.

6. Carl N. Gorman, "Navajo Vision of Earth and Man," *The Indian Historian*, 6, no. 1 (Winter 1973):19.

7. Ethelou Yazzie, ed., *Navajo History* (Rough Rock, Ariz.: Rough Rock Demonstration School, 1971), pp. 9-10.

8. Ibid., pp. 11-12, 13-15, 17-31, 31-34, 35-46, 59-70, 70-72, 74-83.

9. Larry Emerson, "A Tale of Two Worlds," *Sun Tracks*, 1, no. 3 (Spring 1972).

10. Frederick McTaggart, "Mesquakie Stories: The Teachings of the Red Earth People," Ph.D. diss., University of Iowa, 1972, p. 57.

11. Katherine Spencer, *Navaho Chantway Myths* (Philadelphia: American Folklore Society, 1957), p. 24.

12. Ibid., p. 18; McTaggart, "Mesquakie Stories," p. 47.

13. Maggie Bahe, untitled poem, in *Arrows Four: Prose and Poetry by Young American Indians,* ed. T. D. Allen (New York: Washington Square Press, 1974), pp. 90-91; Richard David, untitled poem, Ibid., pp. 95-96.

14. David, untitled poem.

15. Henry Steele Commager, *The Search for a Usable Past* (New York: Alfred A. Knopf, 1967), p. 4.

CHAPTER ONE

1. David M. Brugge, "Pueblo Factionalism and External Relations," *Ethnohistory* (Spring 1969):191-200; Robert W. Young, *The Role of the Navajo in the Southwestern Drama* (Gallup, N.M.: Gallup Independent, 1968).

2. Mary Shepardson, *Navajo Ways in Government*, American Anthropological Association Memoir no. 96 (Menasha, Wis., June 1963), p. 47; Young, *Southwestern Drama*, p. 172.

3. Buck Austin, in Robert W. Young and William Morgan, eds. *Navajo Historical Selections* (Phoenix: Bureau of Indian Affairs, 1954), p. 62.

4. Young, *Southwestern Drama*, p. 18.

5. Fray Alonso de Benavides, *The Memorial of Fray Alonso de Benavides*, trans., Mrs. Edward E. Ayer (Chicago: privately printed, 1916), p. 44; Katherine Spencer, *Reflections of Social Life in the Navaho Origin Myth*, University of New Mexico Publications in Anthropology, no. 3, (Albuquerque, 1947), p. 119; W. W. Hill, *The Hunting and Agricultural Methods of the Navajo Indians*, Yale University Publications in Anthropology, no. 18 (New Haven, 1938).

6. William Y. Adams, "Navajo Ecology and Economy," in *Apachean Culture and Ethnology*, eds., Keith H. Basso and Morris Opler (Tucson: University of Arizona Publications in Anthropology, 1971), p. 79; Hill, *Hunting and Agricultural Methods*, p. 18.

7. Robert W. Young, ed., *The Navajo Yearbook*, vol. 8 (Window Rock: Bureau of Indian Affairs, 1961), pp. 359-65.

8. David M. Brugge, "Navajo Land Usage: A Study in Progressive Diversification," in *Indian and Spanish Adjustments to Arid and Semiarid Environments*, ed., Clark S. Knowlton, Texas Technological College Committee on Desert and Arid Zone Research, Contribution, no. 7 (El Paso, 1964), p. 19; Adams, "Navajo Ecology and Economy."

9. Brugge, "Navajo Land Usage," p. 20.

10. George A. Boyce, "A Primer of Navajo Economic Problems," mimeographed (Window Rock, Ariz.: Navajo Service, Bureau of Indian Affairs, 1942), lists the population growth as follows: 1785—6,000; 1870—10,500; 1900—21,000; 1935—43,500. Boyce, "Primer," p. 7.

11. Gary Witherspoon, "A New Look at Navajo Social Organization," *American Anthropologist* 72, no. 1 (1970).

12. Gerald Thompson, *The Army and the Navajo* (Tucson: University of Arizona Press, 1976), pp. 3-4.

13. Ibid., pp. 4-11.

14. Lawrence Kelly, ed., *Navajo Roundup* (Boulder: Pruett, 1970); Ruth Roessel, ed., *Navajo Stories of the Long Walk Period* (Tsaile, Ariz.: Navajo Community College Press, 1973).

15. Roessel and Johnson, *Navajo Stories*, p. 103; Charlie Mitchell, "A Navaho's Historical Reminiscences," in *Navajo Texts*, eds., Edward Sapir and Harry Hoijer (Iowa City: Linguistic Society of America, 1942), pp. 336-97.

16. Thompson, *The Army and the Navajo*, p. 28, *passim.*

17. "John Smith" and "Rita Wheeler", in Roessel and Johnson, *Navajo Stories.*

18. Thompson, *The Army and the Navajo*, pp. 158-65.

19. See Shepardson, *Navajo Ways;* and Robert W. Young, *A Political History of the Navajo Tribe* (Tsaile, Ariz.: Navajo Community College Press, 1978).

20. Robert W. Young, "The Rise of the Navajo Tribe," in *Plural Society in the Southwest*, eds., Edward H. Spicer and Raymond H. Thompson (New York: Weatherhead Foundation, 1972), pp. 183-85.

21. David F. Aberle, *The Peyote Religion Among the Navaho* (Chicago: Aldine, 1966), pp. 29-33.

22. Frank McNitt, *The Indian Traders* (Norman: University of Oklahoma Press, 1962); William Y. Adams, *Shonto: A Study of the Role of the Trader in a Modern Navaho Community*, Bureau of American Ethnology Bulletin, no. 188, (Washington, D.C., 1963).

23. Young, *Navajo Yearbook*, pp. 48-49.

24. Ibid., pp. 7-11.

25. Ibid., pp. 10, 43, 62; The Inexpert One, "Pollen," in Young and Morgan, *Navajo Historical Selections*, p. 30; Max Hensley's Story, in *Stories of Traditional Navajo Life and Culture*, ed., Broderick Johnson (Tsaile, Ariz.: Navajo Community College Press, 1977), p. 30.

26. Francis Paul Prucha, ed., *Americanizing the American Indian* (Cambridge: Harvard University Press, 1973), pp. 200, 227; see also Young, *Navajo Yearbook;* Young and Morgan, *Navajo Historical Selections;* and Johnson, *Traditional Stories.*

27. Aberle, *Peyote Religion*, pp. 27-29.

28. Young, *Navajo Yearbook*, pp. 146, 148.

29. Adams, "Navajo Economy and Ecology," p. 79.

30. Young, "The Rise of the Navajo Tribe," pp. 184-85; Shepardson, *Navajo Ways*, p. 15.

31. Ruth Underhill, *The Navajos* (Norman: University of Oklahoma Press, 1967), p. 220; Shepardson, *Navajo Ways*, p. 15; Aberle, *Peyote Religion*, pp. 34-36.

32. Aubrey W. Williams, Jr., *Navajo Political Process*, Smithsonian Contributions to Anthropology, vol. 9, (Washington, D.C., 1970), pp. 33-36.

33. Lawrence Kelly, *The Navajo Indians and Federal Indian Policy, 1900-1935* (Tucson: University of Arizona Press, 1968), pp. 39-42.

34. Ibid., pp. 39-43.

35. Ibid.; and Young, "The Rise of the Navajo Tribe," pp. 185-86.

36. Young, "The Rise of the Navajo Tribe," pp. 186-87.

37. Ibid., pp. 187-88.

38. Ibid., pp. 189-90.

39. Kelly, *Navajo Indians*, pp. 61-66.

40. Young, "The Rise of the Navajo Tribe," pp. 190; Kelly, *Navajo Indians*, p. 69.

41. Kelly, *Navajo Indians*, p. 70; Donald C. Parman, *The Navajos and the New Deal* (New Haven: Yale University Press, 1976), pp. 17-20.

42. See Kelly, *Navajo Indians;* Parman, *Navajos and New Deal;* Broderick

Johnson, "Henry Chee Dodge" in *Navajo Biographies,* eds., Broderick Johnson and Virginia Hoffman (Rough Rock, Ariz.: Rough Rock Demonstration School, 1970), pp. 187-212.

CHAPTER TWO

1. David F. Aberle, *The Peyote Religion Among the Navaho* (Chicago: Aldine, 1966), pp. 52-53.

2. Lawrence C. Kelly, *The Navajo Indians and Federal Indian Policy, 1900-1935* (Tucson: University of Arizona Press, 1968), pp. 105-12.

3. Ibid., p. 110.

4. Robert W. Young and William Morgan, eds., *Navajo Historical Selections* (Phoenix: Bureau of Indian Affairs, 1954), p. 60; Robert W. Young, *The Role of the Navajo in the Southwestern Drama* (Gallup, N.M.: Gallup Independent, 1968), pp. 66-67.

5. William H. Zeh, "General Report Covering the Grazing Situation on the Navajo Indian Reservation," in U.S., 71st Congress, 1st session, Senate, Committee on Indian Affairs, *Survey of Conditions of the Indians in the United States,* 1931, pt. 18:9121-32. Report dated, December 23, 1930.

6. For conference transcript, see ibid., pp. 9268-93.

7. Ibid., pp. 9020, 9021, 9119.

8. Ibid., pp. 9654-61.

9. Ibid., pp. 9668-69. Resolution adopted by the New Mexico Wool Growers Association, February 5 and February 6, 1930, Albuquerque, New Mexico.

10. L. Schuler Fonaroff, "Conservation and Stock Reduction on the Navajo Tribal Range," *The Geographical Review* 53, no. 1 (January 1963):200; E. R. Fryer, "The Navajo Service," *Proceedings of the First Navajo Service Land Management Conference* (Window Rock, Ariz.: Navajo Service, Bureau of Indian Affairs, 1937).

11. Fryer, "Navajo Service," p. 5.

12. "Eli Gorman" in Ruth Roessel and Broderick Johnson, ed., *Navajo Livestock Reduction: A National Disgrace* (Tsaile, Ariz.: Navajo Community College Press, 1974), p. 26.

13. John Collier, *On the Gleaming Way* (Denver: Sage Books, 1962), pp. 63-64.

14. Buck Austin, "We Have Lived on Livestock a Long Time," and The Blind Man's Daughter, "The Special Grazing Regulations," in Young and Morgan, *Navajo Historical Selections,* pp. 63, 74; Kay Bennett, *Kaibah: Recollections of a Navajo Girlhood* (Los Angeles: Westernlore Press, 1964), pp. 38-44.

15. Fryer, "Navajo Service," pp. 7-8; W. G. McGinnies, "Stock Reduction and Range Management," in *Navajo Service Land Management Conference,* p. 11.

16. U.S., 75th Congress, 1st session, Senate, Committee on Indian Affairs, *Survey of Conditions of the Indians in the United States,* 1936, pt. 34:17472.

17. Fryer, "Navajo Service," p. 7.

18. See Roessel and Johnson, *Navajo Livestock Reduction,* passim.

19. Hastiin Neez Kimble, "My Thoughts," in Young and Morgan, *Navajo Histori-*

cal Selections, p. 72; Lincoln Perry, Doris Duke Indian Oral History Project, University of New Mexico, tape transcription 313; Ben Morris, Doris Duke Indian Oral History Project, tape transcription 415.

20. *Survey of Conditions,* 1936, p. 17446.

21. Kenneth R. Philp, *John Collier's Crusade for Indian Reform, 1920-1954* (Tucson: University of Arizona Press, 1977), pp. 187-89.

22. Edward H. Spicer, "Sheepmen and Technicians," in *Human Problems in Technological Change,* ed. Edward H. Spicer (New York: Wiley, 1965), p. 195; Donald C. Parman, *The Navajos and the New Deal* (New Haven: Yale University Press, 1976), pp. 25-50.

23. Philp, *John Collier's Crusade,* pp. 188-89.

24. *Survey of Conditions,* 1936, pp. 17497, 17504-7; Parman, *Navajos and New Deal,* pp. 132-59.

25. Parman, *Navajos and New Deal,* p. 159.

26. Ibid., pp. 55-56.

27. "Howard Gorman" in Roessel and Johnson, *Navajo Livestock Reduction,* pp. 72-73; Parman, *Navajos and New Deal,* pp. 75-77.

28. John Collier, *Annual Report of the Commissioner of Indian Affairs,* 1935, reprinted in Wilcomb Washburn, ed., *The American Indian and the United States,* 4 vols. (New York: Random House, 1973), 2:924.

29. *Survey of Conditions,* 1936, pp. 17837-73.

30. Ibid.; Parman, *Navajos and New Deal,* pp. 117-20; Philp, *John Collier's Crusade,* pp. 189-90.

31. Robert W. Young, "The Rise of the Navajo Tribe," in *Plural Society in the Southwest,* eds. Edward H. Spicer and Raymond H. Thompson (New York: Weatherhead Foundation, 1972), pp. 199-200; *Survey of Conditions,* 1936, p. 17608.

32. Parman, *Navajos and New Deal,* pp. 160-63.

33. Young, "The Rise of the Navajo Tribe," pp. 200-301.

34. Ibid., pp. 201, 202; Robert W. Young, *The Navajo Yearbook* (Window Rock, Ariz.: Bureau of Indian Affairs, 1961), pp. 378-82.

35. Young, "The Rise of the Navajo Tribe," pp. 200-1.

36. Ibid., pp. 204-5; Young, *Navajo Yearbook,* pp. 381-82.

37. Young, *Navajo Yearbook,* pp. 382-83. In 1955 Navajo voters approved an indefinite number of terms for the chairman.

38. "Gorman," in Roessel and Johnson, *Navajo Livestock Reduction,* pp. 52-53.

39. Parman, *Navajos and New Deal,* pp. 190-92; and "Morgan's Reconciliation with the Government," pp. 232-63.

40. Ibid.; Aberle, *Peyote Religion, passim.*

41. Katherine Iverson, "Progressive Education for Native Americans: Washington Ideology and Navajo Reservation Implementation," *Review Journal of Philosophy and Social Science,* 3, no. 2 (1979):231-55.

42. Ibid.

43. *Survey of Conditions,* 1936, pp. 17944-45.

44. Paul N. Schmitt, "A Study Showing that Traditional Grade Classifications in Indian Schools of the Southwest Is Impracticable and Misleading," M.S. thesis, University of Kansas, 1936.

45. See Parman, *Navajos and New Deal,* pp. 193-216.

46. Robert Bergman, "Navajo Medicine and Psychoanalysis," *Human Behavior* 2, no. 7 (July 1973):8-15.

47. Jerrold E. Levy, "Navajo Health Concepts and Behavior: The Role of the Anglo Medical Man in the Navajo Healing Process" (Paper prepared for the U.S. Public Health Service, Window Rock, Ariz., August 1, 1963).

48. Paul Mico, "Navajo Perception of Anglo Medicine" (Tuba City, April 16, 1962). See also Alexander H. Leighton and Dorothea C. Leighton, *The Navaho Door* (1944; reprint ed., New York: Russell and Russell, 1966).

49. *Survey of Conditions,* 1931, p. 9217.

50. Parman, *Navajos and New Deal,* pp. 217-31.

51. Ibid., p. 225.

CHAPTER THREE

1. Story in Broderick Johnson, ed., *Navajos and World War II* (Tsaile, Ariz.: Navajo Community College Press, 1978), p. 56.

2. Doris Paul, *The Navajo Codetalkers* (Philadelphia: Dorrance, 1973), pp. 2-3.

3. "Dan S. Benally," in Johnson, *World War II,* p. 75.

4. Paul, *Navajo Codetalkers,* pp. 6-12, 75.

5. "Cozy Stanley Brown," in Johnson, *World War II,* p. 54.

6. Ibid., p. 48; George A. Boyce, *When the Navajos Had Too Many Sheep: The 1940's* (San Francisco: Indian Historian Press, 1974), p. 130.

7. Robert A. Young, "Regional Development and Rural Poverty in the Navajo Indian Area," Ph.D. diss., University of Wisconsin, 1976, pp. 346-47, 258, 274-75.

8. Ibid., p. 276.

9. See Vine Deloria, Jr., "The Disastrous Policy of Termination," in *Custer Died For Your Sins* (New York: Macmillan, 1969), pp. 54-77; Clayton R. Koppes, "From New Deal to Termination: Liberalism and Indian Policy, 1933-1953," *Pacific Historical Review* 46, no. 4 (November 1977):543-66.

10. Broderick Johnson and Virginia Hoffman, "Sam Ahkeah," in *Navajo Biographies* (Rough Rock, Ariz.: Rough Rock Demonstration School, 1970), pp. 215-36.

11. Ibid., p. 237. See also Sam Ahkeah, "A Talk to the Albuquerque Rotary," in U.S., 83rd Congress, 2nd session, *Congressional Record,* March 10, 1954, Senate Appendix A1848.

12. Navajo Tribe, *Navajo Tribal Council Minutes,* February 8, 1954, p. 12.

13. Robert W. Young, *A Political History of the Navajo Tribe* (Tsaile, Ariz.: Navajo Community College Press, 1978), pp. 122-24.

14. Navajo Tribe, *Navajo Tribal Council Resolutions 1922-51* (Window Rock, Ariz.: Navajo Tribe, 1952), p. 528.

15. *Navajo Times,* November 4, 1965.

16. Norman Littell, "Reflections of a Tribal Attorney," 1957, p. 34.

17. Ibid., pp. 6-7.

18. Lee Muck, "Survey of the Range Resources and Livestock Economy of the

Navajo Indian Reservation," mimeographed (Washington, D.C.: Department of the Interior, 1948), pp. 30-32.

19. Edward H. Spicer, "Sheepmen and Technicians," in *Human Problems in Technological Change,* ed., Edward H. Spicer, (New York: Wiley, 1965), p. 199.

20. Robert W. Young, personal interview, February 25, 1974.

21. Littell, "Reflections," p. 25; Navajo Tribe, *Minutes,* February 12, 1954; Young interview.

22. *Williams v. Lee,* 358 U.S. 217 (1959), and *Native American Church v. Navajo Tribal Council* (1959) are both reprinted in Wilcomb Washburn, ed., *The American Indian and the United States,* 4 vols. (New York: Random House, 1973), vol. 4, pp. 2785-87, 2788-91.

23. Littell, "Reflections"; *Adahooniligii,* April 1, 1953; Sam and Janet Bingham, article on Sam Ahkeah, *Navajo Times,* October 19, 1978.

24. Young, "Poverty," pp. 276-77.

25. Robert W. Young, *The Navajo Yearbook* (Window Rock, Ariz.: Bureau of Indian Affairs, 1961), vol. 8, p. 5.

26. Ibid., p. 133.

27. Ibid., pp. 29-33, 21-24.

28. Ibid., pp. 21-24.

29. U.S., 79th Congress, 2nd session, Senate, Committee on Indian Affairs, *Hearings on Navajo Indian Education,* March 14, 1946.

30. U.S., 79th Congress, 2nd session, House, Committee on Indian Affairs, "Statements on Conditions Among the Navajo Tribe," March 9, 1946, May 15, 1946.

31. Young, *Navajo Yearbook,* pp. 43-47; L. Madison Coombs, *Doorway Toward the Light: The Story of the Special Navajo Education Program* (Brigham City, Utah: Bureau of Indian Affairs, 1962).

32. Margaret Szasz, *American Indian Education: The Road to Self-Determination* (Albuquerque: University of New Mexico Press, 1974), pp. 181-82.

33. Young, *Navajo Yearbook,* pp. 56-69.

34. Ibid., p. 65.

35. Ibid., pp. 61, 47-49.

36. Howard Gorman, "Bilingual Education," Rough Rock *News,* January 31, 1973.

37. Navajo Tribal Council Resolution (CAU-43-61), passed August 29, 1961. Navajo Nation, *Navajo Tribal Code,* 3 vols. (Orford, New Hampshire; Equity, 1969), vol. 2, pp. 129-31.

38. George A. Boyce, "Facts About the Navajos," mimeographed (Window Rock, Ariz.: Bureau of Indian Affairs, 1947), p. 10.

39. Young, *Navajo Yearbook,* pp. 67-72.

40. John Adair and Kurt Deuschle, *The People's Health* (New York: Appleton-Century-Crofts, 1970), pp. 29-32.

41. Ibid., p. 33.

42. Young, *Navajo Yearbook,* pp. 73, 77.

43. Ibid., p. 102.

44. Adair and Deuschle, *People's Health,* p. 166.

45. *Young,* Navajo Yearbook, pp. 387, 389.

46. *Adahooniligii,* August-September 1953, June-July 1956.

47. Ibid., May-June 1957.

48. Robert W. Young, *The Navajo Role in the Southwestern Drama* (Gallup, N.M.: Gallup Independent, 1968), pp. 83-85.

49. Richard Van Valkenburg estimated a more rapid decline in Navajo support of chapters than has Aubrey Williams, but this may be due in part to Van Valkenburg's strong antipathy to Collier. Mary Shepardson, *Navajo Ways in Government* (American Anthropological Association Memoir, no. 96 (Menasha, Wis., 1963), p. 83; Aubrey Williams, *Navajo Political Process,* Smithsonian Contributions to Anthropology, no. 9 (Washington, D.C., 1970), p. 38. See also Richard Van Valkenburg, "Navaho Government," *Arizona Quarterly* 1, no. 4 (Winter 1945):63-73; and Solon Kimball, "Future Problems in Navajo Administration," *Human Organization* 9, no. 2 (Summer 1950):21-24.

50. See Navajo Tribe, *Minutes,* January 10, 1953, p. 188.

51. Tribal Council Resolution CJ-20-55, in Navajo Nation, *Navajo Tribal Code,* p. 144; Williams, *Navajo Political Process,* pp. 41-42.

52. Williams, *Navajo Political Process,* pp. 42-43.

53. Ibid., pp. 48-49.

54. Shepardson, *Navajo Ways,* p. 81.

55. Navajo Nation, *Navajo Tribal Code,* pp. 58, 61, 62, 63, 70-70.1.

56. Broderick Johnson and Virginia Hoffman, "Paul Jones," in *Navajo Biographies,* pp. 256-64.

57. Shepardson, *Navajo Ways,* pp. 99-101.

58. Navajo Nation, *Navajo Tribal Code,* p. 75.

59. Ibid., pp. 76-76.1.

60. Williams, *Navajo Political Process,* p. 27.

61. Ibid., pp. 95-96.

62. *Navajo Times,* September 5, 1974.

63. Jane Christian, "The Navajo: A People in Transition," *Southwestern Studies* 2, nos. 2-3 (Fall 1964, Winter 1965):45.

64. Young, *Navajo Yearbook,* p. 389.

65. For a discussion of Public Law 280, see Monroe Price, ed., *Law and the American Indian* (Indianapolis: Bobbs-Merrill, 1972), pp. 210-18.

66. Navajo Tribe, *Minutes,* October 15, 1958, p. 257.

67. Ibid., p. 258.

68. Ibid., October 16, 1958, p. 353.

69. Ibid., October 14-16, 1958, pp. 248-68, 323-55. See also Navajo Nation, *Navajo Tribal Code,* vol. 2, pp. 3-49.

70. Navajo Nation, *Navajo Tribal Code,* pp. 3-4.

71. Ibid., pp. 45-46.3.

72. Young, *Navajo Yearbook,* pp. 267, 269.

73. Young, *Southwestern Drama,* pp. 78-79.

74. Ibid., p. 83.

75. Navajo Tribe, *Council Resolutions, 1922-51,* pp. 301-7, 336-37.

76. Navajo Nation, *Navajo Tribal Code,* pp. 92-94, 96.

77. Navajo Tribe, *Council Resolutions, 1922-51*, p. 295.

78. Young, *Navajo Yearbook*, p. 268.

79. Ibid., pp. 270, 272.

80. Navajo Forest Products Industries, *Annual Report*, 1972-73, pp. 4, 9.

81. Navajo Tribe, *Council Resolutions, 1922-51*, pp. 412, 483.

82. NFPI, *Annual Report*, pp. 11, 15; Young, *Navajo Yearbook*, pp. 181-82.

83. NFPI, *Annual Report*, pp. 16-18; Young, *Navajo Yearbook*, pp. 182-83.'

CHAPTER FOUR

1. See the chapter on Raymond Nakai in Virginia Hoffman and Broderick Johnson, *Navajo Biographies* (Rough Rock, Arizona: Navajo Curriculum Center, Rough Rock Demonstration School, 1970), pp. 322-37.

2. David Aberle, *The Peyote Religion Among the Navaho* (Chicago: Aldine, 1966); Mary Shepardson, *Navajo Ways in Government*, American Anthropological Association Memoir, no. 96 (Menasha, Wis., June 1963), p. 102; Robert W. Young, personal interview, February 25, 1974.

3. *Navajo Times*, August 20, 1964.

4. *Udall* v. *Littell*, 366 F. 2nd 669 D.C. Cir. (1966), reprinted in Monroe Price, ed. *Law and the American Indian* (Indianapolis: Bobbs-Merrill, 1972), pp. 167-70. For Littell's private commentary on this period, see his letters to Thomas M. Storke, the retired publisher of the Santa Barbara *News-Press*. Littell to Storke, April 3, 1964; May 15, 1964; August 17, 1964; October 21, 1966; November 25, 1966; November 30, 1966; February 4, 1967; March 3, 1967; November 27, 1967. Thomas M. Storke Papers, The Bancroft Library, University of California, Berkeley.

5. *Navajo Times*, September 8, 1966, October 13, 1966.

6. Aberle, *Peyote Religion*, pp. 109-10; *Navajo Times*, December 1, 1966. This is my interpretation of the 1966 election and not that of Aberle or the *Navajo Times*.

7. See *Navajo Times* issues, fall 1966.

8. Ibid., June 30, 1966; August 4, 1966; August 25, 1966; June 2, 1966.

9. Ibid., February 23, 1967.

10. Ibid., July 27, 1967.

11. Ibid., December 12, 1968.

12. Ibid.

13. Evan Roberts, "Early History of ONEO" (Paper prepared for the ONEO Supervisory Training Workshop, Farmington, New Mexico, March 11, 1974); *Navajo Times*, October 8, 1964, December 2, 1965.

14. Ibid.

15. These totals do not include the number of people utilizing the new DNA legal aid program, which started as an ONEO operation before becoming an independent entity. Office of Navajo Economic Opportunity, "A History and Report," June-November 1967, pp. 31, 33, 39, 41.

16. Ibid., pp. 35-36, 54.

17. Harry A. Sellery to Allan G. Harper, February 10, 1954. Copy in Navajo Community College Library.

18. Navajo Nation, *Navajo Tribal Code* (Orford, N.H.: Equity, 1969), lists six resolutions passed during this period dealing with this problem (p. 83).

19. Ibid.

20. Navajo Tribe, *Navajo Tribal Council Minutes,* October 9, 1958, p. 125.

21. *Navajo Times,* March 2, 1965, March 16, 1965.

22. Original DNA board member John Rockbridge contributed the new name for the program, which means "Attorneys Who Contribute to the Economic Revitalization of the People." *Law in Action* 1, no. 5 (December 1968).

23. *Navajo Times,* January 5, 1967.

24. Of the ten attorneys hired most recently before that date, three had graduated from Harvard Law School, three from Yale, two from Stanford, and one each from Columbia and Texas. *Law in Action* 1, no. 1 (August 27, 1968).

25. Ibid.

26. Ibid.

27. At Nakai's request, Hardwick had taken over the editorship. An Anglo, he had previously been managing editor of the Gallup *Independent* and an employee of the BIA Navajo Area Education Division. See *Navajo Times,* October 17, 1968, for an example of his criticism of Mitchell and the DNA.

28. Gallup *Independent,* August 9, 1968.

29. Holmes later defended his action, saying, "I had to join the Tribe. I didn't have a choice. My role was to maintain stable government and I couldn't turn on them. I told Mitchell that. I could try to talk to them beforehand, but once they decided, I had to go along." Graham Holmes, personal interview, March 4, 1974.

30. *Dodge v. Nakai,* District Court, District of Arizona (1968), decision of Judge Craig, reprinted in Wilcomb Washburn, ed., *The American Indian and the United States,* 4 vols. (New York: Random House, 1973), 4:2913-18.

31. *Navajo Times,* March 20, 1969.

32. Ibid., May 1, 1969; April 24, 1969; Gallup *Independent,* December 15, 1970. MacDonald's election over Nakai in 1970 made it easier for Mitchell to depart altogether.

33. Gallup *Independent,* June 10, 1970; June 12, 1970; Monroe Price, "Lawyers on the Reservation: Some Implications for the Legal Profession," *The Journal of Law and the Social Order,* reprinted in U.S., 91st Congress, 1st session, *Toward Economic Development for Native American Communities* (Washington, 1969), 1, p. 200. In fairness to Price, it should be added that Luther quoted him somewhat selectively and in at least one place not taking note of intended irony. Price, in fact, argued that the confrontation marked a strengthening of the political process on the reservation and that, on balance, the DNA actually buttressed tribal sovereignty and reinforced the tribal structure.

34. Gallup *Independent,* June 11, 1970; *Law in Action* 2, no. 11 (July 11, 1970).

35. *Law in Action* 4, no. 6 (March 29, 1971).

36. Gallup *Independent,* February 1970 and *passim.*

37. Washburn, *American Indian,* 4:2931-35.

38. Navajo Tribe, "Navajoland: Business Frontier," n.d.

39. *Navajo Times,* April 20, 1967.

40. Ibid., September 10, 1970.

41. David Ralph Graham, *The Role of Business in the Economic Redevelopment of the Rural Community* (Austin: Bureau of Business Research, University of Texas, 1973), pp. 43, 58.

42. Ibid., pp. 48-49, 58-59.

43. Lorraine Turner Ruffing, "Economic Development and Navajo Social Structure" (Paper prepared for the Economic Development Administration, April 1973), pp. 24, 91-92.

44. Ibid., p. 91.

45. Ibid., pp. 92, 99, 109-10.

46. Lorraine Turner Ruffing, "An Alternative Approach to Economic Development in a Traditional Navajo Community," Ph.D. diss. Columbia University, 1972.

47. U.S., 92nd. Congress, 2nd session Senate, Committee on Interior and Insular Affairs, "Problems of Electrical Power Production in the Southwest," (Washington: 1972), pp. 3-9.

48. Graham Holmes, personal interview, March 4, 1974.

49. Ibid.

50. *Diné Baa-Hani,* September 1970; October 1970.

51. The Albuquerque example is courtesy of Francis Becenti, in 1972 a Navajo Community College student.

52. See Nancy Hilding, "American Indian Water Rights on the Rio Grande and Colorado Rivers," unpublished paper, 1973; Daniel H. MacMeekin, "The Navajo Tribe's Water Rights in the Colorado River Basin," U.S., 92nd Congress, 1st session, Part 3 of the Hearings before the Subcommittee on Administrative Practice and Procedure of the Senate Committee on the Judiciary, 1972; Eugene Gade, "Environmental and Economic Issue: The Strip Mining of Black Mesa and the Coal Burning Power Plants in the Southwest," mimeographed, 1971; Monroe E. Price and Gary D. Weatherford, "Indian Water Rights in Theory and Practice: Navajo Experience in the Colorado River Basin," in *American Indians and the Law,* ed. Lawrence Rosen (New Brunswick, N.J.: Transaction Books, 1978), pp. 97-131; Norris Hundley, Jr., "The Dark and Bloody Ground of Indian Water Rights: Confusion Elevated to Principle," *Western Historical Quarterly* (October 1978):455-82.

53. Hilding, "Water Rights," pp. 4-5; Robert Dellwo, "Indian Water Rights: The Winters Doctrine Updated," *Gonzaga Law Review* 6, no. 2 (Spring 1971):215-40.

54. Dellwo, "Indian Water Rights," pp. 232-33.

55. *Navajo Times,* October 21, 1971.

56. Gade, "Environmental and Economic Issue."

57. Ibid.; Eugene Gade, testimony in U.S., 92nd Congress, 1st session, Senate, Committee on Interior and Insular Affairs, "Problems of Electrical Power," p. 207.

58. See U.S., 86th Congress, 2nd session, Senate, Committee on Interior and Insular Affairs, "Proposed Amendments to the 1958 Navajo-U.S. Land Exchange Act," June 22, 1960.

59. Hilding, "Water Rights," pp. 25-26; Price and Weatherford, "Navajo Experience," pp. 110-19.

60. Price and Weatherford, "Navajo Experience," p. 114.

61. MacMeekin, "The Navajo Tribe's Water Rights," p. 777; Price and Rutherford, pp. 116-17.

62. MacMeekin, "The Navajo Tribe's Water Rights," pp. 778-79.

63. Young, *Navajo Yearbook*, p. 130; Richard L. Berkman and W. Kip Viscusi, *Damming the West* (New York: Grossman, 1973), p. 184.

64. Berkman and Viscusi, *Damming the West*, pp. 186-87; U.S., 86th Congress, 2nd session, Joint Committee on Navajo-Hopi Administration, "Legislation Concerning the Navajo Tribe," January 29, 1960, p. 11.

65. Price and Weatherford, "Navajo Experience," pp. 120-24.

66. Ibid., 126-27; *Navajo Times*, May 12, 1966, June 16, 1966.

67. See Committee on Labor and Public Welfare, U.S., 90th Congress, 1st session, Senate, Special Subcommittee on Indian Education, *Indian Education: A National Tragedy—A National Challenge* (Washington: 1969) and Estelle Fuchs and Robert J. Havighurst, *To Live on This Earth: American Indian Education* (Garden City, N.Y.: Anchor Press/Doubleday, 1973).

68. Annie Wauneka, "Statement," U.S., 90th Congress, 1st and 2nd sessions, Senate, Special Subcommittee on Indian Education, Committee on Labor and Public Welfare, Part 3, Flagstaff, Arizona, March 30, 1968, p. 1000.

69. "Centralized vs. Localized Schools," *Navajo Education* (May 1974).

70. *Navajo Times*, May 6, 1965.

71. See Donald A. Erickson and Henrietta Schwartz, "Community School at Rough Rock," mimeographed, 1969.

72. Robert A. Roessel, Jr., "Statement," U.S., 90th Congress, 1st and 2nd sessions, Senate Special Committee on Indian Education, March 30, 1968, p. 1029.

73. Broderick Johnson, *Navajo Education at Rough Rock* (Rough Rock, Ariz.: Rough Rock Demonstration School, 1968), p. 57.

74. Erickson and Schwartz, "Community School," pp. 3.51-3.52.

75. See Robert Bergman et al., "Problems of Crosscultural Educational Research and Evaluation," mimeographed, 1969.

76. See Murray Wax, "Gophers or Gadflies: Indian School Boards," *School Review* (November 1970):62-71; Gloria Emerson, "The Laughing Boy Syndrome," in *School Review* (November 1970):94-98.

77. See the remarks of Massachusetts Institute of Technology linguistics professor Kenneth Hale in the Rough Rock *News*, March 3, 1971.

78. Erickson and Schwartz, "Community School," pp. 2.18-2.19.

79. *Navajo Times*, August 29, 1968.

80. Ibid., February 13, 1969.

81. Navajo Community College Board of Regents, Minutes, June 13, 1968.

82. This paragraph and those following are based essentially on perceptions developed during my three years as an instructor at the school, from September 1969 to June 1972.

CHAPTER FIVE

1. These biographical details are based on material in the *Navajo Times* and information provided by the Chairman's Office. Ada Bluehouse, then the chairman's

secretary and formerly my neighbor at Navajo Community College, provided copies of many of MacDonald's speeches.

2. *Navajo Times,* February 26, 1970.

3. Gallup *Independent,* May 5, 1970; June 2, 1970; June 17, 1970.

4. Ibid., August 25, 1970; *Navajo Times,* August 27, 1970.

5. Gallup *Independent* and *Navajo Times,* September-November 1970.

6. Conclusions are based on election data printed in the *Navajo Times,* December 1, 1966, and Gallup *Independent,* November 14, 1970.

7. *Navajo Times,* January 7, 1971.

8. Graham Holmes, personal interview, March 4, 1974.

9. Gallup *Independent,* October 30, 1970.

10. Lawrence Ruzow, taped commentary, November 1974. I have known Ruzow since his employment as attorney for Navajo Community College during the 1969-70 academic year and had requested his perspective on the role of the general counsel.

11. Ibid.

12. Ibid.

13. James Wechsler (DNA attorney, Window Rock), personal interview, May, 1973; *Diné Baa-Hani,* September-October 1970; August 10, 1971.

14. *Navajo Times,* June 14, 1973; June 28, 1973.

15. Ibid., June 28, 1973.

16. Ibid., June 28, 1973; July 12, 1973.

17. Ibid., October 25, 1973; April 4, 1974; DNA *Newsletter,* October 30, 1973; January 30, 1974.

18. *Navajo Times,* January 15, 1970; September 10, 1970.

19. Ibid., November 7, 1974; June 27, 1974; Gallup *Independent,* September 8-10, 1971; October 8, 1971.

20. Robert W. Young, *The Navajo Yearbook* (Window Rock, Ariz.: Bureau of Indian Affairs, 1961), p. 278; *Navajo Times,* April 19, 1973; March 14, 1974.

21. "Bilingual Education," *Navajo Education* (May 1974).

22. See, for example, "All About How Dennis Todacheeni Came to School," and "The Quest for the Four Parrots"; see "Navajo Area Curriculum Development Project: Social Studies, Grades: Beginners-4 and Grades 5-8" (Window Rock, Ariz.: Navajo Area Office, Bureau of Indian Affairs, August 1970).

23. See Robert D. Wilson, "Assumptions for Bilingual Instruction in the Primary Grades of Navajo Schools," in *Bilingualism in the Southwest,* ed. Paul R. Turner (Tucson: University of Arizona Press, 1973), pp. 143-76.

24. Dillon Platero, personal interview, March 13, 1974.

25. *Navajo Times,* October 24, 1974.

26. Ibid., January 31, 1974; February 6, 1975.

27. Gallup *Independent,* April 18, 1970; *Diné Baa-Hani,* June-July 1970.

28. Gallup *Independent,* December 23, 1970; December 28, 1970; December 15, 1970.

29. Ibid., January 4, 1971; *Navajo Times,* July 26, 1973.

30. Gallup *Independent,* October 7, 1971.

31. Witherspoon, however, only remained briefly as principal of the new school before returning to university teaching.

32. *Navajo Times,* August 23, 1973.

33. Gallup *Independent,* May 19, 1971; *Dine Baa-Hani,* November 1970; June-July 1970; *Navajo Times,* November 9, 1973; November 7, 1974.

34. Donald Erickson and Henrietta Schwartz, "Community School at Rough Rock," mimeographed, 1969. Roessel's tenure would be brief and troubled by financial difficulties. He resigned after only a year on the job.

35. Victor Hackenschmidt, personal interview, May 1973; Gallup *Independent,* September 23, 1970; *Navajo Times,* November 29, 1973; December 13, 1973; January 31, 1974.

36. Katherine Iverson, "Outsiders and Decolonization: Anglo Roles at Navajo Community College," M.A. thesis, University of Wisconsin, 1974.

37. Navajo Division of Education, "Strengthening Navajo Education," Window Rock, Ariz., June 1973.

38. Peter MacDonald, "Strengthening Navajo Education," reprinted in Navajo Division of Education, "Eleven Programs for Strengthening Navajo Education," Window Rock, Ariz., December 1973.

39. *Navajo Times,* September 5, 1974; October 4, 1973.

40. Ibid., September 5, 1974; November 7, 1974.

41. Joshua Fishman, "Bilingual and Biadialectical Education: An Attempt at a Joint Model for Policy Description," as quoted in Bernard Spolsky, "Advances in Navajo Bilingual Education, 1968-72," in *Bilingual Education for American Indians,* ed. Bernard Spolsky, vol. 2 (Navajo), (Washington, D.C.: Bureau of Indian Affairs, 1973), p. 1.

42. *Dine Baa-Hani,* October 1970.

43. *Navajo Times,* December 27, 1974.

44. Gallup *Independent,* October 7, 1971; *Navajo Times,* October 4, 1973.

45. William Harbison, personal interview, February 26, 1974.

46. Gordon Denipah, Navajo Health Authority, personal interview, May 1973.

47. Sid Gilson, personal interview, February 27, 1974.

48. Gallup *Independent,* May 25, 1972; Rough Rock *News,* November 18, 1970.

49. *Navajo Times,* December 5, 1974, and subsequent issues; Lucy Hilgendorf, Navajo Comprehensive Health Planning Agency Advisory Board member, telephone interview, March 10, 1975.

50. *Navajo Times,* September 6, 1973.

51. Ibid., April 25, 1974.

52. Ibid., March 7, 1974; March 14, 1974; March 21, 1974; March 28, 1974; April 18, 1974; April 25, 1974; May 2, 1974; Navajo Health Authority, *Health Resources Directory: Navajo Nation,* Window Rock, Ariz., September 1973.

53. *Navajo Times,* April 23, 1970.

54. Ibid., April 29, 1971.

55. Ibid., January 31, 1974.

56. Ibid., October 25, 1973; January 31, 1974.

57. Ibid., February 21, 1974.

58. Graham Holmes, personal interview, March 4, 1974.

59. El Paso Natural Gas Company and Consolidated Coal Company, "The Burnham Coal Gasification Complex: A Summary for Presentation to Officials of the Navajo Nation," May 24, 1972; *Navajo Times,* February 15, 1973; Bahe Billy

and Philip Reno, "Analysis of Manpower Needs," *Navajo Times,* November 30, 1973.

60. *Navajo Times,* May 10, 1973; July 25, 1973.

61. Ibid., August 9, 1973; August 16, 1973; August 23, 1973; August 30, 1973; December 27, 1973.

62. Peter MacDonald, "Indians Need Their Share, Too" (Address to the Colorado River Water Users Association, December 1972).

63. Peter MacDonald, "The Navajos and the National Energy Crunch," reprinted in *Navajo Times,* February 17, 1972.

64. Peterson Zah, testimony in "Problems of Electrical Power Production in the Southwest," U.S., 92nd Congress, 2nd session, Senate, Committee on Interior and Insular Affairs, Report, 1972, p. 237.

65. Navajo Forest Products Industries, *Annual Report,* 1972-73, pp. 2-3; *Navajo Times,* April 11, 1974.

66. Navajo Nation, *Navajo Tribal Code* (Orford, N.H.: Equity, 1969), pp. 306.2-306.3, 306.10-306.11, 306.17-306.18, 306.20. These pages were added to the code since 1969.

67. Ibid., pp. 173-81, 188-89.

68. David Aberle, "A Plan for Navajo Economic Development," in U.S., 91st Congress, 1st session, Joint Economic Committee, *Toward Economic Development for Native American Communities,* 1969, p. 255.

69. *Navajo Times,* April 4, 1974; March 25, 1971.

70. See Peter MacDonald, "A Ten Year Plan for Navajo Economic Development," June 1972; *Navajo Times* (Window Rock, Ariz.), April 4, 1974.

71. *Navajo Times,* April 4, 1974; September 6, 1973; March 22, 1973.

72. See William Y. Adams, *Shonto: A Study of the Role of the Trader in a Modern Navaho Community,* Bureau of American Ethnology Bulletin, no. 188 (Washington, D.C., 1963); and Frank McNitt, *The Indian Traders* (Norman: University of Oklahoma Press, 1962).

73. See U.S., Federal Trade Commission, *The Trading Post System on the Navajo Reservation,* Staff Report, June 1973; Southwest Indian Development, "Traders on the Navaho Reservation: A Report on the Economic Bondage of the Navaho People," mimeographed (Window Rock, Ariz., 1968); Dan Cronin, "The Trading Post: Exploitation and Dependence of the Navajo," unpublished, 1971.

74. Kent Gilbreath, *Red Capitalism* (Norman: University of Oklahoma Press, 1973), p. 12.

75. Joseph R. Hardy, personal interview, May 25, 1973.

76. Gerald Boyle, "Revenue Alternatives for the Navajo Nation," unpublished, October 1973 (Window Rock, Ariz.), Navajo Office of Program Development, "Feasibility Study of the Tribal Commercial Laundry and Dry Cleaning Enterprise," March, 1974.

77. Navajo Office of Program Development, Development Section, *Annual Report,* (Window Rock, Ariz.), n.d.

78. Office of Navajo Economic Opportunity, "How to Organize and Operate A Co-operative; A Handbook for Chapter Members," 1973, p. 2.

79. Ibid., pp. 4-5, 23-25; *Diné Baa-Hani,* July 7, 1972.

80. Peter MacDonald, "Today Show" interview, NBC Television, January 16, 1975.

81. See various issues of the *Navajo Times,* and also Lynn A. Robbins, "Navajo Labor and the Establishment of a Voluntary Workers Association," *Journal of Ethnic Studies* 6, no. 3 (Fall 1978):97-112.

82. *Navajo Times,* November 30, 1972; December 28, 1972; February 1, 1973.

83. Ibid., March 8, 1973; March 17, 1974.

84. Navajo Nation, *Navajo Tribal Code,* pp. 54-55, 59-60, 64-65, 67-69, 69-70, 70.2.

85. Ibid., pp. 24.1-24.2.

86. Navajo Nation, *Navajo Tribal Code.*

CHAPTER SIX

1. Peter MacDonald, inaugural address, January 7, 1975.

2. Peter MacDonald, comments in response to Peter Iverson's "The Political Career of Peter MacDonald" (Paper delivered at the Annual Dartmouth College Native American Studies Conference, May 8, 1978).

3. *Navajo Times,* October 18, 1973; June 13, 1974.

4. Ibid., April 18, 1974; July 11, 1974.

5. Ibid., July 4, 1974.

6. Ibid., June 20, 1974.

7. Ibid., June 27, 1974.

8. Ibid., August 15, 1974.

9. This analysis is based on vote totals appearing in the *Gallup Independent,* November 14, 1974, the *Navajo Times,* December 1, 1966, and data from the 1966 and 1970 elections.

10. *Navajo Times,* November 14, 1974.

11. El Paso Natural Gas Company, "The Burnham Coal Gasification Project," n.p., n.d.

12. *Navajo Times,* April 17, 1975; April 24, 1975; February 12, 1976; February 19, 1976; September 22, 1977; February 2, 1978; February 9, 1978.

13. Ibid., August 19, 1976; August 26, 1976; July 14, 1977.

14. Ibid., July 14, 1977.

15. Ibid., August 18, 1977.

16. Ibid., August 19, 1976.

17. Ibid., December 23, 1976; December 30, 1976; January 6, 1977; January 20, 1977.

18. Ibid., January 4, 1979.

19. Ibid., April 13, 1978; April 20, 1978; August 10, 1978.

20. Peter MacDonald, "State of the Navajo Nation," February 3, 1977.

21. Washington *Star* article, reprinted in the *Navajo Times,* November 11, 1977; *Business Week* article, December 19, 1977, reprinted in *Navajo Times,* December 29, 1977.

22. Peter MacDonald, "Preconditions for Growth" (Address given at a conference on The Rise of the Southwest: Promise and Problem, Phoenix, April 21, 1977).

23. *Navajo Times*, June 16, 1977; January 25, 1979.

24. Ibid., February 2, 1978; September 28, 1978; October 5, 1978.

25. Navajo Forest Products Industries, *Annual Report*, 1978.

26. *Navajo Times*, June 29, 1978; July 6, 1978.

27. Ibid., April 6, 1978; December 7, 1978.

28. Ibid., February 27, 1975; March 6, 1975; March 13, 1975; March 20, 1975; March 27, 1975; August 27, 1977.

29. J. Lee Correll, "Report Showing Traditional Navajo Land Use and Occupancy of Lands in the 1882 Executive Order Reservation," mimeographed, April 1972, J. Lee Correll and David Brugge, "Historic Use and Occupancy of the Tuba City-Moencopi Area," mimeographed, April 1972; *Navajo Times*, October 24, 1974.

30. Samuel Pete, personal interview, March 13, 1974; *Navajo Times*, December 19, 1974.

31. *Navajo Times*, December 18, 1975; December 25, 1975; September 19, 1976; February 17, 1977; April 7, 1977; May 25, 1978.

32. Ibid., August 31, 1978; October 5, 1978; October 19, 1978; November 9, 1978.

33. Ibid., April 22, 1976; March 30, 1978.

34. Ibid., June 9, 1977; November 16, 1978.

35. Ibid., October 2, 1975; October 9, 1975; December 18, 1975.

36. Ibid., January 6, 1977; January 20, 1977; February 3, 1977; February 17, 1977; March 3, 1977; July 14, 1977; August 25, 1977; May 4, 1978; July 20, 1978.

37. Ibid., March 30, 1978; June 17, 1976; July 22, 1976; January 13, 1977; September 28, 1978.

38. Peter MacDonald, "Education for Survival" (Address given at the State Convention of Delta Kappa Gamma Society International, Clarksville, Ind., April 23, 1977).

39. *Navajo Times*, February 22, 1979.

40. Ibid., March 6, 1975; July 3, 1975; August 21, 1975; October 9, 1975; January 8, 1976; January 22, 1976; September 29, 1977.

41. *Arizona Daily Star* article, reprinted in *Navajo Times*, September 1, 1977.

42. *Navajo Times*, December 8, 1977; December 15, 1977.

43. Ibid., April 27, 1978; August 10, 1978.

44. Ibid., October 2, 1975; September 3, 1976; August 18, 1977; October 6, 1977; April 9, 1978; October 12, 1978.

45. Ibid., October 23, 1975; October 30, 1975; November 7, 1975; January 8, ' 1976; June 10, 1976; August 19, 1976; October 28, 1976; November 4, 1976; November 11, 1976.

46. Ibid., March 4, 1976; March 11, 1976; March 18, 1976; March 25, 1976; April 1, 1976; April 15, 1976; June 3, 1976; June 23, 1976; July 15, 1976; November 4, 1976; November 11, 1976; March 10, 1977.

47. MacDonald, comments to "The Political Career of Peter MacDonald."

48. Ibid.; *Navajo Times*, February 10, 1977.

49. *Navajo Times*, April 7, 1977; April 14, 1977; April 21, 1977; May 12, 1977; May 19, 1977.

50. Ibid., July 1, 1976; August 19, 1976.

51. Ibid., December 23, 1976; August 25, 1977.

52. Ibid., October 27, 1977; November 3, 1977; November 10, 1977; December 1, 1977; December 23, 1977.

53. Ibid., January 26, 1978; February 2, 1978; February 9, 1978; February 16, 1978; February 23, 1978; March 23, 1978; April 20, 1978; May 4, 1978; June 1, 1978; June 8, 1978.

54. Ibid., May 11, 1978; May 18, 1978; December 7, 1978.

CHAPTER SEVEN

1. *Navajo Times,* September 8, 1977; September 15, 1977.

2. Ibid., October 6, 1977.

3. For coverage of the primary campaign, see the *Navajo Times* in May-August, 1978. For an example of the strong criticism aimed at MacDonald, see the letter of Michael Benson in the August 3, 1978, issue. A reply to Benson by Samuel Pete is also included.

4. *Navajo Times,* August 10, 1978.

5. Ibid., August 17, 1978; September 11, 1978; October 26, 1978; November 2, 1978; November 9, 1978.

6. Peter MacDonald, inaugural address, reprinted in *Navajo Times,* January 11, 1979.

7. Michael Benson, "Sovereignty: The Navajo Nation and Taxation" (Window Rock, Ariz.: DNA-People's Legal Services, 1976), pp. 5-13.

8. Ibid., pp. 5-28.

SELECTED
BIBLIOGRAPHY

NAVAJO NATION

Documents and Resolutions

Navajo Nation. *Navajo Tribal Code.* 3 vols. Orford, N.H.: Equity, 1969.
Navajo Tribe. *The Election Law of 1966.* Window Rock, Ariz.: Navajo
    Tribe, 1966.
——. *Navajo Tribal Council Minutes.* January 1952, January 1953, Febru-
    ary 1954, October 1958.
——. *Navajo Tribal Council Resolutions, 1922-51.* Window Rock, Ariz.:
    Navajo Tribe, 1952.
Treaty Between the United States of America and the Navajo Tribe of
    Indians. Las Vegas, Nev.: KC, 1973.

Reports

MacDonald, Peter. "A Ten Year Plan for Navajo Economic Development."
    June 1972.
——. "Background Information Memo: Navajo-Hopi Land Dispute."
    N.d.
Navajo Community College. "Report to the Navajo Tribal Council."
    April 1972.
Navajo Division of Education. "Eleven Programs for Strengthening Navajo
    Education." December 1973.
——. "Strengthening Navajo Education." June 1973.
Navajo Forest Products Industries. *Annual Report.* 1972-73, 1978.

Navajo Health Authority. *Health Resources Directory: Navajo Nation.* September 1973.

Navajo Nation. "Navajo Wool Program." N.d.

Navajo Office of Program Development. "Feasibility Study of the Tribal Commercial Laundry and Dry Cleaning Enterprise." March 1974.

——. "Fifth Quarterly Report." November-December 1973.

"Import Substitution as a Development Strategy." March 1974.

——. Development Section. "Annual Report." 1973.

Navajo Tribal Police Department. "Annual Report." January 1 to December 31, 1971.

Navajo Tribe. "Navajoland: Business Frontier." N.d.

Office of Navajo Economic Opportunity. "A History and Report." June-November 1967.

——. "How to Organize and Operate A Co-operative: A Handbook for Chapter Members." N.d.

Newspapers and Newsletters

Adahooniligii. 1953-56.

Diné Baa-Hani (Hane). 1969-72.

Dinébeiina Nahiilna Be Agaditaha. *Law in Action.* 1968-72.

——. *DNA Newsletter.* 1973-74.

Navajo Education. 1973-74.

Navajo Times. 1964-79.

Office of Navajo Economic Opportunity. *Déé Há-Ne.* 1972-74.

Rough Rock *News.* March 3, 1971; January 31, 1973.

U.S. GOVERNMENT DOCUMENTS

Congressional Hearings and Reports

U.S. Congress. Joint Committee on Navajo-Hopi Administration. "Legislation Concerning the Navajo Tribe." 86th Congress, 2nd session. Washington: Government Printing Office, 1960.

——. House. Committee on Indian Affairs. "Statements on Conditions Among the Navajo Tribe." March 9, 1946; May 15, 1946. 79th Cong., 2d sess. Washington: G.P.O., 1946.

——. Senate. Committee on Indian Affairs. "Hearings on Navajo Indian Education." March 14, 1946. 79th Cong., 2d sess. Washington: G.P.O., 1946.

——. Senate. Committee on Indian Affairs, Subcommittee. "Survey of Conditions of the Indians in the United States." Part 18. 71st Cong., 3d sess. Washington: G.P.O., 1931. Part 34. 75th Cong., 1st sess. Washington: G.P.O., 1936.

——. Senate. Committee on Interior and Insular Affairs. "Navajo and Hopi Indians' Educational and Medical Services." 80th Congress, 2d sess. March 29, 1948. Washington: G.P.O., 1948.

——. Senate. Committee on Interior and Insular Affairs. "Problems of Electrical Power Production in the Southwest." 92d Cong., 2d sess. Washington: G.P.O., 1972.

——. Senate. Committee on Interior and Insular Affairs. "Proposed Amendments to the 1958 Navajo-U.S. Land Exchange Act." 86th Cong., 2d sess. Washington: G.P.O., 1960.

——. Senate. Committee on Labor and Public Welfare. "Hearings Before the Special Subcommittee on Indian Education." 90th Cong., 1st sess. Part 3. March 30, 1968. Washington: G.P.O., 1968.

——. Senate. Committee on Labor and Public Welfare. "Indian Education: A National Tragedy—A National Challenge." 90th Cong., 1st and 2d sess. Washington: G.P.O., 1969.

Other

Ahkeah, Sam. "A Talk to the Albuquerque Rotary." *Congressional Record.* Senate. A1848. 83d Cong., 2d sess. March 10, 1954.

Federal Trade Commission. *The Trading Post System on the Navajo Reservation; Staff Report to the Federal Trade Commission.* June, 1973. Washington: G.P.O., 1973.

NAVAJO HISTORICAL ACCOUNTS

Published

Bennett, Kay. *A Navajo Saga.* San Antonio: Naylor, 1969.

Emerson, Larry. "A Tale of Two Worlds." *Sun Tracks,* 1, no. 3 (Spring 1972).

Johnson, Broderick, ed. *Navajos and World War II.* Tsaile, Ariz.: Navajo Community College Press, 1978.

——. *Stories of Traditional Navajo Life and Culture.* Tsaile, Ariz.: Navajo Community College Press, 1977.

——, and Hoffman, Virginia. *Navajo Biographies.* Rough Rock, Ariz.: Rough Rock Demonstration School, 1970.

——, and Roessel, Ruth, eds. *Navajo Livestock Reduction: A National Disgrace.* Tsaile, Ariz.: Navajo Community College Press, 1974.

Roessel, Ruth, ed. *Navajo Stories of the Long Walk Period.* Tsaile, Ariz.: Navajo Community College Press, 1973.

Sapir, Edward, and Hoijer, Harry, eds. *Navaho Texts.* Iowa City, Iowa: Linguistic Society of America, 1942.

Yazzie, Ethelou, ed. *Navajo History.* Rough Rock, Ariz.: Rough Rock Demonstration School, 1971.

Young, Robert W., and Morgan, William, eds. *Navajo Historical Selections.* Phoenix: Bureau of Indian Affairs, 1954.

Interviews

Ashley, Floyd. Office of Navajo Economic Opportunity. Personal interview, May 1973.

Collins, Rick. DNA Legal Services. Personal interview, May 1973.

Denipah, Gordon. Navajo Health Authority. Personal interview, May 1973.

Fisher, Scott. Navajo Community College. Telephone interview, February 1975.

Gilson, Sid. Gallup Public Health Service Hospital. Personal interview, February 27, 1974.

Hackenschmidt, Linda. Office of Navajo Economic Opportunity. Personal interview, May 1973.

Hackenschmidt, Victor. Window Rock Public Schools. Personal interview, May 1973.

Harbison, William. Gallup Public Health Service Hospital. Personal interview, February 26, 1974.

Hardy, Joseph R. Office of Navajo Economic Opportunity. Personal interview, May 1973.

Hilgendorf, Lucy. Advisory Board, Navajo Comprehensive Health Planning Agency. Telephone interview, March 10, 1975.

Holmes, Graham. Former director, Navajo Area, Bureau of Indian Affairs. Personal interview, March 4, 1974.

Loughlin, Bernice. Gallup Public Health Service Hospital. Personal interview, February 28, 1974.

Pete, Samuel. Navajo-Hopi Land Dispute Commission. Personal interview, March 13, 1974.

Platero, Dillon. Navajo Division of Education. Personal interview, March 13, 1974.

Ruzow, Lawrence, Attorney, Brown, Vlassis and Bain. Taped commentary in response to questions. November 1974.

Wechsler, James. DNA. Personal interview, May 1974.

Young, Robert W. University of New Mexico. Personal interview, February 25, 1974.

Other

Duke, Doris. Indian Oral History Project. Albuquerque: University of New Mexico Library.

Warren, David. Seminar presentation. Center for the History of the American Indian. October 30, 1973.

NEWSPAPERS

Akwesasne Notes, Early autumn 1972.

Gallup *Independent,* 1968-72.

Los Angeles *Times,* March 4, 1973.

New York *Times,* July 8, 1972.

Wassaja, March 1975.

LETTERS

Sellery, Harry A. Letter to Allan G. Harper. February 10, 1954. Navajo Community College library collection of Navajo materials.

PAPERS

Thomas M. Storke Papers. The Bancroft Library, University of California, Berkeley.

UNPUBLISHED MATERIALS

Arthur, Harris. "Evaluation of Navajo Opinion and Input on the Development of the Navajo Irrigation Project." N.d.

Benson, Michael. "Sovereignty: The Navajo Nation and Taxation."

Window Rock, Ariz.: DNA-People's Legal Services, 1976.

Bergman, Robert, et al. "Problems of Crosscultural Educational Research and Evaluation." Mimeographed. 1969.

Boyce, George A. "Facts About the Navajos." Mimeographed. Window Rock, Ariz.: Bureau of Indian Affairs, 1947.

——. "First Annual Report on Education to the Navajo Tribe." Mimeographed. Window Rock, Ariz.: Bureau of Indian Affairs, 1945.

——. "A Primer of Navajo Economic Problems." Mimeographed. Window Rock, Ariz.: Navajo Service, Bureau of Indian Affairs, 1942.

Boyle, Gerald. "Revenue Alternatives for the Navajo Nation." October 1973. Navajo Community College, Tsaile, Ariz.

Correll, J. Lee. "Report Showing Traditional Navajo Use and Occupancy of Lands in the 1882 Executive Order Reservation." Mimeographed. April 1972.

——, and Brugge, David. "Historic Use and Occupancy of the Tuba City-Moencopi Area." Mimeographed. April 1972.

Cronin, Dan. "The Trading Post: Exploitation and Dependence of the Navajo." Navajo Community College, 1971.

Diné Coalition. "Coal Gasification Is Something Else." N.d.

El Paso Natural Gas and Consolidation Coal Company. "The Burnham Coal Gasification Complex: A Summary for Presentation to Officials of the Navajo Nation." May 24, 1972.

——. "The Burnham Coal Gasification Project." N.d.

Erickson, Donald, and Schwartz, Henrietta. "Community School at Rough Rock." Mimeographed. 1969.

Fowler, Mitchell. "Navajos Not Satisfied!" N.d.

Gade, Eugene. "Environmental and Economic Issue: The Strip Mining of Black Mesa and the Coal Burning Power Plants in the Southwest." Mimeographed. 1971.

Hackenschmidt, Victor. "Elementary Education Improvement Program." Mimeographed. 1973.

Hilding, Nancy. "American Indian Water Rights on the Rio Grande and Colorado Rivers." 1973.

Iverson, Katherine. "Anthropologists and Social Change." 1974.

Iverson, Peter. "The Political Career of Peter MacDonald." Paper presented to the annual Dartmouth College Native American Studies Conference, May 8, 1978.

Levy, Jerrold E. "Navajo Health Concepts and Behavior: The Role of the

Anglo Medical Man in the Navajo Healing Process." Window Rock, Ariz.: U.S. Public Health Service, August 1, 1963.

Littell, Norman. "Reflections of a Tribal Attorney." 1957. Copy on file in the Navajo Tribal Museum library.

MacDonald, Peter. "Comments in Response to Iverson's, 'The Political Career of Peter MacDonald'." May 8, 1978.

——. "Education for Survival." Address to the State of Indiana convention of Delta Kappa Gamma. April 23, 1977.

——. "Inaugural Address." January 7, 1975.

——. "Preconditions for Growth." Address to "The Rise of the Southwest: Promise and Problem Conference." Phoenix, Ariz., April 21, 1977.

Mico, Paul. "Navajo Perception of Anglo Medicine." Mimeographed. Tuba City, Navajo Wealth Education Project, PHS. Indian Hospital, April 16, 1962.

Muck, Lee. "Survey of the Range Resources and Livestock Economy of the Navajo Indian Reservation." Mimeographed. Washington, D.C.: Department of the Interior, 1948.

Roberts, Evan. "Early History of ONEO." Paper prepared for the ONEO Supervisory Training Workshop, Farmington, New Mexico, March 11, 1974.

Ruffing, Lorraine Turner. "Economic Development and Navajo Social Structure." Wash. Report prepared for the Economic Development Administration, April 1973.

Southwest Indian Development, "Traders on the Navaho Reservation: A Report on the Economic Bondage of the Navaho People." Mimeographed. Window Rock, Ariz., 1968.

Spolsky, Bernard, and Holm, Wayne. "Literacy in the Vernacular: The Case of the Navajo." University of New Mexico, Navajo Reading Study Progress Report, no. 8. Mimeographed. March 1971.

Tedlock, Dennis. "Learning to Listen: Oral History as Poetry." Paper presented at Answers Without Questions: An Evaluation and Critique of Oral History, annual meeting of the Organization of American Historians, Chicago, April 1973.

Walker, Hugh. "The Problems of a Cross-Cultural Medical Care Among the Navajo."

Warren, David. "Cultural Studies in Indian Education." Position paper prepared for Research and Cultural Studies, Development Section,

Institute of American Indian Art, Santa Fe, n.d.
Werner, Oswald, and Begishe, Kenneth. "Ethnoscience in Applied Anthro-
pology." Mimeographed. 1970. Copy supplied to author by Prof.
Werner, Northwestern University.

THESES AND DISSERTATIONS

Holm, Wayne. "Some Aspects of Navajo Orthography." Ph.D. disserta-
tion, University of New Mexico, 1972.
Iverson, Katherine. "Outsiders and Decolonization: Anglo Roles at Navajo
Community College." M.A. thesis, University of Wisconsin, 1974.
Iverson, Peter. "The Evolving Navajo Nation: Diné Continuity Within
Change." Ph.D. dissertation, University of Wisconsin, 1975.
McTaggart, Frederick. "Mesquakie Stories: The Teachings of the Red
Earth People." Ph.D. dissertation, University of Iowa, 1972.
Philp, Kenneth. "John Collier and the American Indian, 1920-45." Ph.D.
dissertation, Michigan State University, 1971.
Ruffing, Lorraine Turner. "An Alternative Approach to Economic
Development in a Traditional Navajo Community." Ph.D. dissertation,
Columbia University, 1972.
Schmitt, Paul N. "A Study Showing that Traditional Grade Classifica-
tions in Indian Schools of the Southwest Is Impracticable and Mis-
leading." M.S. thesis, University of Kansas, 1936.
Young, Robert A. "Regional Development and Rural Poverty in the
Navajo Indian Area." Ph.D. dissertation, University of Wisconsin,
1976.

BOOKS

Aberle, David. *The Peyote Religion Among the Navaho.* Chicago: Aldine,
1966.
Adair, John, and Deuschle, Kurt. *The People's Health.* New York:
Appleton-Century-Crofts, 1970.
Adair, John, and Worth, Sol. *Through Navajo Eyes.* Bloomington:
Indiana University Press, 1972.
Adams, William Y. *Shonto: A Study of the Role of the Trader in a Modern*

Navaho Community. Washington, D.C.: Bureau of American Ethnology, 1963.

Allen, Perry, ed. *Navajoland, U.S.A.* Window Rock, Ariz.: Navajo Tribe, 1968.

Bailey, L. R. *The Long Walk.* Los Angeles: Westernlore Press, 1964.

Beatty, Willard, ed. *Education for Action.* Washington, D.C.: Bureau of Indian Affairs, 1944.

——. *Education for Cultural Change.* Washington, D.C.: Bureau of Indian Affairs, 1953.

Benavides, Fray Alonso de. *The Memorial of Fray Alonso de Benavides.* Trans. Mrs. Edward E. Ayer. Chicago: privately printed, 1916.

Bennett, Kay. *Kaibah: Recollections of a Navajo Girlhood.* Los Angeles: Westernlore Press, 1964.

Berkman, Richard L., and Viscusi, W. Kip. *Damming the West.* New York: Grossman, 1973.

Boyce, George A. *When the Navajos Had Too Many Sheep: The 1940's.* San Francisco: Indian Historian Press, 1974.

Chien, Chiao. *Continuation of Tradition in Navajo Society.* Taipei: Institute of Ethnology, Academia Sinica, 1971.

Clark, Ann Nolan. *Little Herder in Spring.* Washington, D.C.: Bureau of Indian Affairs, 1940.

Collier, John. *From Every Zenith.* Denver: Sage Books, 1963.

——. *On the Gleaming Way.* Denver: Sage Books, 1962.

Commager, Henry Steele. *The Search for a Usable Past.* New York: Alfred A. Knopf, 1967.

Condie, Leroy. *All About How Dennis Todacheeni Came to School.* Albuquerque: Navajo Social Studies Project, College of Education, University of New Mexico, and Division of Education, Navajo Area, Bureau of Indian Affairs, n.d.

——. *The Quest for the Four Parrots.* Albuquerque: Navajo Social Studies Project, College of Education, University of New Mexico, and Division of Education, Navajo Area, Bureau of Indian Affairs, 1970.

Coombs, L. Madison. *Doorway Toward the Light: The Story of the Special Navajo Education Program.* Brigham City, Utah: Bureau of Indian Affairs, 1962.

Deloria, Vine, Jr. *Behind the Trail of Broken Treaties.* New York: Delta Books, 1974.

——. *Custer Died For Your Sins.* New York: Macmillan, 1969.

Downs, James F. *Animal Husbandry in Navajo Society and Culture.* University of California Publications in Anthropology, no. 1. Berkeley, 1964.

Fuchs, Estelle, and Havighurst, Robert J. *To Live on This Earth: American Indian Education.* Garden City, N.Y.: Anchor Press/Doubleday, 1973.

Gilbreath, Kent. *Red Capitalism.* Norman: University of Oklahoma Press, 1973.

Gordon, Suzanne. *Black Mesa: The Angel of Death.* New York: John Day, 1973.

Graham, David Ralph. *The Role of Business in the Economic Redevelopment of the Rural Community.* Austin: Bureau of Business Research, University of Texas, 1973.

Hill, W. W. *The Hunting and Agricultural Methods of the Navajo Indians.* Yale University Publications in Anthropology, no. 18. New Haven, 1938.

Hoffman, Virginia, and Johnson, Broderick. *Navaho Biographies.* Rough Rock, Ariz.: Navajo Curriculum Center, Rough Rock Demonstration School, 1970.

Iverson, Peter. *The Navajos: A Critical Bibliography.* Bloomington: Indiana University Press, 1976.

Johnson, Broderick. *Navaho Education at Rough Rock.* Rough Rock, Ariz.: Rough Rock Demonstration School, 1968.

Johnson, Broderick and Virginia Hoffman. *Navajo Biographies.* Rough Rock, Arizona: Rough Rock Demonstration School, 1970.

Kane, Robert L., and Kane, Rosalie A. *Federal Health Care (With Reservations!).* New York: Springer, 1972.

Kelly, Lawrence C. *Navajo Indians and Federal Indian Policy, 1900-1935.* Tucson: University of Arizona Press, 1968.

——, ed. *Navajo Roundup.* Boulder: Pruett, 1970.

Kluckhohn, Clyde, and Leighton, Dorothea. *The Navaho.* Rev. ed. New York: Anchor, 1962.

Krug, Julian. *Report on the Navajo.* Washington, D.C.: Bureau of Indian Affairs, 1948.

Leighton, Alexander H., and Leighton, Dorothea C. 1944. Reprint ed. *The Navaho Door.* New York: Russell and Russell, 1966.

Link, Martin, ed. *A Century of Progress.* Window Rock, Ariz.: Navajo Tribe, 1968.

McNickle, D'Arcy. *Native American Tribalism: Indian Survivals and Re-*

newals. New York: Oxford University Press, 1973.

McNitt, Frank. *The Indian Traders.* Norman: University of Oklahoma Press, 1962.

Meriam, Lewis, et al. *The Problem of Indian Administration.* Baltimore: Johns Hopkins University Press, 1928.

Mitchell, Emerson Barney Blackhorse. *Miracle Hill.* Norman: University of Oklahoma Press, 1967.

Ness, Gayl D., ed. *The Sociology of Economic Development.* New York: Harper & Row, 1970.

Newcomb, Franc Johnson. *Hosteen Klah.* Norman: University of Oklahoma Press, 1964.

Parman, Donald C. *The Navajos and the New Deal.* New Haven: Yale University Press, 1976.

Parsons, Talcott. *The Social System.* Glencoe, Ill.: Free Press, 1951.

Paul, Doris. *The Navajo Codetalkers.* Philadelphia: Dorrance, 1973.

Philp, Kenneth R. *John Collier's Crusade for Indian Reform, 1920-1954.* Tucson: University of Arizona Press, 1977.

Price, Monroe, ed. *Law and the American Indian.* Indianapolis: Bobbs-Merrill, 1972.

Prucha, Francis Paul, ed. *Americanizing the American Indian.* Cambridge: Harvard University Press, 1973.

Roessel, Ruth, ed. *Navajo Studies.* Many Farms, Ariz.: Navajo Community College Press, 1971.

Sasaki, Tom. *Fruitland, New Mexico: A Navaho Community in Transition.* Ithaca, N.Y.: Cornell University Press, 1960.

Shafer, Boyd C. *Nationalism: Interpreters and Interpretations.* Washington, D.C.: American Historical Association, 1959.

Shepardson, Mary. Navajo Ways in Government. American Anthropological Association Memoir, no. 96. Menasha, Wis., June 1963.

Shepardson, Mary, and Hammond Blodwen. *The Navajo Mountain Community.* Berkeley: University of California Press, 1970.

Snyder, Louis L. *The Meaning of Nationalism.* New Brunswick, N.J.: Rutgers University Press, 1954.

Spencer, Katherine. *Navaho Chantway Myths.* Philadelphia: American Folklore Society, 1957.

——. *Reflections of Social Life in the Navajo Origin Myth.* University of New Mexico Publications in Anthropology, no. 3. Albuquerque, 1947.

Spicer, Edward H., and Thompson, Raymond H., eds. *Plural Society in the Southwest.* New York: Weatherhead Foundation, 1972.

Stanford Research Institute. *Tourist Potential on the Navajo Indian Reservation.* Palo Alto, Calif., August 1955.

Szasz, Margaret. *American Indian Education: The Road to Self-Determination.* Albuquerque: University of New Mexico Press, 1974.

Thompson, Gerald. *The Army and the Navajo.* Tucson: University of Arizona Press, 1976.

Underhill, Ruth. *The Navajos.* Norman: University of Oklahoma Press, 1967 (rev. ed.)

Vansina, Jan. *Oral Tradition: A Study in Historical Methodology.* Chicago: Aldine, 1965.

Washburn, Wilcomb, ed. *The American Indian and the United States.* 4 vols. New York: Random House, 1973.

Williams, Aubrey W., Jr. *Navajo Political Process.* Washington, D.C.: Smithsonian Contributions to Anthropology, vol. 9, 1970.

Wilson, John P. *Military Campaigns in the Navajo Country, Northwestern New Mexico, 1780-1846.* Santa Fe: Museum of New Mexico Press, 1967.

Young, Robert W. *A Political History of the Navajo Tribe.* Tsaile, Arizona: Navajo Community College Press, 1978.

——. *The Role of the Navajo in the Southwestern Drama.* Gallup, New Mexico: Gallup Independent, 1968.

——, ed. *The Navajo Yearbook,* vol. 8. Window Rock: Bureau of Indian Affairs, 1961.

Young, Stella, ed. *Navajo Native Dyes: Their Preparation and Use.* Washington, D.C.: Bureau of Indian Affairs, 1940.

ARTICLES

Aberle, David. "A Plan for Navajo Economic Development." In *Toward Economic Development for Native American Communities.* U.S. Congress. Subcommittee on Economy in Government of the Joint Economic Committee. 91st Congress, 1st session. Washington, D.C.: Government Printing Office, 1969.

Adams, William Y. "Navajo Ecology and Economy." In *Apachean Culture and Ethnology,* edited by Keith H. Basso and Morris Opler. Tucson: University of Arizona Publications in Anthropology, no. 21, 1971.

——. "Navajo Social Organization." *American Anthropologist* 73, no. 1 (1971):273.

Bahe, Maggie. Untitled poem, pp. 90-91. In *Arrows Four: Prose and Poetry by Young American Indians,* edited by T. D. Allen..New York: Washington Square Press, 1974.

Barth, Fredrik. "On the Study of Social Change." *American Anthropologist* 69, no. 6 (1967). Reprinted as "Studying Social Change," pp. 239-52. In *The Meaning of Culture,* edited by Morris Freilich. Lexington, Mass.: Xerox, 1972.

Bergman, Robert. "Navajo Medicine and Psychoanalysis." *Human Behavior* 2, no. 7 (July 1973):8-15.

Boas, Franz. "Northern Elements in the Mythology of the Navajo." *American Anthropologist* 10, no. 11 (November 1897):371-76.

Brugge, David M. "Navajo Land Usage: A Study in Progressive Diversification," pp. 16-24. In *Indian and Spanish Adjustments to Arid and Semiarid Environments,* edited by Clark S. Knowlton. El Paso: Texas Technological College Committee on Desert Arid Zone Research, 1964.

——. "Pueblo Factionalism and External Relations." *Ethnohistory* (Spring 1969):191-200.

Burge, Moris. "The Navajos and the Land: The Government, The Tribe, and the Future." *National Association on Indian Affairs Bulletin,* no. 26 (February 1937).

Christian, Jane. "The Navajo: A People in Transition." *Southwestern Studies,* 2, nos. 2-3 (Fall 1964, Winter 1965).

Conn, Stephen. "Bilingual Legal Education," pp. 115-21. In *American Indian Education,* edited by R. Merwin Deever et al. Tempe: Arizona State University, June 1974.

David, Richard. Untitled poem, pp. 95-96. In *Arrows Four: Prose and Poetry by Young American Indians,* edited by T. D. Allen. New York: Washington Square Press, 1974.

Dellwo, Robert. "Indian Water Rights: The Winters Doctrine Updated." *Gonzaga Law Review* 6, no. 2 (Spring 1971):215-40.

Dippie, Brian W. "This Bold But Wasting Race: Stereotypes and American Indian Policy." *Montana* 23 (January 1973):2-13.

Dobyns, Henry. "Therapeutic Experience of Responsible Democracy," pp. 268-94. In *The American Indian Today,* edited by Stuart Levine and Nancy O. Lurie. Baltimore: Penguin, 1968.

Downs, James F. "The Cowboy and the Lady: Models as a Determinant of the Rate of Acculturation Among the Piñon Navajo." Kroeber Anthropological Society Papers, no. 29 (Fall 1963). Reprinted in *Native Americans Today,* edited by Howard M. Bahr; Bruce A. Chadwick; and Robert C. Day. New York: Harper & Row, 1972.

Emerson, Gloria. "The Laughing Boy Syndrome." *School Review* (November 1970):94-98.

Erickson, Donald. "Custer Did Die For Our Sins!" *School Review* (November 1970).

Fonaroff, L. Schuler. "Conservation and Stock Reduction on the Navajo Tribal Range." *The Geographical Review* 53, no. 1 (January 1963): 200-23.

Frank, Andre Gundar. "The Development of Underdevelopment," pp. 3-17. In *Dependence and Underdevelopment,* edited by James D. Cockroft; Andre Gundar Frank; and Dale L. Johnson. New York: Anchor, 1972.

Fryer, E. R. "The Navajo Service." In *Proceedings of the First Navajo Service Land Management Conference.* Window Rock, Ariz.: Navajo Service, Bureau of Indian Affairs, 1937.

Gorman, Carl N. "Navajo Vision of Earth and Man." *The Indian Historian* 6, no. 1 (Winter 1973).

Hundley, Norris, Jr. "The Dark and Bloody Ground of Indian Water Rights: Confusion Elevated to Principle." *Western Historical Quarterly* (October 1978):455-82.

Iverson, Katherine. "Progressive Education for Native Americans: Washington Ideology and Navajo Reservation Implementation." *Review Journal of Philosophy and Social Science* 3, no. 2 (1970):231-55.

Iverson, Peter. "Legal Counsel and the Navajo Nation Since 1945." *American Indian Quarterly* 3, no. 1 (Spring 1977):1-15.

——. "Legal Services and Navajo Economic Revitalization." *Journal of Ethnic Studies* 4, no. 3 (Fall 1976):21-34.

——. "Peter MacDonald." pp. 222-42. In *American Indian Leaders: Studies in Diversity,* edited by R. David Edmonds. Lincoln, Nebraska: University of Nebraska Press, 1980.

——. "The Rise of Navajo Nationalism." In *Identity and Awareness in the Minority Experience,* edited by George Carter and Bruce Mouser. La Crosse: University of Wisconsin-La Crosse Institute for Minority Studies, 1975.

Jorgensen, Joseph. "The Indians and the Metropolis," pp. 66-113. In *The American Indian in Urban Society,* edited by Jack O. Waddell and O. Michael Watson. Boston: Little, Brown, 1971.

Kimball, Solon. "Future Problems in Navajo Administration." *Human Organization* 9, no. 2 (Summer 1950):21-24.

Koppes, Clayton R. "From New Deal to Termination: Liberalism and Indian Policy, 1933-1953," *Pacific Historical Review* 46, no. 4 (November 1977):543-66.

MacMeekin, Daniel. "The Navajo Tribe's Water Rights in the Colorado River Basin." U.S., 92nd Congress, 1st session, Senate, Judiciary Committee. In "Administrative Practices and Procedures Relating to Protection of Indian Natural Resources." Washington, D.C.: Government Printing Office, 1972.

McGinnies, W. G. "Stock Reduction and Range Management." *Proceedings of the First Navajo Service Land Management Conference.* Window Rock, Ariz.: Navajo Service, Bureau of Indian Affairs, 1937.

Mitchell, George, et al. "A New Concept on the Navajo," pp. 24-39. In *American Indian Education,* edited by R. Merwin Deever. Tempe: Arizona State University, June 1974.

Murphy, Penny. "A Brief History of Navajo Literacy," pp. 4-25. In *Analytical Bibliography of Navajo Reading Materials,* edited by Bernard Spolsky; Agnes Holm; and Penny Murphy. Washington, D.C.: Bureau of Indian Affairs, 1970.

Parman, Donald L. "J. C. Morgan: Navajo Apostle of Assimilation." *Prologue* 4, no. 2 (Summer 1972):83-98.

Porvasnik, John. "Traditional Navajo Medicine." *GP* 36, no. 4 (October 1967):181-82.

Price, Monroe. "Lawyers on the Reservation: Some Implications for the Legal Profession," *The Journal of Law and the Social Order.* Reprinted in U.S., Congress, Joint Economic Committee, *Toward Economic Development for Native American Communities.* Vol. 1. Washington, D.C.: Government Printing Office, 1969, pp. 191-222.

——, and Weatherford, Gary D. "Indian Water Rights in Theory and Practice: Navajo Experience in the Colorado River Basin," pp. 97-131. In *American Indians and the Law,* edited by Lawrence Rosen. New Brunswick, N.J.: Transaction Books, 1978.

Reeve, Frank D. "The Government and the Navaho, 1846-1858." *New Mexico Historical Review* 14, no. 1 (1939):82-114.

Reno, Philip. "Manpower Planning for Navajo Employment: Training for Jobs in a Surplus-Labor Area." *New Mexico Business* (December 1970):8-16.

Robbins, Lynn A. "Navajo Labor and the Establishment of a Voluntary Workers Association." *Journal of Ethnic Studies* 6, no. 3 (Fall 1978): 97-112.

Rosenfelt, Daniel. "Indian Schools and Community Control." *Stanford Law Review* 25, no. 4 (April 1973):492-550.

Sasaki, Tom, and Adair, John. "New Land to Farm: Agricultural Practices Among the Navajo Indians of New Mexico," pp. 97-111. In *Human Problems in Technological Change,* edited by Edward H. Spicer. New York: Wiley, 1965.

Shepardson, Mary. "Comments on Legal Services and the Tribal Courts" (Transcript of remarks at the Arrowhead Conference on Law and Legal Services on Indian Reservations, September 1967), pp. 161-67. In *Law and the American Indian,* edited by Monroe Price. Indianapolis: Bobbs-Merrill, 1972.

——. "Problems of the Navajo Tribal Courts in Transition." *Human Organization* 24, no. 3 (Fall 1965):250-53.

Spicer, Edward H. "Sheepmen and Technicians," pp. 185-207. In *Human Problems in Technological Change,* edited by Edward H. Spicer. New York: Wiley, 1965.

Spolsky, Bernard. "Advances in Navajo Bilingual Education, 1968-72," pp. 1-5. In *Bilingual Education for American Indians,* vol. 2 (Navajo) Edited by Bernard Spolsky. Washington, D.C.: Bureau of Indian Affairs, 1973.

——. "Navajo Language Maintenance: Six Year Olds in 1969." *Language Sciences,* no. 13 (December 1970):19-24.

Van Valkenburg, Richard. "Navaho Government." *Arizona Quarterly* 1, no. 4 (Winter 1945):63-73.

Vogt, Evon. "The Navaho," pp. 275-336. In *Perspectives in Indian Culture Change,* edited by Edward H. Spicer. Chicago: University of Chicago Press, 1961.

Wax, Murray. "Gophers or Gadflies: Indian School Boards." *School Review* (November 1970):62-71.

Wilson, Robert D. "Assumptions for Bilingual Instruction in the Primary Grades of Navajo Schools," pp. 143-76. In *Bilingualism in the Southwest,* edited by Paul R. Turner. Tucson: University of Arizona Press, 1973.

Witherspoon, Gary. "A New Look at Navajo Social Organization." *American Anthropologist* 72, no. 1 (1970):55-65.

Young, Robert W. "The Origin and Development of Navajo Tribal Government," pp. 371-411. In *The Navajo Yearbook,* vol. 8, edited by Robert W. Young. Window Rock, Ariz.: Bureau of Indian Affairs, 1961.

——. "The Rise of the Navajo Tribe." In *Plural Society in the Southwest,* edited by Edward H. Spicer and Raymond H. Thompson. New York: Weatherhead Foundation, 1972.

——. "A Sketch of the Navajo Language," pp. 430-510. In *The Navajo Yearbook,* vol. 8, edited by Robert W. Young. Window Rock, Ariz.: Bureau of Indian Affairs, 1961.

INDEX

Aberle, David, 11, 30, 87, 166
Adair, John, 66
Adams, V. Allen, 96
Adams, William, 5
Advisory Committee: actions taken by, 81, 86, 92, 95-97, 127; creation of, 70; instructions to, 78-79
AFL-CIO, 173, 206
Ahkeah, Sam: actions taken by as chairman, 52, 55, 85; biography of, 51-52; campaign by against Paul Jones, 71-72; comment by on stock reduction, 23; testimony of, 62
Alamo, 129, 182
Albuquerque Indian school, 13, 63
Allen, Marie, 155
Allen, Perry, 214, 217
Allison, Art, 192-93
American Indian movement, 173-74, 195, 212
Ames Brothers Ford, 135
Anderson, Clinton, 113
Anderson, Larry, 217
Andrus, Cecil, 185
Aneth: controversy in oil fields, 183, 187-88, 212; impact of oil strike, 68, 77, 220; votes by in elections, 87, 130

Apache County, 72, 202, 206, 224
Arizona Public Service Company, 79, 191-92
Arizona v. California, 108-9
Armex Corporation, 101, 216
Arthur, Chester, 195
Arthur, Harris, 185
Arviso, Katherine, 148
Ashurst, Henry F., 19, 25
Aspinall, Wayne, 112-13
Atcitty, James, 212, 214
Atcitty, Thomas, 149-50, 200-201

Babbitt, Bruce, 217
Babbitt, David, 12
Babbitt, William, 12
Bailey, F. Lee, 208, 210-11
Bain, C. Randall, 132, 196
Barber, Elmer, 161
Barnes, Duard, 95
Beatty, Willard, 40-41
Becenti, Herbert, 62
Becenti, Hoskie T., 205
Becenti, Tom, 137
Beclabito, 160, 186
Begay, Allen, 148
Begay, Edward T., 135
Begay, Fleming, 171

About the Author

PETER IVERSON is Assistant Professor of History at the University of Wyoming in Laramie. His earlier publications include *The Navajos: A Critical Biography*.